# Daniel

*Westminster Bible Companion*

---

*Series Editors*

Patrick D. Miller
David L. Bartlett

# Daniel

C. L. SEOW

Westminster John Knox Press
LOUISVILLE • LONDON

Some Scripture quotations are the author's translations.

*Book design by Publishers' WorkGroup*
*Cover design by Drew Stevens*

*First edition*

Published by Westminster John Knox Press
Louisville, Kentucky

This book is printed on acid-free paper that meets the American National Standards Institute Z39.48 standard. ♾

PRINTED IN THE UNITED STATES OF AMERICA

03 04 05 06 07 08 09 10 11 12 — 10 9 8 7 6 5 4 3 2 1

**Library of Congress Cataloging-in-Publication Data**

Seow, C. L. (Choon Leong)
Daniel / C.L. Seow.—1st ed.
p. cm. — (Westminster Bible companion)
Includes bibliographical references.
ISBN 0-664-25675-9 (alk. paper)
1. Bible. O.T. Daniel—Commentaries. I. Title. II. Series.

BS1555.3 .S46 2003
224'.5077—dc21 2002072364

For Hui-Ling, “wise and clever,” my joy

# Contents

# Series Foreword

This series of study guides to the Bible is offered to the church and more specifically to the laity. In daily devotions, in church school classes, and in listening to the preached word, individual Christians turn to the Bible for a sustaining word, a challenging word, and a sense of direction. The word that scripture brings may be highly personal as one deals with the demands and surprises, the joys and sorrows, of daily life. It also may have broader dimensions as people wrestle with moral and theological issues that involve us all. In every congregation and denomination, controversies arise that send ministry and laity alike back to the Word of God to find direction for dealing with difficult matters that confront us.

A significant number of lay women and men in the church also find themselves called to the service of teaching. Most of the time they will be teaching the Bible. In many churches, the primary sustained attention to the Bible and the discovery of its riches for our lives have come from the ongoing teaching of the Bible by persons who have not engaged in formal theological education. They have been willing, and often eager, to study the Bible in order to help others drink from its living water.

This volume is part of a series of books, the Westminster Bible Companion, intended to help the laity of the church read the Bible more clearly and intelligently. Whether such reading is for personal direction or for the teaching of others, the reader cannot avoid the difficulties of trying to understand these words from long ago. The scriptures are clear and clearly available to everyone as they call us to faith in the God who is revealed in Jesus Christ and as they offer to every human being the word of salvation. No companion volumes are necessary in order to hear such words truly. Yet every reader of scripture who pauses to ponder and think further about any text has questions that are not immediately answerable simply by reading the text of scripture. Such questions may be about historical and geographical details or about words that are obscure or so loaded with meaning that one cannot tell at a glance what is at stake. They may be about the fundamental meaning of a passage or about what connection a particular text might have to our contemporary world. Or a teacher preparing for a church school class may simply want to know: What should I say about this biblical passage when I have to teach it next Sunday? It is our hope that these volumes, written by teachers and pastors with long experience studying and teaching Bible in the church, will help members of the church who want and need to study the Bible with their questions.

The New Revised Standard Version of the Bible is the basis for the interpretive comments that each author provides. The NRSV text is presented at the beginning of the discussion so that the reader may have at hand in a single volume both the scripture passage and the exposition of its meaning. In some instances, where inclusion of the entire passage is not necessary for understanding either the text or the interpreter's discussion, the presentation of the NRSV text may be abbreviated. Usually, the whole of the biblical text is given.

We hope this series will serve the community of faith, opening the Word of God to all the people, so that they may be sustained and guided by it.

# Abbreviations

| | |
|---|---|
| *ANET* | *Ancient Near Eastern Texts Relating to the Old Testament.* Edited by J. B. Pritchard. 3d ed. Princeton, N.J.: Princeton University Press, 1969. |
| *Ant.* | *Antiquitates judaicae.* Josephus. |
| B.C.E. | Before the Common Era (same as B.C.) |
| C.E. | Common Era (same as A.D.) |
| *COS* | *The Context of Scripture.* Edited by W. W. Hallo and K. L. Younger. 3 vols. Leiden: Brill, 1997. |
| *DSST* | *The Dead Sea Scrolls Translated.* Edited and translated by F. García Martinez. Leiden: Brill, 1994. |
| *1 En* | *1 Enoch* (a pseudepigraphical work; fourth century B.C.E.) |
| Jdt. | Judith (an apocryphal book; late second century–first century B.C.E.) |
| *Jub* | *Jubilees* (a pseudepigraphical work) |
| 1–2 Macc. | 1 & 2 Maccabees (apocryphal books; between late second century and early first century B.C.E.) |
| NAB | *The New American Bible* |
| NIV | *New International Version* |
| NRSV | New Revised Standard Version |
| Sir. | Sirach (an apocryphal book; early second century B.C.E., before 180) |
| Tob. | Tobit (an apocryphal book; third century B.C.E.) |
| Wis. | Wisdom of Solomon (an apocryphal book; late first century B.C.E. or early first century C.E.) |

# Introduction

The book of Daniel has fascinated readers through the ages. In particular, the stories of Daniel and his friends in the first half of the book have inspired great works of art: frescoes and sculptures in Roman catacombs, ornamentations on architectural structures of churches, colorful illustrations on medieval manuscripts, and masterpieces by some of the greatest artists in history, including Rubens, Rembrandt, and Michelangelo. In music, too, the stories have had their impact, including in the last century Benjamin Britten's *The Burning Fiery Furnace*, Louis Gruenberg's musical score of *The Daniel Jazz*, Louis Armstrong's rendition of *Shadrach, Meshach, and Abednego*, not to mention the now-popular church musical, *It's Cool in the Furnace*. These stories are staples in many church school curricula, where Daniel and his friends are held up as models of courageous faith.

One wonders, however, if these stories contain more than entertainment value and the platitudinous lessons in the hit–children's video series, *Veggie Tales*. One must ask, too, how these tales are related, if at all, to the second half of the book, with its visions of bizarre monsters, linen-clad angels, and perplexing numerology. Among Christian interpreters, the book has often been viewed as one that predicts specific events in the New Testament. So the translators of the old King James Version take the divine being that the friends of Daniel encountered in the fiery furnace to be "*the* Son of God" (3:25), and the one who is to come with the clouds of heaven is called "*the* Son of Man" (7:13). By the same token, the stone hewn not by human hands that is expected to crush empires (2:24–35, 44–45) has been taken to refer to the advent of Christ or the establishment of the church. For still others, the evil power depicted in the visions of chapters 7–12 is none other than the antichrist, and the book is believed to be about the end of the world and the ultimate victory of good over evil. Yet, to imagine that the original recipients of the book might have been content to accept that all these predictions had nothing to do with them whatsoever but with events that will come to pass long after their time is a bit difficult.

This commentary attempts to read Daniel with an eye on its theological message for the original audience but also on the relevance of that message for the contemporary community of faith. The book's chief theological contribution comes in its perspective on the sovereignty of God and how that sovereignty may be manifested on earth through God's faithful servants. Before outlining that theology, however, this introduction first considers various matters pertaining to the book's place in the canon; its provenance, compositional history, and literary genres; and the occasion that gave rise to the book in largely its present form.

## THE BOOK IN THE CANON

The book of Daniel has its name because the stories and visions that it contains largely revolve around a man named Daniel. The first half of the book (chaps. 1–6) contains stories about the experiences of Daniel and his friends in the courts of foreign kings; they refer to Daniel in the third person. The second half (chaps. 7–12) contains visions reportedly received *by* Daniel; they are told in the first person.

Reflecting an emphasis on the stories of the first half of the book, the received text of the Hebrew Bible places Daniel in the third major portion of the canon: the Writings. Accordingly, the book usually takes its place after Esther, a court narrative set in the Persian period, and before Ezra-Nehemiah, an account of the experiences of Jewish exiles upon their return to Judea. That placement reflects the historical setting of the book and suggests how one might read the book; Daniel is about the experience of displacement, as in Esther, but it also anticipates the restoration of the displaced people of God, as in Ezra-Nehemiah.

In contrast to the Hebrew Bible, the Greek translation of the Old Testament that became the authoritative text among Christians reflects an emphasis on the second half of the book, the visions of chapters 7 to 12, placing Daniel in the second portion of the canon, the Prophets. In most modern Christian editions of the Bible, therefore, the book is found after Ezekiel, a book with which it has many literary, thematic, and theological affinities, as it contains visions of what the restored community of faith might be after the painful experience of destruction and displacement. Inasmuch as the book of Daniel is concerned to impart visions of what that community of faith would and should be, Daniel is rightly regarded as a prophet, as he appears in one of the Qumran fragments, Matthew 24:15, and some early Jewish sources.

The differences between the Hebrew text of Daniel and the Greek text are not simply a matter of placement within the canon, however. One important difference is that the Greek text is considerably longer, containing additional materials not found in the Hebrew Bible. These extra sections include (1) the Prayer of Azariah and the Hymn of the Three Jews found after Daniel 3:23; (2) the story of Susanna placed before chapter 1 in some Greek versions but after chapter 12 in others; and (3) the story of Bel and the Dragon placed at the end of the book. These passages, commonly called *Additions to Daniel*, were apparently never a part of the Hebrew text. Despite some reservations about their authenticity by some early Christian interpreters, they were regarded as part of the book of Daniel by the Western Church until the split between the Protestants and the Catholics in the sixteenth century C.E. The Protestants rejected them as apocryphal, but the Catholic Church reaffirmed their authority at the Council of Trent in 1546, designating them as deuterocanonical.

## THE LEGENDARY DANIEL

Daniel, the *persona dramatis* of the book, is first named in 1:6 without any background information whatsoever about his origin. The prophets of the Old Testament are typically introduced by their father's name, profession, or place of origin, but Daniel is simply called "Daniel," without other personal details about him, as if the original reader would have already known who he was.

The book of Ezekiel, a work from the early sixth century B.C.E., mentions a Daniel, along with Noah and Job, as persons of exemplary righteousness (Ezek. 14:14, 20). Daniel was apparently also known to the audience of Ezekiel as a paragon of wisdom, for the arrogant prince of Tyre reportedly believed himself "wiser than Daniel" (Ezek. 28:3). In the book of Jubilees from the second century B.C.E., one reads of a legendary hero named Daniel, a renowned figure from before the Flood (*Jub* 4:20). Such a legendary Daniel from hoary antiquity is not known elsewhere in the Bible. A Daniel, however, is known from a story from the ancient city of Ugarit (present-day Ras Shamra on the Mediterranean coast of Syria) about a man from long ago who trusted his gods and was apparently known for his righteousness and wisdom. The Daniel of Canaanite lore worshiped a god named El (hence the name Daniel, etymologically explained as "My judge is El"). El was depicted in Ugaritic literature as an ancient figure, "the father of years," an epithet that echoes Daniel's vision of the deity as an "Ancient One" (literally "the Ancient of Days"), who sits enthroned as chief god, presiding over the divine court (see Dan. 7:13). In Canaanite mythology, El is consistently depicted as a divine king, whose will was made known to humanity through dreams and visions and whose message was imparted to others through intermediaries. The portrayal of God in the book of Daniel is similar. The legendary Daniel, known from long ago but still remembered as an exemplary character in the exilic period and beyond, serves as the principal human "hero" in the biblical book that now bears his name. In accordance with his reputation from antiquity, he is portrayed as righteous and wise. He is seen as an intermediary who is able to interpret dreams and, thus, convey the will of the transcendent God to humans (so chaps. 1–6). He is also a recipient of visions from on high that are interpreted for him by heavenly intermediaries (so chaps. 7–12).

## THE ORIGIN OF THE BOOK

The traditional attribution of the book to Daniel is a presumption derived from the fact that the accounts of the visions in chapters 7 to 12 are related in the first person. Yet, the first half of the book refers to Daniel in the third person, with the only first-person narrative coming from Nebuchadnezzar in 4:1–27, 34–37. In the latter case, the first-person narrative is unquestionably a literary artifice. In fact, the initial first-person account in chapter 7 is introduced in the third person: "Then he [Daniel] wrote down the dream" (which is then recounted in the rest of the book in the first person).

The traditional view also holds that the book was composed during the period of its historical setting, during the last days of the Babylonian Empire and the early Persian period in the sixth century B.C.E. Such a dating of the book is belied by a number of internal oddities, though, most notably a series of historical problems. First, the book begins by referring to Nebuchadnezzar's invasion of Jerusalem in the third year of the reign of Jehoiakim (609–598 B.C.E.), the year 606 B.C.E. (see 1:1). According to Jeremiah 25:1, however, Nebuchadnezzar did not come to power until the fourth year of Jehoiakim's reign in 605 B.C.E. The one-year difference is admittedly slight and may be accounted for in various ways. More serious is the fact that no attack on Jerusalem by Nebuchadnezzar is recorded prior to 598 B.C.E. (2 Kgs. 24:1–16). Following that attack on Jerusalem, Nebuchadnezzar brought Jehoiakim as a captive to Babylon along with "the vessels of the house of the LORD," which were then put in the palace of Babylon (2 Chr. 36:7; compare Dan. 1:2). The Babylonian Chronicles, which meticulously record the exploits of Nebuchadnezzar, confirm this event in 598 B.C.E. and others like it, but no record exists of an attack on Jerusalem in 606 B.C.E. or thereabouts. The account in Daniel 1:1–2 is difficult to reconcile with all the historical data known from elsewhere in the Bible. Coordinating the information with what is known from extant historical records is also difficult.

Second, the book speaks of King Belshazzar as the successor and son of Nebuchadnezzar (5:1, 2, 30; 7:1). Yet, Belshazzar was not the son of Nebuchadnezzar but of Nabonidus. Nebuchadnezzar was succeeded by his son Amel-Marduk, who ruled for about two years (562–560 B.C.E.), before Neriglissar usurped the throne (560–556 B.C.E.). Neriglissar was briefly succeeded by his son Labashi-Marduk (556 B.C.E.), who was murdered, and his throne was assumed by the usurper Nabonidus (556–539 B.C.E.), the father of Belshazzar. So Belshazzar could not strictly have been the "son" of Nebuchadnezzar, and he was never called "king" in any of the records.

Third, the book speaks of Darius the Mede, the son of Ahasuerus (9:1). According to the book, this Darius became king as the Babylonian Empire fell (5:31) and he organized the kingdom into 120 satraps (6:1), but the historical records make no mention of a Mede named Darius, and the Babylonians were defeated not by the Medes but by the Persians. A Darius in the sixth century—Darius I Hystaspes (522–486 B.C.E.)—like the Darius of the book of Daniel organized the empire into satrapies. Darius I, though, was not a Mede but a Persian, and he is so characterized elsewhere in the Bible (Ezra 4:5, 24; 6:14; Neh. 12:22).

For some interpreters, such discrepancies, if not reconciled or explained away in some fashion, discredit the book altogether, as in the case of the anti-Christian philosopher Porphyry in the third century C.E. Porphyry argued that a book with historical inconsistencies cannot be an inspired or authoritative work. Ironically, traditional scholarship also makes that assumption, thus allowing Porphyry to define the terms of debate. Interpreters of this persuasion concede in effect that the authenticity of the book rides on the accuracy of every last historical detail.

Such an approach may well be valid if the book had been written as a historiographic work, if its purpose were to present a factual account of the Babylonian-Persian period. By the same token, if Shakespeare's play *Julius Caesar*, set in the early period of the Roman Empire but written centuries later, were intended as a historiographic work, one might not think it very reliable. Likewise, if one were to take Leonardo da Vinci's *The Last Supper* to be a historical depiction of the time of Jesus as it really was, one might easily discredit the artist because of the anachronisms and other historical discrepancies in that painting. Still, these works have value, and they do teach something about history. To be sure, certain characters in Shakespeare's play are historically verifiable, but others are purely fictitious. The play should be judged as literature, not history. Its purpose is to entertain, and is compelling to that extent. Similarly, the value of Leonardo da Vinci's painting of the Last Supper is not dependent on the historical precision of the work, for historiography was never its intent. Rather, its purpose was to instruct and inspire. The worth of the painting should be considered in light of its purpose, even if that is not explicitly addressed. So, too, the value of the book of Daniel as scripture does not depend on the historical accuracy of the props on its literary stage, but on the power of its theological message. The authority of the book as scripture lies in its power to inspire and shape the community of faith. The book of Daniel functions as scripture inasmuch as it instructs the community as to the ways of God and the ways that community members should conduct themselves before the sovereign God.

The presence of historical discrepancies by no means suggests that the work is totally devoid of historical information. Indeed, in contrast to the discrepancies in details from the period of its historical setting in the sixth and fifth centuries, the book is remarkably precise in its allusions to certain events in the Ptolemaic and Seleucid periods down to the time just before the death of Antiochus IV Epiphanes, at the end of 164 B.C.E. This is particularly evident in the overview of history in 11:2–45. While this historical recitation paints the Persian and early Hellenistic periods in the broadest strokes, the recitation becomes more and more detailed as it reaches the end. The Persian period is accounted for by way of an awkward reference to four kings ruling after Darius the Mede (11:2), whereas in fact thirteen rulers reigned for over two centuries. Similarly, the epochal conquest of Alexander the Great and the complicated history of the struggle among his successors and various pretenders to the throne are glossed over in merely two verses (11:3–4). By contrast, the history of the conflict between the Seleucids and the Ptolemies is recounted in pedantic detail, virtually every bit of which may be corroborated by other sources (11:5–20). Then the reign of Antiochus IV Epiphanes, a period of about a decade (175–164 B.C.E.), is rehearsed in 11:21–45. The difference is astounding. Whereas the period from the Persian Empire to the immediate successors of Alexander are touched upon in merely three verses, the decade-long reign of Antiochus IV is covered in twenty-four. Clearly, the interests of the passage's author and probably its audience are focused on that decade. That a writer in the sixth century might have been so fuzzy about the historical details of that time but so careful and accurate about events centuries later is difficult to believe. Moreover, whereas the events in the decade leading up to the sacking of the temple in 167 B.C.E. and its immediate aftermath are remarkably accurate (11:21–39), the portrayal of the eventual demise of Antiochus in 11:40–45 is largely at odds with what one knows from other sources. The projected war between the Ptolemies and the Seleucids simply never occurred (11:40–43) and Antiochus did not die in Palestine (see 11:44–45) but in Persia. The conclusion that one should draw from the historical overview in 11:2–45 seems inevitable: that account must have been completed near the end of the reign of Antiochus but some time before his death in December 164 B.C.E., or at least before the information of his death reached Palestine, probably in the spring of 163 B.C.E.

## HOW THE FINAL FORM OF THE BOOK CAME ABOUT

The possibility of a fairly precise date for the last three chapters does not imply that all parts of the book originated in that same period. Indeed, nothing in the first half of Daniel requires a date of origin in the second century. In the first half of the book, the Jews are persecuted, but they seem to have had opportunities to succeed and they apparently harbored hope of positively influencing the government under whose rule they were subject. The foreign despots, while hardly benign, are not necessarily recalcitrant or entirely malevolent. Nebuchadnezzar bows down to Daniel when the former's dream is explained to him (chap. 2), he acknowledges the God of the Jews, issues an edict forbidding blasphemy against that God (chap. 3), and even repents of his ways (chap. 4). Belshazzar rewards Daniel for his interpretation of the mysterious writings on the wall, even though that interpretation is purely a word of doom (chap. 5). Darius the Mede, who is most sympathetic to Daniel, issues a decree that people throughout his domain should tremble before Daniel's God (chap. 6). Moreover, the suffering of the Jews in the first half of Daniel comes not so much from evil rulers as from the fact that the Jews are exiles and minorities in a foreign land. They are persecuted for their religious practices and because of the petty jealousies of their peers, but Daniel and his friends do succeed under the patronage of the foreign kings. Nothing like this type of narrative is found in the second half of the book, where the atrocities are that of a singularly arrogant and evil oppressor, Antiochus Epiphanes.

A review of the book's compositional history must take into consideration its bilingualism, namely, the fact that 1:1–2:4a and 8:1–12:13 are in Hebrew, but 2:4b–7:28 are in Aramaic. A number of scholars have proposed plausibly that most of the court tales of Daniel 1–6 once circulated independently in the late Persian and early Hellenistic periods. The accounts may also contain significant elements from earlier sources, but the stories themselves were probably already known in substantially their present forms by the late fourth or early third century. Such a dating is corroborated to some extent by the linguistic evidence. In general, the Aramaic of this portion of Daniel appears to be typologically more advanced than the Aramaic of the sixth and fifth centuries and possibly even of the Aramaic of the Samaria Papyri from the first half of the fourth century, but the Aramaic is more conservative than the dialects dating from 200 B.C.E. onward. The presence of three Greek loanwords in the book (all in chapter 3) does not contradict this dating, for Greek loanwords are well attested in Aramaic inscriptions from Palestine already in the late Persian period.

Daniel 7, which is also written in Aramaic, has some obvious literary and thematic connections with the Aramaic passages of chapters 2–6. Indeed, distinct echoes appear in chapter 7 of the dreams of Nebuchadnezzar in chapters 2 and 4 and the vision of Belshazzar in chapter 5. The chronological sequence followed through Daniel 1–6 is broken, however, as the vision of Daniel begins with the first year of the reign of Belshazzar, whose death is already accounted for at the end of chapter 5. Thus, chapter 7 seems, on the one hand, extraneous to chapters 1–6 and, on the other hand, deliberately linked to them. Even though chapter 7 picks up on the scheme of four regimes in chapter 2, the four regimes referred to in Daniel 7 are not the four regimes within the chronological framework of Daniel 1–6 (that is, Nebuchadnezzar, Belshazzar, Darius the Mede, and Cyrus) but four empires, the fourth being the Hellenistic domain out of which eventually came the "little horn," a reference to Antiochus Epiphanes. The most likely explanation for this discrepancy is that Daniel 7 is a reinterpretation of the vision in Daniel 2 in the light of the atrocities perpetrated by Antiochus.

The existence of a collection comprising the Aramaic portions of the book seems likely, with Daniel 7 being the latest component added to that collection, perhaps to provide a new interpretive context for the narratives. Beyond that conclusion, one might speculate that a Hebrew composition constituting the bulk of chapters 8–12 was subsequently added to the Aramaic anthology, with literary and theological cues coming from chapter 7. Whereas chapter 7 is cosmic and implicit, however, chapter 8 is nationalistic and explicit. Indeed, chapter 8 represents a specific application of the mythological symbols in chapter 7. From here on out, the visions are much more directly concerned not with the exploits of individual Jews in the dispersion, as in chapters 1–6, but with the survival of the Jewish people and their faith in the face of the greatest threat to confront them since the destruction of Jerusalem in the sixth century.

This threat of a loss of national identity may account for the linguistic shift from Aramaic, still the language of international relations in those days, to the rejuvenated national language of the Jewish people. The author of the Hebrew composition in 8:1–12:4, thus, added the new materials to the earlier Aramaic anthology (2:4b–7:28). In addition, a Hebrew introduction (1:1–2:4a) has been put at the beginning. Finally, to this whole work, a postscript (12:5–13) was later added (probably some time in the spring of 163 B.C.E.) to update the final revelation in 10:1–12:4.

## LITERARY GENRES

The first six chapters of the book comprise a series of narratives about the encounters of Jews in the foreign court. As such, the beginning of Daniel is similar to two other biblical stories: the story of Joseph in the court of Pharaoh in Egypt and the story of Esther in the Persian court. One may, indeed, think of the narratives in Daniel in terms of these two variations of the tales of Jews in the foreign court. As in the Joseph story, chapters 2, 4, and 5 tell of a triumph of a lowly and forgotten captive over the established experts in the interpretation of divine mysteries in the land of his sojourning. In each case, the challenge is posed in the form of a mystery that troubles the foreign king, the mystery coming in the form of dreams in the Joseph story and in Daniel 2 and 4, and in the form of an ominous inscription on the wall in Daniel 5. None of the king's experts is able to solve the problem. Rather, the lowly captive brings the resolution through wisdom that is divinely granted. In consequence, the captive sage is rewarded.

As in the Esther story, chapters 3 and 6 concern a threat of death that is brought about when the Jews are set up by outsiders. The crisis in Daniel 3 evolved because faithful Jews would not bow down to any symbol of power except their God, a situation reminiscent of Mordecai's refusal to bow down before another human being. In Daniel 6, the issue is that a faithful Jew would continue the practice of his faith regardless of a governmental prohibition. In both stories, the faithful Jews are restored and even rewarded.

Befitting an introduction, Daniel 1 reflects elements of both variations of the genre. Distinct echoes of the Joseph story are present in the account about youthful captives who survive through their God-given wisdom, as are reminiscences of Esther in the motif of the captives' refusal to compromise their identity even in the face of grave danger. Like the faithful Jews in both the Joseph and Esther stories, therefore, the captives in Daniel 1 are rewarded.

Taken together, these tales of the Jews in the foreign court offer a sort of anthology of various situations that the faithful may encounter as a people living under foreign domination. The Jews in these stories are a people that have no power except through whatever gifts they may receive from their God and their faith in the power of God to deliver them. Their rulers may be autocratic, as Nebuchadnezzar and Belshazzar were, or they may be more like Darius, who was generally benign but lacking the courage to stand up to political pressures. The autocrats may be open to change, like Nebuchadnezzar, or they may be recalcitrant, like Belshazzar. Sympathetic foreign officials, like the wardens charged with supervision of the young captives in chapter 1, may appear, but pressures also exist for the majority in the population to conform to the imperialist demand of the captors, as in chapter 3, or the malicious schemes of jealous colleagues, as in chapter 6. Such is life for a minority people trying to live out their faith under the domination of others. These stories in Daniel 1–6 offer an assurance that faithfulness amid such trials is not only possible but necessary, for the power of God may indeed be manifest through the faithful lives of God's suffering servants.

When one moves beyond the first six chapters, however, one encounters not a variety of situations but one: an environment of terrible oppression by an arrogant and blasphemous tyrant. Here, too, a reader finds a very different genre of literature. Chapters 7 through 12 offer a distinct focus on cosmic realities, expressed in the idioms and symbolisms of myth—that is, language and symbolisms about the conflict of supramundane powers of order and chaos. A persistent emphasis emerges on the disclosure, if only incompletely, of heavenly plans. This type of literature is best exemplified in the New Testament in the Apocalypse of John (that is, the book of Revelation), the word "apocalypse" being derived from the Greek noun meaning "revelation." Since a number of such texts are attested in antiquity (mostly from 200 B.C.E. to 300 C.E.), scholars have been able to identify the primary characteristics of such literature, the most important being (1) use of first person in the account of visions, typically in the name of a pseudonymous seer; (2) coded language, such as animal symbolisms and numerology; (3) interpretation of visions by celestial intermediaries; (4) the periodization of history, culminating in decisive triumph of good over evil; and (5) emphasis on the disclosure of divine mystery. All these traits are present in Daniel 7–12.

Such writings typically originated with groups that perceive themselves to be disenfranchised and powerless in the face of overwhelming evil. Hence hope beyond the limitations of this world is emphasized. The apocalyptic thinkers of antiquity pointed beyond mundane and temporal realities in order to provide a meaningful theological perspective on history. The overwhelming presence of evil in the world prompted them to conclude that this world may not be the only arena in which God acts. History seemed to be marching on inexorably, as if the power of God were not a factor at all, only human power, machinations, alliances, and intrigues.

In the face of such a crisis of theological confidence, the author of Daniel reconsiders history. To the author, evil, which seems to dominate this world, has taken on cosmic proportions. Indeed, creation seems to have been undone, the chaotic monsters of the world seem to have been unleashed once again, and God seems to have lost all dominion, as even a mere "little horn" like Antiochus dares to impose his arrogant reign of terror on the world (Dan. 7). Recalling the ancient myth of a rebellion in heaven, the author speaks of the rise of Antiochus in terms of a daring ascent to take the place of the Most High in the heavenly council, even sweeping down some of the hosts of heaven in the process; Antiochus dares to march against Jerusalem, long considered by Israel to symbolize the abiding presence of God, desecrating the sanctuary and imposing a sanction on religious festivities (Dan. 8). Jeremiah's prophecy of the end of desolation after seventy years has to be radically reinterpreted to mean seventy jubilee periods (Dan. 9). History is allowed to run its course. Then, at the climax of the visions—in the last revelation to the seer (Dan. 10–12)—one finds an overview of events leading up to the time of Antiochus. That history gives the impression that human decisions and actions determined all that is happening: humans scheme and plot as they strive to assert control over one another. Yet, the account is preceded by an assertion that celestial powers represent the people of God and they are arrayed against their counterparts representing the other nations (10:20–21). The entire historical recitation is dubbed a documentation of "truth," the word "truth" being one used of the faithfulness of God (11:2). Those introductory notices provide the theological lens for reading the overview: despite the impression that the historical overview makes, the battles are being fought not only on earth, but also in heaven. So the recitation ends as it begins with the appearance of the angel Michael, Israel's protector, who is expected to deliver those who are still alive at the end (12:1). Yet even those who are not alive would not be left out, for there is hope beyond life in this world and time—there is the possibility of resurrection (12:2).

## THE OCCASION OF THE BOOK

Whatever its literary history, the book of Daniel in substantially its present form was almost doubtlessly completed during the reign of Antiochus Epiphanes. Although he had been sent to Rome in 189 B.C.E., following the defeat of his father by the Romans, Antiochus rose to become king in 175 B.C.E. through a series of improbable coincidences (see commentary at 11:21–39). Then Jason, the treacherous brother of the High Priest Onias III, came to Antiochus with an offer to buy the high priesthood for a substantial sum of money, with a promise to turn Jerusalem into a Hellenist polis (1 Macc. 1:10–15; 2 Macc. 4:7–22). Strapped for funds to pay the hefty indemnity to Rome and to defray the expenses for his military adventures, Antiochus eagerly agreed. His commitment to the deal was only good until a higher bid came along, however. When Menelaus, a subordinate of Jason, later offered the king a higher prize for the high priesthood, Antiochus seized that new opportunity. So Menelaus became the high priest, embezzling funds from the temple to pay his patron (2 Macc. 4:23–32). When Onias tried to expose him, Menelaus had him assassinated (2 Macc. 4:33–34; compare Dan. 9:26). That year was 171 B.C.E., regarded by the author of the book as the beginning of the desolation of the sanctuary and the end of legitimate sacrifice, a period of desolation that would last about twenty-three hundred days—until the rededication of the temple in December 164 B.C.E. (8:13–14), probably the beginning of the last week of years alluded to in 9:27. Meanwhile, Antiochus became increasingly atrocious in his acts. Following his attack on Egypt in 169 B.C.E., he invaded Jerusalem to rob the temple to meet his financial needs (1 Macc. 1:15, 20–28, 63), the allusion from Daniel 11:28. The following year, he attacked Egypt again, although it would not be "as it was before" (11:29). This time, he was humiliated by the Romans and forced to withdraw (11:30). Jason, upon hearing rumors that Antiochus was dead, revolted (2 Macc. 5:5–10). Already enraged by his public humiliation at the hands of the Romans, Antiochus ordered merciless reprisal (11:30; compare 2 Macc. 5:15–17). His mercenary troops stormed the city, massacring its inhabitants. The fortification was razed and in its place a citadel called the Akra was erected overlooking the temple mount and defended by Gentile mercenaries and renegade Jews (1 Macc. 1:33–35). The temple was desecrated. An altar to Zeus Olympius was set up, upon which a pig was reportedly sacrificed. The Jews were forbidden to keep the Sabbath or celebrate the festivals (1 Macc. 1:45–46; 2 Macc. 5:6). Torah scrolls were desecrated (1 Macc. 1:56; compare probably Dan. 8:12). The desolation that began with the murder of Onias at the beginning of the last week of years (171 B.C.E.) has now reached its nadir midway through that "week" of years, 167 B.C.E. (see Dan. 9:27). In response to that crisis, the author composed the apocalypse that is now in the latter half of the book, combining it with the anthology of stories of exiled Jews in foreign courts.

The anonymous author is probably to be associated with those referred to in the book as *maśkîlîm* "the wise" (1:4 [NRSV "versed"]; 11:33, 35; 12:3, 10), apparently promoters of understanding and insight. Verbs of the same root also appear several times in the book (1:17; 7:8; 9:13, 22, 25). From elsewhere in the Bible, one gathers that a *maśkîl* is one who seeks God (Pss. 14:2; 53:2), trusts God (Prov. 16:20), is thoughtful regarding the weak (Ps. 41:1) and prudent in speech and action (Prov. 10:5, 19; 14:35; 17:2; 19:14; 21:12; Amos 5:13). The *maśkîlîm* appear to be people without power of their own; whatever power or success they have, they have only by the will of God (1 Sam. 18:14–15) or through the trust they gain from those in power (Prov. 14:35). Daniel and his friends are portrayed as *maśkîlîm* in all these senses. Furthermore, one gathers from 11:32–33 that the *maśkîlîm* in the second century B.C.E. are distinguished from those who betray the covenant with God, namely, the renegade Jews who side with the Seleucids. Yet they may not necessarily be identified with those loyal to God who "stand firm and take action" (11:32), a probable allusion to the active-resistance movement known as the *ḥăsîdîm* (1 Macc. 2:42; 7:13–17). The distinction is suggested by the disjunction at the beginning of 11:33, a disjunction not rendered in NRSV: "*But* as for the *maśkîlîm* among people, they will bring understanding to many . . ." (author's translation, emphasis added). Although sharing with the *ḥăsîdîm* a commitment to the traditional Jewish faith and practices (1 Macc. 1:62–64; 2:29–38), the *maśkîlîm* apparently did not follow the way of zealotry. Rather, apart from their role in promoting understanding, they are described in entirely passive terms in 11:33–35: they fall, they are in captivity and plundered for days, they are helped a little, they are joined by others, and they are to be refined, purified, and cleansed. Their model of faithful conduct may have been the suffering servant in Isaiah 40–55, the faithful servant of God who would act prudently (*yaśkîl*) even amid great suffering in order that "many" who witness that steadfast faithfulness might also perceive and understand (see Isa. 52:13; 41:20). So, too, Daniel expects the *maśkîlîm* to stumble, even as the suffering servant is expected to stumble (Isa. 59:10, 14). Yet, these *maśkîlîm* will be vindicated, even if they should die, for they will lead many to righteousness (Dan. 12:3), just as the suffering servant will "make many righteous" (Isa. 53:11). Indeed, they will shine brightly like stars in the sky (Dan. 12:3), even as it is said of the suffering servant: "Out of his suffering one will see light" (author's translation of Isa. 53:11, according to readings in the Qumran manuscripts and the Greek version).

## THEOLOGICAL PERSPECTIVE

The reader has a preliminary glimpse of the theological perspective of the book in the introductory chapter, for the Hebrew text identifies a threefold giving by God: God *gave* (NRSV "let . . . fall") King Jehoiakim of Judah into the hand of Nebuchadnezzar (1:2); God also literally *gave* Daniel "to grace and mercies" (1:9; NRSV "allowed . . . to receive favor and compassion"); and God *gave* Daniel and his friends the "knowledge and skill" that allowed them to preserve their faith (1:17). This emphasis on God's giving at the outset should immediately signal that the book is primarily about God's power and activity and only secondarily about any human model of excellence. Daniel and his friends succeed only because God has given them "to grace and mercies" and God had given them the wherewithal to cope with their challenges with their faith intact. The sovereignty of God implies complete divine freedom, for the God who gave people into a situation of suffering (1:2), presumably as a divine judgment of sin (see 9:4–19), is also the God who delivers them from their terrible plight (1:9, 17); the God of judgment is at once the God of grace.

The theme of the sovereignty of God, introduced at the very beginning of the book, is one that recurs in the book, where the deity is repeatedly called "the God of gods" (2:47; 11:36), "the Lord of kings" (2:47), and "the Most High God" (3:26; 4:2, 17, 24, 25, 32, 34; 5:18, 21; 7:18, 22, 25 [twice], 27). That sovereign God is the one who gives kingship and power and glory "to whom[ever] he will[s]" (4:17, 25, 32; 5:21). On the one hand, divine sovereignty means that all human powers, even the oppressive and wicked ones—like the autocratic Nebuchadnezzar (1:1; 2:37, 38; 4:25, 31), the sacrilegious Belshazzar (5:18, 21), and the evil Antiochus Epiphanes—derive their power ultimately from the divine Sovereign (see 2:21; 4:17, 25, 32; 5:21). On the other hand, divine sovereignty also means that God may give power even to the powerless, indeed, to the lowliest of mortals (2:47; 4:17, 25). Indeed, through the lowly and seemingly powerless God's reign may be manifest on earth, if only in an incomplete way.

Arguably the most poignant portrayal of divine sovereignty in the book is the vision described in 7:9–10. The setting is that of a heavenly assembly room where thrones are set in place, the allusion being made here to the notion of the divine council known in ancient Canaanite mythology but also in earlier biblical literature (1 Kgs. 22:19, 23; Isa. 6:1–13; 40:1–11). Yet, only the Ancient One takes his throne; no mention of other gods in this celestial court is made, only a plurality of thrones. At issue in the chapter is the monstrosity of evil power that has become so overwhelming, as if the forces of chaos are threatening once again to dominate the world. Yet the text affirms that sovereign God is still firmly in control in the court, even if some of those monsters will continue to be around for "a season and a time" (7:12). The threat of chaos in the world will not yet be eliminated completely, but it will be watched, contained, and countered in the interim.

The agent through whom the divine Sovereign will counter the persistent threat of evil will come "with the clouds of heaven" (7:13). In Canaanite mythology as in the Bible, the imagery of one who comes in a cloud is used to depict divine appearance to deliver people in distress (Deut. 33:26; Pss. 18:10; 68:4, 33; 104:3; Isa. 19:1). Yet, the text is clear that this one who comes with the clouds of heaven appears not as a deity but as a mortal, literally, "one like a son of man"—someone who unexpectedly receives God's special attention and care (Pss. 8:5; 144:3; Job 25:6), someone from whom one does not ordinarily expect salvation (Ps. 146:3). Yet, to him, this mere mortal, "dominion and glory and kingship" are given. Not only that, in contrast to the temporal reign of the kings of the empires (see Dan. 7:12), what is given to this mortal champion will be enduring: it shall not pass away and it shall never be destroyed (7:14). The Aramaic vocabulary here is suggestive. Unlike the dominion of kings that shall be made to pass away (2:21; 4:31; 5:20; 7:12), this particular dominion will not pass away. Moreover, unlike the tree symbolizing Nebuchadnezzar's arrogant power that is destroyed (4:23), this reign is like the reign of God that "shall never be destroyed" (6:26).

The doxology in which those words affirming the indestructibility of God's reign are found comes at the heels of Daniel's survival in the lions' den. Darius praises "the living God" (6:26) and affirms the eternal, everlasting character of God's reign precisely because Daniel, who is called the "servant of the living God" (6:20) has survived, for God has sent an angel to shut the mouth of the lions so that they could not "hurt" or "harm" him (vv. 22, 23; both words translate the same Aramaic verb rendered as "destroy"). That is, the "indestructibility" of the servant of the living God (6:20) is evidence of the indestructible reign of the living God (6:26). The survival of the faithful, if ever so vulnerable, servants of God is testimony to the eternal character of the reign of God! Indeed, the eternal reign of the sovereign God is manifest not in the power of the world's rulers but in the survival of faith.

This view of the indestructible reign of God is in accord with the characterization of the regime that God will set up instead of the worldly regimes that come and pass away, an eternal regime "that shall never be destroyed" (2:44). That regime, the fifth one in Nebuchadnezzar's dream in chapter 2, is symbolized by the stone hewn not by human hands from a mountain (2:45), a mountain that, in the prophecy of a prophet of the exile (Isa. 51:1–2), yields the displaced people of God: the exiles are hewn from the mountain that is Abraham and Sarah. To Daniel, these displaced ones represent the abiding reign of God, even if they are powerless and lowly. Indeed, as Daniel would have it, they who are hewn from the mountain without human hands will grow to be a great mountain that fills all the earth (2:35). Chapter 2 ends with Nebuchadnezzar, who is called "king of kings," confessing Daniel's God as "God of gods" and "Lord of kings" (2:47). Indeed, the "king of kings" falls upon his face, as a statue might (compare 1 Sam. 5:1–5), doing obeisance before Daniel the lowly exile (Dan. 2:46–47). In the king's gesture, the prophecy is already coming to pass: imperial kingship collapses before the "stone" hewn not by human hands, and that stone immediately begins to grow, for Daniel is promoted and his friends with him (2:48–49). The stone does not yet fill the earth, but prophecy has been set in motion for the sovereign God to transfer "the kingdom, the power, the might, and the glory" (2:37) from imperial ruler to God's lowly servant. The God who makes kings pass away (NRSV "deposes kings") and "sets up kings" (2:21) has, indeed, given power to Daniel, apparently power as manifested in his wisdom and insight (2:23).

In Daniel 7, the power that will not pass away and will never be destroyed is given to the one who comes with the clouds, now a demythologized figure that is incarnated, as it were, in human form, as "a son of man," who comes to the presence of the deity and is presented before the deity (7:13). Yet, when the vision is interpreted in 7:18, an individual is not the one who receives the eternal reign but "the holy ones of the Most High," and that point is reiterated in 7:22, which affirms that judgment has been rendered in favor of "the holy ones" and that they are the ones who receive kingship. Thus, the agent of God's will has not only been demythologized; the agent of God has been democratized. The one is the many; the many are the one. The equation of the singular one who is like a mortal with plural "holy ones" seems odd, for the designations "holy ones" and "holy one" have, up to this point in the book, always referred to celestial beings, members of the heavenly host of the Most High (4:13, 17, 23). So, too, the "holy one" in 8:13 would refer to a member of the divine entourage in heaven. Yet the text speaks of the war that Antiochus would wage against "the holy ones" (7:21) and he would prevail over and overcome these "holy ones" (7:21, 25). In any case, by the time one gets to 7:27, one reads of "the people of the holy ones of the Most High." Here it seems that the identities of the celestial holy ones and the terrestrial holy ones (the people of God) have virtually coalesced, the latter being understood as a reflex of the former, a microcosm of the heavenly macrocosm. The champion who comes with the clouds of heaven has first been demythologized, for the divine rider of clouds has been identified as one who comes as a mortal. Then that same figure is democratized and "remythologized," as it were, so that that one who comes is now symbolic of the people, who are being identified with the celestial host!

The purpose of this bold theological move is not merely to exalt the Jewish people. Rather, and more importantly, that identification of the celestial with the terrestrial conveys in a powerful way heaven's involvement with earth. Thus, the encroachment of the little horn against Jerusalem is portrayed, again in terms reminiscent of mythology, as a rebellious act against the Most High and the host of heaven, and the earthly victory of the invader is expressed as the casting down of "some of the host and some of the stars" (8:9–10). Despite the mythological language, the allusion is clearly to the defeat of the defenders of the Jewish faith (8:12–14), as further explication in the chapter makes plain: the victims of the attack are called "the people of the holy ones" (8:24), but also "numerous" (v. 24, NRSV "the powerful") and the "many" (v. 25), a pair of words that elsewhere characterize the people of God (Exod. 1:9) but also the celestial host (Joel 2:11). The point is that atrocities like those committed by Antiochus are not merely committed against mortals, they touch even the heavens; they involve the heavenly host, the commander of the (heavenly) host (Dan. 8:11), even the commander of the commanders of the host prince (8:25). The divine realm is certainly not above the fray! For the author of the apocalyptic visions in Daniel, the celestial commanders of the host are very much involved with their earthly counterparts in their struggle against the forces of chaos and destruction, the principalities and the powers, whether mundane or supramundane (10:13–21). Thus, even if history seems to be dictated by human alliances, schemes and intrigues (11:2–45), divine forces are nevertheless fighting for the good of humanity and protecting God's people (see 12:1). God alone is sovereign of history—the one who determines times and seasons (2:21; 7:12)—and God is intimately and actively involved with humanity in their struggles, as they face the terrors of this world.

God is certainly holy and transcendent in the book of Daniel, for God is repeatedly called "the King of heaven" (4:37), "the Lord of heaven" (5:23), "the God of heaven" (2:18, 19, 37, 44), "God in heaven" (2:28), or even, simply, "Heaven" (4:26). Yet that transcendence did not imply a

God too remote to be concerned with human affairs. Indeed, the text makes a point of contrasting the theology of the outsiders who know of the power of divine beings but do not believe that they are with mortals on earth (2:10–12) with the notion that Daniel's God, the God of heaven, nevertheless deigns to intervene on behalf of mortals on earth (2:18–23).

The transcendent God does reveal divine mysteries to humans and God does respond to the plight of mortals on earth, although faith in God is not predicated upon God's ability to do so. As the friends of Daniel insist to Nebuchadnezzar, even in the face of death, "If our God whom we serve is able to deliver us from the furnace of blazing fire and out of your hand, O king, let him deliver us. But if not, be it known to you, O king, that we will not serve your gods and we will not worship the golden statue that you have set up" (3:17–18). Worship of God is not utilitarian, and God is wholly free to deliver or not to deliver. In that case, of course, God does intervene wondrously on behalf of the faithful, for while the Jews were in the fiery furnace, a divine being—literally one like the appearance of a son of the gods—appeared with them in the midst of the fire. The imagery is poignant, for the text does not speak of deliverance *from* the fire but that a divine being—God's surrogate presence—is literally with those who are endangered; God is with them *in* the fire. So, too, in the story of Daniel in the lions' pit: God sent an intermediary into the pit to keep Daniel from destruction (6:22, 23). In that reliable divine involvement in life's trials and tribulations, people of faith can be assured that the reign of God, even if it is not fully realized in one's own time and place—even if it is not evident by earthly expectations of power—will never pass away and will never be destroyed. On the contrary, God's reign will continue to grow until it fills all the earth (compare Acts 1:8). No promise of ease in life is made, no assurance of freedom from trials and tribulations, no removal of the threat of terror and death—only a hope held out of vindication even after death, a resurrection hope (12:1–4). Though the kingdom is already in some sense here and already given to those hewn from the mountain not by human hands, the kingdom is still not yet. One can understand because God has revealed (12:10), yet still not fully understand (12:8). In the meantime, one can only live life even in "a time of anguish" and pray for deliverance (12:1), perhaps in the words of the quintessential "Son of Man" in the Bible, who taught his followers to pray to a transcendent God, a God who is in heaven: "And lead us not into temptation, but deliver us from evil: For thine is the kingdom, and the power, and the glory, for ever. Amen" (Matt. 6:13, KJV).

# 1. Daniel and His Friends at the Babylonian Court
## *Daniel 1:1–21*

**1 In the third year of the reign of King Jehoiakim of Judah, King
Nebuchadnezzar of Babylon came to Jerusalem and besieged it. 2 The Lord
let King Jehoiakim of Judah fall into his power, as well as some of the vessels of the house of God. These he brought to the land of Shinar, and placed
the vessels in the treasury of his gods.**

**3 Then the king commanded his palace master Ashpenaz to bring some
of the Israelites of the royal family and of the nobility, 4 young men without
physical defect and handsome, versed in every branch of wisdom, endowed
with knowledge and insight, and competent to serve in the king's palace;
they were to be taught the literature and language of the Chaldeans. 5 The
king assigned them a daily portion of the royal rations of food and wine.
They were to be educated for three years, so that at the end of that time
they could be stationed in the king's court. 6 Among them were Daniel,
Hananiah, Mishael, and Azariah, from the tribe of Judah. 7 The palace master gave them other names: Daniel he called Belteshazzar, Hananiah he
called Shadrach, Mishael he called Meshach, and Azariah he called
Abednego.**

**8 But Daniel resolved that he would not defile himself with the royal
rations of food and wine; so he asked the palace master to allow him not
to defile himself. 9 Now God allowed Daniel to receive favor and compassion from the palace master. 10 The palace master said to Daniel, "I am
afraid of my lord the king; he has appointed your food and your drink. If he
should see you in poorer condition than the other young men of your own
age, you would endanger my head with the king." 11 Then Daniel asked the
guard whom the palace master had appointed over Daniel, Hananiah,
Mishael, and Azariah: 12 "Please test your servants for ten days. Let us be
given vegetables to eat and water to drink. 13 You can then compare our
appearance with the appearance of the young men who eat the royal
rations, and deal with your servants according to what you observe." 14 So
he agreed to this proposal and tested them for ten days. 15 At the end of ten
days it was observed that they appeared better and fatter than all the young**

**men who had been eating the royal rations. [16]So the guard continued to withdraw their royal rations and the wine they were to drink, and gave them vegetables. [17]To these four young men God gave knowledge and skill in every aspect of literature and wisdom; Daniel also had insight into all visions and dreams.**

**[18]At the end of the time that the king had set for them to be brought in, the palace master brought them into the presence of Nebuchadnezzar,**
**[19]and the king spoke with them. And among them all, no one was found to compare with Daniel, Hananiah, Mishael, and Azariah; therefore they were stationed in the king's court. [20]In every matter of wisdom and understanding concerning which the king inquired of them, he found them ten times better than all the magicians and enchanters in his whole kingdom. [21]And Daniel continued there until the first year of King Cyrus.**

Chapter 1 serves as an introduction to the stories of Daniel and his friends in chapters 1–6 and, one may argue, even as an introduction to the entire book (see the introduction on "How the Final Form of the Book Came About"). Daniel 1 sets the stage for the narrator to begin addressing the question of how God may continue to function in and through history, even though history seems to have failed as the obvious arena of divine activity. At the outset, the narrator locates the story in a particular historical setting, namely, the Babylonian captivity (vv. 1–2). Indeed, the entire chapter is framed by two chronological notices (vv. 1, 21). The book begins with the third year of Jehoiakim's reign (606 B.C.E.) when, according to the narrator, the captivity began; chapter 1 ends with the first year of the reign of Cyrus (539 B.C.E.), the ruler of the Medes and Persians, who brought about the fall of the Babylonian Empire. That period, too, is presumed by the first half of the book, where the events are set within four reigns, beginning with Nebuchadnezzar in chapter 1 and ending with a mention of the reign of Cyrus in chapter 6. The Edict of Cyrus (see 2 Chr. 36:22–23; Ezra 1:1–4), issued in the first year of his reign, set in motion the return of the Jews from their exile in Babylon. Daniel the faithful Jew will still be around when the mighty Nebuchadnezzar is long gone.

Within that chronological framework an important theological affirmation recurs, although that fact is obscured in most English translations. The narrator claims that the God who literally *gave* (NRSV "let") Jehoiakim into the hand of Nebuchadnezzar (v. 2) also *gave* (NRSV "allowed") Daniel literally "to grace and mercies" (v. 9) and *gave* the four young men "knowledge and skill" to cope with their predicament before the Babylonian king (v. 17). God's sovereign will and power, as expressed in this threefold giving, is the theological thread that holds the literary unit together. One gathers, therefore, that the God who brought about the exile is the very same one who enabled Daniel and his friends to survive and even to thrive amid a hostile environment. The God of judgment is, paradoxically, also the God of grace. The opening chapter of Daniel is first and foremost about God's sovereignty and freedom and only secondarily about a model of righteous and faithful human conduct.

## HISTORICAL SETTING AND A THEOLOGICAL PROBLEM Daniel 1:1–2

The stories in the book of Daniel are set in the context of Israel's defeat and consequent exile. The details of that historical setting are, however, difficult to coordinate with other biblical passages (2 Kgs. 24:1–25:20; 2 Chr. 36:5–21; Jer. 39:1–40:6; 52:1–34) and extrabiblical sources for a number of reasons:

1. According to other passages in the Bible, Nebuchadnezzar did not officially begin to reign until the fourth year of Jehoiakim's reign.
2. Although Babylonian records indicate that Nebuchadnezzar led a number of expeditions into Palestine when he was a crown prince, no attack on Jerusalem is mentioned.
3. All sources indicate a siege of Jerusalem in 597 B.C.E., during the reign not of Jehoiakim but of Jehoiachin and then, again, in 586 B.C.E., long after Jehoiakim had died.

Such discrepancies prompted the third-century (C.E.) philosopher Porphyry and his intellectual successors to question the historical veracity of the book altogether, while apologists (both ancient and modern) have proffered various ways to harmonize the data. The notice in verses 1–2 appears, however, to be merely a telescoping of various events that led up to the eventual dispersion of the Israelites in the sixth century. In any case, the notice serves its purpose well by providing a narrative setting to tell the stories of individuals who are trying to live out their convictions in a world dominated by those who do not share their faith. It is a world in which the will of God is difficult to discern in the face of seemingly insurmountable political power. At all events, the significance of the historical context is ultimately not to provide one with raw historical data for the sake of knowledge alone. Rather, its significance is primarily theological. The narrative suggests that God's will is being worked out amid the messiness of human history, even when the experience of exile and oppression obscure that will.

The humiliation that Jerusalem suffered at the hands of the

Babylonians in the sixth century brought about an unparalleled theological crisis. Jerusalem, long portrayed as the abode of Israel's God, was besieged and sacked by a foreign army, worshipers of a pagan god. What's more, Nebuchadnezzar, whose name bears the name of the Babylonian god Nabu (Nebo in Isa. 46:1), was the victorious conqueror of the city. Unlike the besieging of the city by the Assyrians at the end of the eighth century B.C.E. (2 Kgs. 18:13–20:19; Isa. 36–37), there was no miraculous deliverance, no reprieve for Judah in the sixth. The invaders entered the city in 586 B.C.E., and the sacred vessels in the temple that were not destroyed were carried away to a distant land (see 2 Chr. 36:5–6), where they were subsequently desecrated (see Dan. 5:2–3, 23). According to the narrator, the Babylonian conqueror had taken these vessels—veritable emblems of divine presence in Israel—from "the house of God" and brought them to his homeland and placed them in "the house of *his* god" and "the house of the treasury of *his* god" (1:2 author's translation, emphasis added). The repetition of the word "house" (three times) and "his god" (twice), evident in the Hebrew text but not in the Greek versions followed by NRSV, underscores the theological crisis that this event created for those who believed in the God of Israel and Judah. The twofold reference to "his god" stands over against "the God" of the Jerusalem temple. The vessels from the house of God are now in the house of Nebuchadnezzar's god and, indeed, they have been ignominiously relegated to the house of the treasury of that god. More than a military defeat for the nation, therefore, Nebuchadnezzar's aggression posed a profound theological problem. This precise theological problem, highlighted by the Hebrew wordplay at the outset, indicates how one is to read the chapter and the rest of the book. The opening words suggest that this story—and, indeed, the entire book of Daniel—is not so much about human beings, faithful and heroic though some of them may be, but about God's will and power in world history.

The narrator asserts that it was the Lord who literally *gave* (NRSV "let") Jehoiakim king of Judah into the hands of Nebuchadnezzar (v. 2), meaning that Israel's God was really in control of the whole operation, despite the awesome and overwhelming power of the Babylonian king, worshiper of Nabu. This response to destruction in Israel is conventional. To those suffering in exile, however, such a claim probably would have sounded hollow in the face of reality, unless God could be shown to be still in control and quietly at work behind the scenes. Here, as Calvin appropriately observed long ago, the narrator is asserting the providence and judgment of the sovereign God: God intentionally gave Jehoiakim (and his people) into the power of an outsider! That narrator would, in fact, return to other aspects of the sovereign God's *giving* as the story unfolds (vv. 9, 17).

Nebuchadnezzar's homeland is called "the land of Shinar" (v. 2), a reference to the southeastern region of present-day Iraq. That region had the reputation of being a place of idolatry and general wickedness (Zech. 5:11). Arrogant humans once endeavored to construct direct access to God there by erecting the infamous tower of Babel (Gen. 11:1–9). They could not, of course, reach their objective in heaven, despite all their efforts. Instead, the deity descended from heaven to punish them for their sinful arrogance and, in consequence, humanity was scattered and people no longer spoke one common language as before. Now, however, Nebuchadnezzar King of Babylon (the Hebrew has, literally, "king of Babel") is trying to show God up. Nebuchadnezzar comes from Babel to Jerusalem and seizes the sacred vessels from God's house. Military power dares to defy the power of God. The king of Babel even tries to reverse the consequences of God's judgment at Babel by imposing a common language on one and all (v. 4). God had willed the dispersion of people from Babel, according to Genesis 11, but Nebuchadnezzar brings them back to the land of Shinar. God had willed many languages, but Nebuchadnezzar would have them learn the language of Babylon (Babel). Anyone familiar with the tower of Babel story, as the original audience of Daniel no doubt was, would surely wonder how God would respond to this new challenge to the divine will from the king of Babel. Thus, the primary theological question that the book addresses is laid out immediately, if only implicitly, in verses 1 and 2: How will the will of God be fulfilled in the face of such a manifestation of arrogant and hostile human power?

## OPPORTUNITIES AND TEMPTATIONS TO COMPROMISE Daniel 1:3–8

There is a modern ring to the story in verses 3–8. The triumphant imperialist government offers scholarships to the brightest and the best among the vanquished. This act is clearly not one of pure generosity, for the scholarships are reserved for those who are most likely to benefit the government directly. The opportunity would be given only to the elite, specifically, young men who are physically in the best condition and who are already intellectually equipped to benefit the government—"to serve in the king's palace" (v. 4). These youngsters are to be "without physical defect," the same condition required of those who are dedicated to God's service as priests (Lev. 21:16–24) and of animals offered up to God as sacrifice (Lev. 22:19–21). Apparently, Nebuchadnezzar expects that the Israelites who are brought before him should be of the same quality as those presented before Israel's God. Importantly, these youngsters are also described as *maśkîlîm* (NRSV "versed"), a term that is used later in the book for those who are "wise" enough to bring understanding to many, even at the price of their own suffering and death (11:33, 35; 12:3, 10). These are the people of discernment who will teach many and ultimately bring many to righteousness (12:3). That Nebuchadnezzar should seek people with these qualities to serve his own imperial agenda is ironic, for these precise characteristics describe the people who will be instrumental in the fulfillment of the will of God.

The young men are to be taught "the literature and language of the Chaldeans" (v. 4), the term "Chaldean" being used in this instance in the ethnic sense, referring to the Babylonians (5:30; 9:1; Jer. 24:5; 25:12; Ezek. 1:3). The youngsters are to be educated for three years which, according to some ancient Persian and Greek sources, was the standard period for higher education that typically began when the boys were fourteen years old and lasted until they were sixteen or seventeen.

Mixed in with the opportunity for education are temptations, for the youngsters are provided with daily rations from what the Hebrew text describes as "the delicacies of the king and the wine that he drinks" (v. 5). Among those selected are four lads with perfectly good Jewish names, each of which bears some reference to their God: Daniel ("my judge is God"), Hananiah ("the Lord is gracious"), Mishael ("who is what God is?"), and Azariah ("the Lord has helped"). But they, like many young people pursuing education in foreign countries, are given strange-sounding foreign names. Whatever their original meanings may have been, the foreign names of the four youths sound utterly nonsensical in Hebrew: Belteshazzar (Daniel), Shadrach (Hananiah), Meshach (Mishael), and Abednego (Azariah). Scholars have tried to make sense of these names, finding Babylonian or Old Persian etymologies for each of them, but none of the reconstructions is completely convincing. The names in their present forms are simply meaningless in Hebrew and no doubt sounded that way to the original readers of the book. Still, the narrator does not seem to object to them and, throughout the book, these foreign names are used alongside the Jewish ones. Elsewhere in the Old Testament, too, no objection to foreign names seems to have been raised. Joseph in Egypt was given the Egyptian name Zaphenath-Paneah. Esther, whose name is derived from the Mesopotamian goddess Ishtar, is the adopted name of a Jewish young woman named Hadassah (Hebrew for "Myrtle") and her uncle's name, Mordecai, recalls the Babylonian god Marduk. Among the early leaders of the restoration was one named Zerubbabel, a name of Babylonian origin. As we know from various Aramaic and cuneiform documents, Jews scattered throughout Mesopotamia and Egypt often assumed foreign names, even names that originally were linked with pagan gods.

The narrator of the book of Daniel apparently shares this indifference about Jews having foreign names. Still, the text says pointedly that the names of these four youths were assigned by the palace master, who was chief of the imperial charges (v. 7). That the language used for the assignment of names is different from what we find elsewhere in the Bible is also noteworthy; in other places, the Hebrew typically has an idiom that means, literally, "call a name" or "call by name." Here the verb is not "to call" but "to determine." The verb is used twice in verse 7, although this fact is lost in the NRSV translation, literally: "And he *determined* for them . . . and he *determined* for Daniel . . ." (NRSV "The palace master gave. . . . Daniel he called"). In using this particular vocabulary, the narrator sets the reader up for Daniel's response, for the first Hebrew word in verse 8 is the very same one, literally, "and he determined." Yet, in verse 8, Daniel—not the chief warden—makes a determination: "And Daniel *determined* upon his heart" (NRSV "But Daniel resolved"). The similar vocabulary used in verses 7–8 starkly underscores the difference in subjects. Whereas the chief warden determined names for Daniel and his friends, Daniel determined in his own heart that he was not going to "defile" himself. Daniel accommodated to what the chief warden had determined (his foreign name), but he himself determined to draw a line somewhere in order not to compromise himself. In the end, it seems, it is up to Daniel to determine upon his heart who he is and to remember to whom he ultimately owes his allegiance.

The language of corruption or defilement is noteworthy, too, for it suggests that at issue is one's moral and religious self. Imperial largesse for education and the imposition of meaningless names are not perceived as threats to one's moral identity in the way that consumption of the king's delicacies and wine seems to be. One wonders, however, what about this food and this wine makes them so unacceptable, so defiling. Technically, the Torah's dietary laws are not violated. Certainly, wine is nowhere forbidden, except for Nazirites (Num. 6:1–4). Even early Jewish interpreters recognized that the law did not explicitly prohibit their consumption. One might speculate that something about the ingredients of the delicacies or the manner of their preparation has rendered them ritually unacceptable to pious Jews, but the rejection of the wine would still be unexplained. Perhaps this food and drink had been offered to idols previously, although that would not explain the acceptability of the vegetarian portions that surely would have been offered as well. The text does not, in fact, give any explicit reason for

Daniel's rejection of the delicacies. What the narrative does say clearly and repeatedly, though, is that the delicacies and wine are *from the king* (vv. 5, 8, 13, 15, 16). The rations are clearly a special privilege that the king has extended to these elite youngsters. Indeed, biblical and extra-biblical records note that such rations were assigned to Jehoiachin and members of the royal household while they were in exile in Babylon and, as far as we know, Jehoiachin accepted his daily rations (see 2 Kgs. 24:30; *ANET*, p. 308). Especially in the face of the deprivations and sufferings of exile, turning down such royal offerings is surely no easy matter. For good reason, therefore, Calvin took these temptations for Daniel and his friends to be such that, if accepted, would cause them a loss of their Jewish identity. Daniel accepted and endured the training in Chaldean language and literature and the bearing of a foreign name, but he was determined to reject the temptation of these privileges. Perhaps the narrator intends to portray Daniel as being more faithful than Jehoiachin, the scion of the house of David in exile. Whatever the reason, for Daniel, a diet of legumes (literally "seeds") and water instead of the tempting offerings of the king was apparently one way to remain faithful in the face of the overwhelming power of the Babylonians (compare Tob. 1:10–11; Jdt. 12:1–4). For Joseph in Egypt, resistance to the temptation of his master's wife was a matter of principle, a "statement" of who he was. For Daniel, the resistance to the temptation of the king's pleasurable delicacies and wine was a "statement" of who he was. The king's offer in this regard was dangerous because of its consequences (the loss of identity), and Daniel's determination to resist the temptation enabled him to be in solidarity with the wretchedness of the other captives. In his will to resist, therefore, Daniel identifies himself with others in their desperate straits.

Such a manner of resistance to "the world" remains a viable one for many people today; some people choose vegetarianism or fasting as ways to express their conscience and their faith. The issue here is not the preferability of vegetarian diets or water or, for that matter, anything else that one consumes, but a matter of conscience and identity. By the same token, some people today may reject the "consumption" of certain products for various ethical reasons—because of the ingredients, the way the goods have been manufactured, the exploitation of others in the process, the effect of the production of these goods on the environment, and so forth. Such an ethical stance is determined not by a rigid law that is universally applied, but by one's own sense of what defines one's moral self. So, too, one may observe that Daniel made a personal decision to reject a privilege; he determined upon his heart to resist this privilege as something that would somehow corrupt him (v. 8).

## DANIEL'S RESISTANCE AND THE GRACE OF GOD
## Daniel 1:9–17

The narrator never loses sight of the theological focus implicitly laid out at the beginning. The text immediately goes on to show that God made Daniel's decision work (v. 9). The NRSV translation does not adequately convey the theological profundity of the Hebrew. The text says, literally, "God gave Daniel for grace and mercies before the chief warden" (v. 9). In the first place, the language of divine intervention here echoes verse 2, where the deity is said to have given Jehoiakim into the hand of the Babylonians. The God who *gave* Jehoiakim into the power of the Babylonians also *gave* Daniel and his friends, literally, "to grace and mercies." The sovereignty of God is thus affirmed; the theological paradox of divine judgment and grace is maintained. Despite the obvious power of the Babylonians, or any other human power for that matter, God is the narrator's "lord." Even in the land of Shinar, the infamous place of wickedness, God is at work and ever providing. Moreover, the reference to "grace and mercies" points not so much to the favor of the chief warden (as the NRSV suggests: "favor and compassion from the palace master") but to the "grace and mercies" of God before the prison warden. Indeed, one may compare this text with the story of Joseph in Egypt, a story that has many parallels with the accounts of Daniel's experience. Joseph was also in captivity in a foreign land, but the Lord was with him, extending "grace" (the same Hebrew word is used in Dan. 1:8) to him and showing him favor in the eyes of the prison warden (Gen. 39:21). So, too, the story in Daniel 1 implies that God was with Daniel, granting him "grace and mercies *before* the chief warden." As in the Joseph story, so in the first chapter of Daniel, one learns that God's will is being worked out even amid adverse circumstances.

The narrator then proceeds to show how the "grace and mercies" were manifest in the case of Daniel and his friends. First comes the chief warden's noncommittal response to Daniel's proposal. The chief warden admits to fear of the king, his "lord" (contrast the chief warden's "my lord" in v. 10 with the narrator's "Lord" in v. 2!). The chief warden does not, however, react adversely to the request, as one might expect an imperial official to do. He does not report the matter to his superiors, which would no doubt have resulted in Daniel's death. He does not reject the idea, and that seems to suffice for the moment. Sometimes, it seems, even a passive and neutral response of a timid unbeliever may turn out to be a manifestation of divine grace and mercy.

In any case, through the words of the chief warden, the narrator subtly shifts the reader's attention from Daniel's own determination in his heart to the situation of all four youngsters. Nothing is said of the reactions of Daniel's friends, but they are obviously drawn into the picture. The noncommittal response of the chief warden apparently allows Daniel to continue his quest through another avenue, this time through the guard appointed by the chief (v. 11). The proposal to have a short trial period for Daniel's plan to work seems reasonable and poses little risk for the guard (v. 13). So the guard subscribes to the idea and the plan is given a chance (v. 14). By now, one sees how good may be brought about in the subtlest ways. Daniel is said to have made the determination in his heart, but others are drawn willy-nilly to take a stand. The chief warden who was charged with the care of these youngsters and his appointee are both drawn, if ever so tentatively, into the decision. Daniel's friends are obviously drawn into the decision, even though their voices are never heard. And this episode all began with a single person's determination upon his heart (v. 8) and, of course, the providence of God who gave that person "to grace and mercies" (v. 9). That's how God's will for greater good is achieved sometimes: taking one person's initiative of faith, a determination "upon the heart," together with the grace and mercies of God. In this way, a simple, quiet, passive resistance—in this case the mere forgoing of a privilege—may lead to the working out of God's will for many.

The result of the test is beyond human expectation, for the four youngsters who were not fed the royal rations turn out to be better off than those who were fed (v. 14). The linkage with the Joseph story is evident again, for the terms used of the four delicacy-deprived youngsters echo the description of the fat cows in Pharaoh's dream that represented years of plenty (Gen. 41:2, 18). Of the lads who had not eaten from the riches of the king's table, the text says, literally, "their appearance was beautiful and fat of flesh" (v. 15). Without risk, then, the guard exempted the four from having to eat the king's provisions. Instead, the guard gave the youths their vegetarian portions (v. 16).

Yet, that particular diet is not the central point of the story. The narrator makes this point by moving from the guard's giving of legumes (v. 16) to God's giving of knowledge and success as regards all "literature and wisdom" (v. 17). Here again, the narrator's focus is not so much the faithful and righteous conduct of any human being—what they should eat or what they should drink. Rather, the providence of God (see Matt. 6:25–34), the God of judgment who gave Jehoiakim into the hand of Nebuchadnezzar (v. 2), is the very God of grace who gave Daniel "to grace and mercies" (v. 9). The point is not the triumph of vegetarianism or even the triumph of piety or the triumph of wisdom, therefore, but the triumph of God. Because of God's providence, not Nebuchadnezzar's, the four youths are blessed with knowledge and success pertaining to "every aspect of literature and wisdom" (v. 17). Nebuchadnezzar's scholarship program was intended to bring selected youngsters to specialized wisdom and knowledge of Babylonian literature. The narrator insists, however, that God is the one who gives these things and, lest there be any misunderstanding, the text has it that God's giving applies to "every aspect of literature and wisdom," presumably including anything that one may acquire from the Babylonian academy.

The four youngsters are not all blessed equally with gifts, however. Daniel is singled out as one with "insight into all visions and dreams" (v. 17), which are the concern of the rest of the book. Daniel is portrayed here as a mediator of divine revelation, a vehicle of the prophetic word (see Num. 12:6). Hence he is appropriately called a prophet in the New Testament (Matt. 24:15). He is viewed as one of the *maśkîlîm*, people of discernment, who make a difference in the world not by any manifestation of power, but by the power of insight and by their teaching of understanding to many, even though they themselves may stumble as they do so (see Dan. 11:33–35). In the end, God triumphs over evil power in this manner: not by military might, but by the mediation of divine will through the quiet faith of God's people, even the lowly and seemingly powerless, and not by wisdom contrived and sought after by mortals, but by the gift of wisdom that comes only by God's sheer grace.

## DANIEL'S FINAL EXAMINATION AND ITS RESULTS
## Daniel 1:18–21

The final examination comes when all the selected youngsters are presented before Nebuchadnezzar. The result is that the four who had not compromised themselves fared better than the others, and so they are given positions in the imperial administration. Indeed, not only are they at the top of their class, they far exceeded the experts in the Babylonian academy.

Many readers will no doubt recognize echoes throughout the chapter of the story of Joseph in Egypt (Gen. 37; 39–44). The original readers of the book, who must have been thoroughly familiar with the traditions, doubtless discerned them also. Like Joseph, Daniel finds himself in a foreign land—the former in Egypt, the latter in Mesopotamia. Joseph is said to have been handsome, as were Daniel and his friends. Joseph was tempted by Potiphar's wife, but he resisted her seduction; Daniel was tempted by the rations of delicacies and wine from the king's table, but he resisted them. God showed Joseph grace and favor in the sight of the prison warden; God gave Daniel "to grace and mercies" before the chief warden. Just as Joseph had a foreign name, so Daniel and his friends were given foreign names. Joseph was so gifted that he outperformed all the Egyptian sages and magicians. Daniel and his friends were so gifted that they were "ten times better" (Dan. 1:20) than the Babylonian sages and experts. The story of Joseph makes the theological point that God acted quietly behind the scenes through Joseph to bring about salvation to people even when they were living in hostile conditions. What was true for Joseph in Egypt was true for Daniel in Mesopotamia, for the same God acted quietly in each instance.

Daniel is said to have continued in Babylon "until the first year of King Cyrus" (v. 21). The significance of this chronological notice lies in the fact that it marked the end of the Babylonian captivity and the return of the temple appurtenances that were carried off to Babylon (see 2 Chr. 36:22–23; Ezra 1:7, 11). Daniel would outlast Nebuchadnezzar and his Babylonian successors. Indeed, beyond the Babylonian period that serves as the historical setting of the story, one sees God's will being worked out in similar ways—through individuals who were willing to stand up for what they believed. In the second century B.C.E., Antiochus Epiphanes invaded Palestine and sacked the temple in Jerusalem that had been rebuilt to replace the one that the Babylonians had destroyed. In a reign of absolute terror, Antiochus desecrated the temple, taunted the Jews, and attempted to force them to eat forbidden food (1 Macc. 1:10–64; 2 Macc. 6–7). Many in Israel stood firm in their faith, however, and resolved not to compromise themselves, preferring to be put to death (1 Macc. 1:62–63). For many scholars, the reign of Antiochus was the time when the book of Daniel was composed; the stories in Daniel were told or retold to encourage Jews in their resistance to the "Nebuchadnezzar" of their generation. Whatever its provenance, the story of Daniel's resistance would certainly have resonated with the Jews in the time of Antiochus. We know that Daniel and his friends were already known by the time of the book of Maccabees as models of faith (1 Macc. 2:59–60). That story has continued for generations to edify people, not only about the possibility of living faithfully amid the messiness of human history, but especially about the mysterious and quiet working out of the sovereign God's will in that history. The story is about the triumph of God not through ordinary manifestations of power, but through God's manifold *giving*—even amid suffering, even amid signs of powerless, even amid the threat of death.

# 2. Nebuchadnezzar's Dream

## *Daniel 2:1–49*

1 In the second year of Nebuchadnezzar's reign, Nebuchadnezzar
dreamed such dreams that his spirit was troubled and his sleep left him. 2 So
the king commanded that the magicians, the enchanters, the sorcerers, and
the Chaldeans be summoned to tell the king his dreams. When they came
in and stood before the king, 3 he said to them, "I have had such a dream
that my spirit is troubled by the desire to understand it." 4 The Chaldeans
said to the king (in Aramaic), "O king, live forever! Tell your servants the
dream, and we will reveal the interpretation." 5 The king answered the
Chaldeans, "This is a public decree: if you do not tell me both the dream
and its interpretation, you shall be torn limb from limb, and your houses
shall be laid in ruins. 6 But if you do tell me the dream and its interpretation, you shall receive from me gifts and rewards and great honor. Therefore
tell me the dream and its interpretation." 7 They answered a second time,
"Let the king first tell his servants the dream, then we can give its interpretation." 8 The king answered, "I know with certainty that you are trying to
gain time, because you see I have firmly decreed: 9 if you do not tell me the
dream, there is but one verdict for you. You have agreed to speak lying and
misleading words to me until things take a turn. Therefore, tell me the
dream, and I shall know that you can give me its interpretation." 10 The
Chaldeans answered the king, "There is no one on earth who can reveal
what the king demands! In fact no king, however great and powerful, has
ever asked such a thing of any magician or enchanter or Chaldean. 11 The
thing that the king is asking is too difficult, and no one can reveal it to the
king except the gods, whose dwelling is not with mortals."

12 Because of this the king flew into a violent rage and commanded that
all the wise men of Babylon be destroyed. 13 The decree was issued, and the
wise men were about to be executed; and they looked for Daniel and his
companions, to execute them. 14 Then Daniel responded with prudence and
discretion to Arioch, the king's chief executioner, who had gone out to execute the wise men of Babylon; 15 he asked Arioch, the royal official, "Why
is the decree of the king so urgent?" Arioch then explained the matter to

Daniel. [16] So Daniel went in and requested that the king give him time and
he would tell the king the interpretation.

[17] Then Daniel went to his home and informed his companions,
Hananiah, Mishael, and Azariah, [18] and told them to seek mercy from the
God of heaven concerning this mystery, so that Daniel and his companions
with the rest of the wise men of Babylon might not perish. [19] Then the mys-
tery was revealed to Daniel in a vision of the night, and Daniel blessed the
God of heaven.

20 Daniel said:

"Blessed be the name of God from age to age,
for wisdom and power are his.
21 He changes times and seasons,
deposes kings and sets up kings;
he gives wisdom to the wise
and knowledge to those who have understanding.
22 He reveals deep and hidden things;
he knows what is in the darkness,
and light dwells with him.
23 To you, O God of my ancestors,
I give thanks and praise,
for you have given me wisdom and power,
and have now revealed to me what we asked of you,
for you have revealed to us what the king ordered."

[24] Therefore Daniel went to Arioch, whom the king had appointed to
destroy the wise men of Babylon, and said to him, "Do not destroy the wise
men of Babylon; bring me in before the king, and I will give the king the
interpretation."

[25] Then Arioch quickly brought Daniel before the king and said to him:
"I have found among the exiles from Judah a man who can tell the king the
interpretation." [26] The king said to Daniel, whose name was Belteshazzar,
"Are you able to tell me the dream that I have seen and its interpretation?"
[27] Daniel answered the king, "No wise men, enchanters, magicians, or
diviners can show to the king the mystery that the king is asking, [28] but
there is a God in heaven who reveals mysteries, and he has disclosed to
King Nebuchadnezzar what will happen at the end of days. Your dream and
the visions of your head as you lay in bed were these: [29] To you, O king, as
you lay in bed, came thoughts of what would be hereafter, and the revealer
of mysteries disclosed to you what is to be. [30] But as for me, this mystery
has not been revealed to me because of any wisdom that I have more than
any other living being, but in order that the interpretation may be known
to the king and that you may understand the thoughts of your mind.

[31] "You were looking, O king, and lo! there was a great statue. This statue
was huge, its brilliance extraordinary; it was standing before you, and its
appearance was frightening. [32] The head of that statue was of fine gold, its
chest and arms of silver, its middle and thighs of bronze, [33] its legs of iron,
its feet partly of iron and partly of clay. [34] As you looked on, a stone was cut

out, not by human hands, and it struck the statue on its feet of iron and clay
and broke them in pieces. 35 Then the iron, the clay, the bronze, the silver,
and the gold, were all broken in pieces and became like the chaff of the
summer threshing floors; and the wind carried them away, so that not a
trace of them could be found. But the stone that struck the statue became
a great mountain and filled the whole earth.

36 "This was the dream; now we will tell the king its interpretation.
37 You, O king, the king of kings—to whom the God of heaven has given the
kingdom, the power, the might, and the glory, 38 into whose hand he has
given human beings, wherever they live, the wild animals of the field, and
the birds of the air, and whom he has established as ruler over them all—
you are the head of gold. 39 After you shall arise another kingdom inferior
to yours, and yet a third kingdom of bronze, which shall rule over the
whole earth. 40 And there shall be a fourth kingdom, strong as iron; just as
iron crushes and smashes everything, it shall crush and shatter all these.
41 As you saw the feet and toes partly of potter's clay and partly of iron, it
shall be a divided kingdom; but some of the strength of iron shall be in it,
as you saw the iron mixed with the clay. 42 As the toes of the feet were part
iron and part clay, so the kingdom shall be partly strong and partly brittle.
43 As you saw the iron mixed with clay, so will they mix with one another
in marriage, but they will not hold together, just as iron does not mix with
clay. 44 And in the days of those kings the God of heaven will set up a kingdom that shall never be destroyed, nor shall this kingdom be left to another
people. It shall crush all these kingdoms and bring them to an end, and it
shall stand forever; 45 just as you saw that a stone was cut from the mountain not by hands, and that it crushed the iron, the bronze, the clay, the silver, and the gold. The great God has informed the king what shall be
hereafter. The dream is certain, and its interpretation trustworthy."

46 Then King Nebuchadnezzar fell on his face, worshiped Daniel, and
commanded that a grain offering and incense be offered to him. 47 The king
said to Daniel, "Truly, your God is God of gods and Lord of kings and a
revealer of mysteries, for you have been able to reveal this mystery!"
48 Then the king promoted Daniel, gave him many great gifts, and made him
ruler over the whole province of Babylon and chief prefect over all the wise
men of Babylon. 49 Daniel made a request of the king, and he appointed
Shadrach, Meshach, and Abednego over the affairs of the province of
Babylon. But Daniel remained at the king's court.

Daniel 2 contains an account of Nebuchadnezzar's dream of a gigantic, multipartite statue—a dream that is explicated by Daniel, with a tantalizing prediction about earthly royal power being replaced by the eternal rule of God. Numerous attempts have been made to identify the various regimes represented by the various parts of the statue that Nebuchadnezzar saw in the dream. In this regard, the greatest controversy among interpreters has always revolved around the identity of the fourth regime, represented by the fourth part of the statue. That regime is of particular interest because the text claims that God will bring about yet another reign at that time—one that will negate all the others but that will itself be enduring (v. 44).

The dominant view among commentators through the ages is that the four parts of the statue represent four empires that will emerge successively, each one beginning only after its predecessor is completely diminished. Yet, apart from the certainty that the first is the Babylonian kingdom of Nebuchadnezzar, no consensus on the referents of the rest of the statue has emerged. For most interpreters in antiquity and still some today, the fourth power must mean the Roman Empire, and so the second must be Medo-Persian and the third Hellenistic. For many modern scholars, however, the fourth must be the Hellenistic Empire, and so the second and third refer to Media and Persia, respectively. In any case, these great powers represented by the four parts of the statue, according to Daniel's explication of the dream, will be crushed by a stone hewn "not by human hands" from a mountain, a stone that will itself become a mountain filling all the earth (vv. 35, 45). Divine intervention is clearly meant in this imagery—as suggested, too, by the same expression "not by human hands" in 8:25—but interpreters cannot agree if this stone that symbolizes the reign of God would be an individual (such as the Jewish messiah or Christ in his first or second advent) or a corporate entity (the Jewish nation or the church).

The story echoes earlier biblical traditions. Most widely recognized in this regard are the similarities between this story and the story of Joseph in Egypt, especially Genesis 41. In Daniel as in the Joseph story, we have a foreign ruler whose spirit is troubled by a dream, the failure of professional diviners to assuage the ruler's anxiety, a young Hebrew captive accomplishing what the experts could not, the faithful captive attributing his success to God, and the rewarding of the captive and his promotion to a position of enormous influence in the kingdom of his sojourning. Thus, like young Joseph in the second year of his sojourn in Egypt, Daniel in the second year of his exile would enlighten his mighty captor and save others from certain death.

Read in light of the Joseph story, one may consider Daniel's success all the more remarkable. Not only does Daniel outperform a more diverse team of consultants than Joseph did, but the assignment at hand is far more difficult. Whereas the Egyptian ruler had asked only for the interpretation of his dreams, the Babylonian king demands to know both the content of the dream and its interpretation, a point that is reiterated throughout the story (vv. 5, 6, 7, 9, 26, 30, 36). Yet, the purpose is not merely to show that this captive novice has made fools of his captors so comically. Much more is at stake in this narrative than the skillful interpretation of dreams by a wise and pious courtier. More so than the Joseph story, Daniel 2 calls attention to the triumph of divine wisdom and foreknowledge conveyed through a lowly exile, a faithful servant of God. The story illustrates the sovereignty of God, who humbles the mighty and exalts the lowly.

In this regard, the Daniel narrative is particularly reminiscent of the poems of Isaiah 40–55, where one finds an unmistakable emphasis on the wisdom and foreknowledge of Israel's God over against the idols of the foreign nations (Isa. 41:21–29; 43:9; 45:19; 46:10; 48:5–6, 16). To the poet of Isaiah 40–55, Israel's God is the one "who frustrates the omens of liars, and makes fools of diviners; who turns back the wise, and makes their knowledge foolish; who confirms the word of his servant and fulfills the prediction of his messengers" (Isa. 44:25–26a). The Chaldeans have too much confidence in their knowledge and wisdom, the poet observes, but their diviners will finally not be able even to save themselves (Isa. 47:5–15, especially vv. 10, 13–14). The God of the Jewish exiles, by contrast, is able to reveal things concealed in darkness (Isa. 45:3), secrets that are hidden and yet unknown to humanity (Isa. 48:6), for Israel's God is sovereign over light and darkness (Isa. 45:7; compare 42:16). Such, too, is the God to whom Daniel prays, for his God "reveals deep and hidden things; he knows what is in the darkness, and light dwells with him" (Dan. 2:22). In the poems of Isaiah 40–55, the gods of the nations, unable to declare the things that will happen before they happen, are challenged to produce witnesses to vindicate themselves, so that those who hear the testimonies may say, "It is true" (Isa. 43:9). In Daniel 2, while the Chaldean experts are impotent in the face of Nebuchadnezzar's challenge and readily admit so, Daniel insists that his God is able to reveal mysteries and make known what will be in the future (Dan. 2:28). Eventually, after Daniel is able to bear witness to things that are to happen before they happen, the Chaldean king is the one who confesses what is true: "Truly, your God is God of gods and Lord of kings and a revealer of mysteries, for you have been able to reveal this mystery!" (Dan. 2:47). Thus, just as the poet in Isaiah 40–55 predicted the prostration of foreign rulers before the exiles (Isa. 43:14; 49:7, 23), one finds Nebuchadnezzar prostrating before Daniel, the Jew in the service of a foreign ruler (Dan. 2:46–47).

The poet in Isaiah 40–55 envisioned that the exiles would eventually humble their adversaries and become to them like a new sledge, threshing mountains to dust and crushing hills like chaff, so that the wind would carry them off and scatter them (Isa. 41:15–16). Similar idioms are used in Daniel 2 of the stone that would crush the mighty powers of the world. Indeed, even though the foreign powers are represented by metals, they will become "like chaff of the summer threshing floor," carried off by a wind until not a trace of them is left (Dan. 2:35). Daniel speaks of a stone hewn "not by human hands" coming "from the mountain" (Dan. 2:45), a stone that will itself grow to be a great mountain filling the whole earth. Here the imagery of the stone hewn from the mountain may ultimately be derived from the earlier exhortation to faithful Jews during the Babylonian exiles: "Look to the mountain from which you were hewn, yea, to the quarry from which you were dug" (Isa. 51:1b author's translation). Such literary and rhetorical allusions must surely be taken into consideration as one endeavors to understand the account of the dream and its interpretation.

Daniel 2 has a prehistory. Clues of redaction are apparent throughout: the king is intolerant of any attempt to buy time (v. 8), yet he readily grants Daniel reprieve (v. 16); Daniel appeared directly before the king in verse 16, but he has to be introduced by Arioch in verse 25; Daniel's three friends appear suddenly in verse 17, where they are referred to by their Hebrew names, have no part to play in the rest of the story, but are mentioned again in verse 49, this time by their foreign names. Some have posited plausibly that the oracle concerning the statue may have had an earlier—probably Mesopotamian—origin and may have once served as political propaganda of some sort. Accordingly, that oracle may have been incorporated into the present narrative, which itself is modeled after the Joseph story and given a new meaning. The chapter's purpose now, it is often suggested, is to demonstrate the superiority of wisdom properly conceived, namely, the superiority of wisdom that comes from God and the important place of piety. That view presumes the subordination of the dream oracle to the narrative—to the extent that the dream oracle itself is nothing more than an illustration of the sage's God-given wisdom. Yet the prediction of the coming reign of God culminates in the dream oracle and seems to be at the heart of the entire chapter. The preceding narrative, including the doxology, leads up to it, leaving interpretive cues along the way; the conclusion of the story illustrates the preliminary fulfillment of the oracle. Drawing on various sources and alluding to antecedent traditions, the narrator apparently corroborates the message of comfort proffered to Babylonian exiles in the sixth century by the poet of Isaiah 40–55: God is the sovereign of history, even if that sovereignty is not readily evident amid political realities. Indeed, the will of God will be effectuated through the ministrations of God's lowly servant.

The chapter may be divided into five sections that move smoothly from one to the next. The first (vv. 1–12) explains the circumstances that led to a life-and-death crisis for Daniel and his friends. The second (vv. 13–23), which explains Daniel's involvement in resolving the problem, revolves around a beautifully crafted and theologically profound prayer that provides a necessary preface to the interpretation of the dream. The third (vv. 24–35) is an account of the dream, the revelation of which was the first part of Nebuchadnezzar's demand. The fourth (vv. 36–45) relates Daniel's interpretation of the dream, thus fulfilling the second part of Nebuchadnezzar's demand. The last section (vv. 46–49) is not only the conclusion of the story; it shows how Daniel's prediction is immediately, if only partially, being fulfilled. The five sections build on one another until the chapter reaches its denouement at the end.

## THE CRISIS
## Daniel 2:1–12

The story is set in the second year of Nebuchadnezzar's reign (v. 1). This chronological datum poses a problem for many interpreters because Daniel and his companions were supposed to go through training for three years and so would not yet have completed their education in the Babylonian academy (1:5); indeed, they did not have their final examination until the end of that three-year period (1:18). Yet one may make sense of this chronological notice in its present literary-canonical context. That Daniel had not yet completed the program that the Babylonians had designed is true, but that fact makes his successful interpretation of Nebuchadnezzar's dream all the more remarkable. His success cannot be attributed to Babylonian education and cannot be explained in terms of his education at all. The chronological notice highlights a comic irony in the narrative: a mere trainee in the Babylonian academy will outperform all the full-fledged experts; a lowly exile will enlighten his mighty captor. Yet, the point is not merely that the novice has made a fool of the experts, which admittedly is a common motif in stories of this sort. More importantly, the point is a theological one: Daniel's success is owing neither to his personal gifts nor to his Chaldean education, but to the wisdom and the power of God alone.

Moreover, it is significant that the story is placed so early in Nebuchadnezzar's career. The king has only recently come to power after a decisive battle against the remnant of the Assyrian army and its allies at Carchemish (605 B.C.E.). That battle, in fact, assured Nebuchadnezzar his place as king of the new empire. He had every reason to be confident in the second year of his reign, but he was not. He was troubled by his dream and could not sleep. The king is terrified, despite all the impressions of absolute power that the story portrays. The king is depicted at the outset as a man desperate for answers. Then, of all people, a novice and exile brings a divinely provided solution to the king's troubling dream.

Unlike the dreams of King Abimelech of Gerar (Gen. 20:1–18) and King Solomon (1 Kgs. 3:3–15), where the meaning of the dream is plain and requires no interpretation, the dream of Nebuchadnezzar requires explication by an intermediary. In this and other ways, Nebuchadnezzar's dream is most like that of Pharaoh in the story of Joseph. In the latter story, Pharaoh had a series of dreams and because of them "his spirit was troubled" (Gen. 41:8). So, too, Nebuchadnezzar had a dream and "his spirit was troubled" (vv. 1, 3). Interestingly, even though only one dream is at issue in Nebuchadnezzar's case (see vv. 3, 4, 5, 28), the Hebrew text in verse 1 actually refers to the king's *dreams*, thus echoing Pharaoh's two dreams in the Joseph story. Pharaoh's dreams came during the second year of Joseph's sojourn in Egypt (Gen. 41:1). Likewise, Nebuchadnezzar's dream came during Daniel's second year in exile. Pharaoh summoned his "magicians" and sages to court, only to learn that none of them could explain his dreams (Gen. 41:8). Nebuchadnezzar, too, called for his experts, including "magicians" but also "enchanters, sorcerers, and Chaldeans." Nebuchadnezzar is apparently taking no chances. He summons consultants in the various professional guilds of diviners from Egypt to Mesopotamia. Not only is his conference of experts more comprehensive than Pharaoh's, his assignment for these experts is far more challenging than what Pharaoh had given his consultants. Pharaoh only asked that they provide the interpretation of his dreams, but Nebuchadnezzar demanded more: he wanted to know both the contents of the dream and its interpretation.

The king's initial charge to the Chaldeans seems innocuous enough. He tells them that he had a dream and that his spirit is troubled "to know the dream," as the Hebrew text has it (Dan. 2:3). The NRSV translation, which has the king troubled "by the desire to understand it," is too free and obscures the ambiguity that may have been intended. One is not told why the king would not or could not provide the substance of his dream, as Pharaoh did. Perhaps he had simply forgotten what he had dreamed. Perhaps he was withholding that information to see if these experts were really any good at their jobs, a view that finds some support in verse 9. Perhaps the narrator wants to show that Daniel was even more gifted than Joseph. Perhaps the point is that the king is an utterly unreasonable person. Whatever the case, the Chaldeans are oblivious to the nature of the king's request, no doubt thinking that when the king says, "to know the dream," he means to know only its interpretation (so also NRSV "to understand it"). The Chaldeans do not quite grasp the point of the king's twofold demand until verse 10.

A number of extant dream-books were found in Mesopotamia, veritable reference works that the ancient diviners consulted on every conceivable dream scenario. Perhaps for that reason, the Chaldeans are so confident that they will have an answer for the king; the standard tools of the trade were available readily, and all the Chaldeans needed to do was to check their secret resources. Nebuchadnezzar proclaims in no uncertain terms, however, that they are required to tell him the dream *and* its interpretation, adding both a deadly threat for failure (v. 5) and a promise of reward for success (v. 6). When they ask, again, for an account of the dream (v. 7), the king impatiently accuses them of trying to use delay tactics and of conspiracy and deceit (vv. 8–9). He is unrelenting in his twofold demand for content and interpretation (vv. 5, 6, 7, 9).

After the king has asked three times for both the content and the interpretation of the dream (vv. 3, 5–6, 8–9), the Chaldean charlatans finally understand and are forced to admit the limits of their ability (vv. 10–12). They are understandably at wits' end. They recognize both the limits of their expertise and the unreasonable nature of the king's demand. No one on earth can do such a thing, they cry. No king, no matter how great and powerful, has ever made such a request, one that is so obviously impossible for mortals to meet. Those who remember the story of Joseph no doubt recall that even Pharaoh did not demand such a humanly impossible task. Only divine beings can do what the king is demanding, the Chaldeans admit, but they add quickly that the gods could not be there, since the gods do not dwell with mortals (v. 11). So they make no appeal whatsoever for divine help. At their response, the king goes into a violent rage and orders the execution of all the sages of Babylon, including those who, like Daniel and his friends, know nothing about the king's conference with his consultants (v. 12).

## DANIEL STEPS FORWARD
## Daniel 2:13–23

Daniel and his friends, though they are apparently still apprentices at the Babylonian academy, are considered to be among the sages to be executed. Despite the obvious danger, Daniel has the presence of mind and the temerity to speak to the "chief executioner" (v. 14), the title here being similar to the Hebrew one used of Potiphar, "the captain of the guard" in the Joseph story (Gen. 39:1). Daniel gingerly inquires about the uncompromising nature of the decree, and it is explained to him. His response to the explanation is entirely unexpected, however: he immediately goes before the king (Dan. 2:16). Whereas the text notes Daniel's caution in his approach to the "chief executioner" in verse 14, nothing is said about his attitude in his approach to the king. The narrator simply notes his direct approach: Daniel went and he requested (v. 16). He is apparently not well recognized enough to have been brought as a consultant with the other sages, but he dares to go before the king without being summoned. Such an act would no doubt have constituted a violation of palace protocol and would likely have been a capital offense (see Esth. 4:11). Recognizing the impropriety of Daniel's action, therefore, a few commentators have conjectured that Daniel only requested that the chief executioner go before the king on his behalf. Whether or not it is plausible that a Jewish exile like Daniel might have had such easy access to the despot, the narrator would have the reader believe that Daniel did it and was miraculously spared. Esther, another Jew living under the rule of foreigners, likewise risked her life by appearing before the Persian king without being summoned and, in doing so, eventually saved many lives. So, too, Daniel's life-risking action would preserve lives (Dan. 2:18). His quiet confidence stands out against the obsequiousness of the Chaldean charlatans. Surprisingly, the king is willing to grant Daniel's outright request for more time, whereas the Chaldeans had been readily accused of using delay tactics. Moreover, Daniel manages to confer with his friends, here called by their Jewish names, without being charged with conspiracy. Reading this story in its present context—following the story in chapter 1—one may properly understand that a quiet but powerful force is at work that the narrator does not spell out explicitly. The sovereign deity who "gave Daniel to grace and mercies" (so the Hebrew in 1:9) is apparently still in control of events in human history. Appropriately, therefore, Daniel asks his companions to pray for God's "mercies" (the Aramaic equivalent of the Hebrew word in 1:9) concerning the "mystery." Moreover, they are to pray not only for their own salvation from the threat at hand, but for the rest of the sages of Babylon (2:18).

Contrast the perspective of Daniel and that of the Chaldeans, who begin with confidence in their own ability to uncover the truth of Nebuchadnezzar for him (v. 4), but end up admitting that no one on earth can do it (v. 11). They recognize that the gods can do so, but they do not consider that avenue because they thought that the gods were not with mortals. The Chaldeans would count only on their wisdom to solve their predicament. "*We* will reveal the interpretation," they claim (v. 4, emphasis added). Daniel, by contrast, believes that the matter is a divine mystery that can be known only if God were to reveal it. Although he refers to the deity as "the God of the heaven," an epithet of the wholly transcendent God, he does not hesitate to seek divine mercies for matters on earth. The theology of the Chaldeans emphasizes divine transcendence (God is far away) over a theology of divine immanence (God is with us), but Daniel's theology balances both the realities of divine transcendence and immanence. God is at once wholly transcendent ("of heaven"), but still present to help mortals (with us).

Daniel is obviously portrayed as a pious Jew, but much more than a subtle call for trust in the power of prayer is present here. His doxology is similar in form and diction to others found elsewhere in the Bible, but it is not a mere pious interlude or interpolation here in the narrative, as it is often suggested. Indeed, the hymn in verses 20–23 both summarizes the theological issues raised so far in the narrative and anticipates the interpretation of the dream. The doxology here may even be theologically pivotal to the entire passage. His prayer provides the theological premise upon which the following account depends. Indeed, the theology of history that is explicated in Daniel's interpretation of the dream cannot be adequately understood apart from this prayer.

The "name of God" that Daniel blesses (v. 20) is not merely the divine appellation. The "name of God" is, in fact, a way of referring to the presence of God that does not compromise the notion of radical transcendence. So Israel's hymnic tradition contains many references to the divine name as synonymous with the very presence of God: "Praise the name of the LORD" (Pss. 113:1; 135:1), "Sing praises to his name" (Pss. 68:4; 135:3), "to give thanks to the name of the LORD" (Ps. 122:4). In the Deuteronomic tradition, the "name of the LORD" is a veritable extension of divine presence set in the temple by none other than God (Deut. 12:5, 21; 14:24; compare 2 Sam. 7:13; 1 Kgs. 8:16–20). In this way (among others), the theologians in Israel were able to speak of the simultaneous transcendence and immanence of God. God is so transcendent that even the highest of heavens cannot contain God, yet God's presence amid humanity is made possible by the divine "name" (see 1 Kgs. 8:27–29). So the narrator says that Daniel blessed "the God of heaven" (Dan. 2:19), but the quotation of the prayer begins with the blessing of "the name of God" (v. 20). To bless the name of God is to bless God. To bless God is to reciprocate the blessings that one receives from God by returning a gift of praise.

The hymn returns to the issues that the narrative has implicitly raised so far. Wisdom, which the experts summoned by Nebuchadnezzar are supposed to have, and power, which is presumed to belong to the king, are, in fact, God's to give: "for wisdom and power are his" (v. 20b). Nebuchadnezzar accuses the Chaldean sages of trying to "gain time" (v. 8) and waiting for time to change (v. 9), and Daniel has to request the king to give him a period of time (v. 16). The hymn makes clear now, however, that God "changes times and seasons" (v. 21a). Whereas the

Chaldeans bid the king to "live forever" (v. 4), Daniel's hymn blesses the name of God "forever and ever" (v. 20a, NRSV "from age to age"). Indeed, the doxology asserts that the king himself is subject to the authority and power of God, for God is the one who "deposes kings and sets up kings" (v. 21b). God is the true source of wisdom and knowledge, which the king's dream requires in order to be known; God reveals secrets and mysteries, and the wisdom and power of God are just what Daniel will mediate.

The deity who is at once transcendent and willing to be present is, for Daniel, none other than the God of his ancestors (v. 23a), a God who deigns to relate to a particular people. This divine designation "God of my ancestors" is significant, inasmuch as its very first appearance in the Bible is in connection with God's self-revelation: God was revealed to Moses as "the LORD," the distinctive name of Israel's God, the God of their ancestors (Exod. 3:13–16; 4:5). That divine designation would recur, too, in the Deuteronomic tradition as a constant reminder of the ancient bond that Israel had with God. In the context of Daniel's doxology, then, one is to understand that "the God of the ancestors," whose self-revelation to Moses enabled Moses to confront Pharaoh's awesome power, is now revealing again, this time through his servant in exile, who is to confront yet another powerful and oppressive ruler in history. The God of heaven (Dan. 2:19) is the God of Israel's ancestors (v. 23), a transcendent God who nevertheless relates to a particular people and intervenes in history to deliver them. So the doxology begins with the affirmation that wisdom and power belong *to God* (v. 20), but ends with wisdom and power given *to Daniel* (v. 23), who is now enabled to address the king. Calvin calls attention to the juxtaposition of wisdom and power, even though Daniel is but a captive standing before his mighty captor. The doxology implies that God's wisdom and power will be mediated through human agents, even through those who are lowly and powerless. The narrative so far is sufficient to show how God's wisdom may be manifest through a lowly exile. How God's power will similarly be manifest remains to be seen.

## THE DREAM DESCRIBED
## Daniel 2:24–35

On the basis of this divine revelation—so the "therefore" at the beginning of verse 24 implies—Daniel now asks to be brought before the king. The chief executioner's introduction of Daniel ("a man who can tell the king the interpretation") and the king's query ("are you able to tell me the dream . . . and its interpretation?") together provide the opportunity for Daniel to attribute the revelation to God. Daniel concurs with the judgment of the Chaldean diviners that the king's demand is impossible for human beings to meet (v. 27). He points out, however, that a transcendent God reveals such mysteries, and that this God has disclosed to Nebuchadnezzar things to come (v. 28). Here Daniel is like Joseph (Gen. 41:16) in that he, too, attributes the revelation of mystery to God.

The text is emphatic that the dream concerns something that will happen later: "what will happen at the end of days" (Dan. 2:28), "what would be hereafter" (v. 29), "what is to be" (v. 29), "what shall be hereafter" (v. 45). The English expression "at the end of days" (also in 10:14) sounds like a reference to the end of history or the end of time. The word translated as "end" may, however, simply mean "hereafter" or "the future." Hence, the expression here may be understood as, literally, "in the hereafter of days" (v. 28), an unspecified time in the future. Certainly, that is how the related Hebrew phrase is used in Genesis 49:1; Numbers 24:14; Deuteronomy 4:30; 31:29, all of which are rendered in the NRSV as "in days to come" or "in time to come." Already in Daniel 1:18, the expression "at the end of days" simply means sometime later. The Hebrew expression is also used of the distant future (Isa. 2:2; Mic. 4:1), but such usage does not detract from the fact that the basic reference is to some unspecified time in the future and not necessarily to the end of time or the end of history. These things described by Daniel are said to be already in the king's mind, only now to be retrieved, as it were, and clarified for the king (Dan. 2:29, 30). Daniel then proceeds to tell the king the content of the dream, thus fulfilling the first part of the king's demand.

According to Daniel, the king's dream is of an enormous "statue," a word used for images erected to represent the presence of gods and kings. Because the statue in Nebuchadnezzar's dream symbolizes royal power, a royal statue is likely meant. Such images were erected primarily for propagandistic reasons, the power and majesty of the king being conveyed by their typically intimidating size and splendor. Sometimes they were set up in conquered territories as reminders of the might of the victorious kings and their gods. Moreover, some were composed of different types of materials, mostly different metals in combination with alabaster or stone.

The statue in Nebuchadnezzar's dream is gigantic, extraordinarily brilliant, and awe-inspiring (v. 31). Yet, its splendor is not sustained throughout. Indeed, the splendor seems to dissipate: the head of the statue is made of gold, but the upper torso and arms are of silver, the lower torso and thighs are of bronze, the legs of iron, and the feet are partly of iron and partly of clay. A stone cut "not by human hands," an expression that occurs also in 8:25 and meaning probably that it originates by divine will and power (see also Job 34:20), strikes the statue at its weakest point, namely, its feet, which are partly made of clay. Thereupon, the entire statue not only collapses, but even disintegrates. All its components—even the metals—fall to the ground (Dan. 2:35) and are so finely shattered that they are blown away like chaff by the wind, so that not a trace of them could be found. The imagery is reminiscent of the prophecy in Isaiah 41:15–16 of the foreign nations that humiliate Israel eventually being reduced to chaff and blown away by the will of the Lord. That parallel is important for understanding Nebuchadnezzar's dream. The stone that is cut not by human hands then becomes a great mountain that fills the whole earth, an image that echoes prophetic visions of Jerusalem glorified as the symbol of the Lord's abiding reign (Isa. 2:2–3; 11:9; Mic. 4:1–2).

## THE DREAM INTERPRETED
## Daniel 2:36–45

Daniel then proceeds to interpret the dream, thus fulfilling the second part of the king's demand. Nebuchadnezzar is addressed directly as "king, the king of kings" (v. 37). This redundant address summarizes in a preliminary way the substance of Daniel's interpretation. At issue in the exposition, it seems, is kingship, which is what the statue represents. At the outset, the text moves ironically from Daniel's address of the king as "king of kings" to suggest that his kingship is, in fact, derived. The king who is called "king of kings" has been given kingship by an even greater king, the God of heaven (v. 37) and "the Lord of kings" (v. 47). God is the lord of the "king of kings"! Nebuchadnezzar's kingship is but a microcosm of true power, an earthly reflex of a greater power that is the source of "the kingdom (or, better, 'kingship'), the power, the might, and the glory" (v. 37). Finally the God of heaven gives kingship, power, and glory. So in the New Testament, Jesus teaches his disciples to pray to God *in heaven*, saying, "Thy kingdom come. Thy will be done in earth, as *it is* in heaven. . . . For thine is the kingdom, and the power, and the glory, for ever. Amen" (Matt. 6:9–13, KJV). Daniel's exposition will, in fact, lead to the affirmation of a greater kingship than a mere human one, a kingship that "shall stand forever" (v. 44).

Moreover, the description of Nebuchadnezzar's dominion in verse 38 echoes the account of the creation of humanity in Genesis 1:26. According to that creation account, humanity has been made in God's "image" (the same word for the statue in Daniel) and granted dominion over all of

God's creation—the fish of the sea, birds of the air, cattle, wild animals, and creeping things. Humanity was created to represent divine presence on earth, just as a royal statue in an earthly domain might represent the presence of an imperial ruler. To be sure, Nebuchadnezzar has extraordinary power as "king of kings" with dominion over peoples as well as other creatures of the world, the wild animals and the birds of the air (Dan. 2:38). Yet, his dominion is derived from a greater king. The "king of kings" is, after all, a mortal created by God to reflect divine dominion.

Although designated "king of kings," Nebuchadnezzar is only part of a larger image: he is its head—"the head of gold" (v. 38). His place in history is not forever, as the Chaldeans suggested in their salutation in verse 4. After him will come another reign (v. 39). Daniel does not say what the second regime refers to, except to say that it will be somehow "inferior" to Nebuchadnezzar's, presumably as silver is "inferior" to gold. A third reign of bronze "shall rule over the whole earth" and a fourth will be strong like iron, utterly destroying "all these" (v. 40).

No consensus exists among scholars on the historical referents of the four regimes represented by the composite royal statue. Many hold that four successive "kingdoms"—four empires—are meant, yet the text does not say that the Babylonian Empire is the golden head but that King Nebuchadnezzar is: "You are the head of gold" (v. 38). So the passage should be about kings, as the royal statue suggests, rather than empires per se. Even granting that the narrator means Babylon when Nebuchadnezzar is addressed, however, none of the other kingdoms or kingships is identified, and herein lies the interpretive difficulty. Some scholars hold that the three regimes beyond Nebuchadnezzar's refer to the "kingdoms" of the Medes, Persians, and Greeks, while others think of the Medo-Persian, Greek, and Roman empires.

Moreover, while the second regime clearly comes after the first (v. 39), nothing is said about how long each regime is supposed to last. The idea that the vision is about successive empires spanning centuries is belied by the fact that the fourth one is supposed to utterly destroy "all these" (v. 40), implying that preceding regimes will still exist when the fourth reign emerges. Perhaps, then, the text is referring not to four different empires over several centuries, but to four reigns/kingships. Indeed, the word translated as "kingdom" in the NRSV is the same word for "kingship" or "reign." The word is found elsewhere in the book for the reign of Nebuchadnezzar (4:26, 32, 36), the reign of Belshazzar (5:18, 26, 28; 8:1), the reign of Darius (6:26, 28), the reign of Cyrus (6:28), and the eternal reign of God (4:3, 34; 7:27). Thus, the passing of Nebuchadnezzar's reign mentioned in 4:28 is not the end of the Babylonian kingdom per se, for Nebuchadnezzar, according to the book's own historiography, is succeeded by his "son"

Belshazzar, whose own reign would end with the accession of "Darius" the Mede (6:1). Accordingly, then, the second regime is that of Belshazzar, who is indeed portrayed as inferior to Nebuchadnezzar (see 5:22–29). If so, the third regime would be that of Darius the Mede (6:1, 28) and the fourth of "Cyrus the Persian" (6:28). So the four regimes are the four reigns that one finds in Daniel 1–6.

Although the second regime is said to be inferior to Nebuchadnezzar's, no such thing is said of the others—just as none of the other kings in Daniel 1–6 except Belshazzar's kingship is portrayed as being inferior to Nebuchadnezzar's. The third power will, in fact, be broad in scope: it "shall rule over the whole earth" (Dan. 2:39). This assertion is, in fact, implicitly corroborated later in the book by the edict of Darius the Mede—the third ruler in the book—to "all peoples, nations, and languages that inhabit the earth," invoking his own dominion over them (see 6:25–26). Darius the Mede, the third ruler after Nebuchadnezzar and the inferior Belshazzar, has dominion over all the earth. The fourth reign then must be the fourth and last king explicitly mentioned in chapters 1–6, namely, "Cyrus the Persian" (6:28), who is portrayed in the book as the last king in whose reign Daniel served (1:21). As historians might point out, in the reign of Cyrus, the regimes of Belshazzar (the de facto ruler of Babylon when it fell at the hands of the Persian army) and the last Median kings were destroyed once and for all. Thus, historically, Cyrus the fourth power did destroy "all these" (2:40).

The Greek historian Herodotus, who notes the different ethnic background of the Persians and the Medes, reports that Cyrus himself was a product of mixed marriage, which was, of course, an anathema to the Jews. The narrator may well be alluding to this background, for in Cyrus himself and in his political coalition, there was a "mixing of human seed" (v. 43). In any case, Cyrus was the one who brought about the unification of the mighty Persians and the Median kingdom that was disintegrating—thus, an alliance of two unequal powers, a mixing of the strong with the brittle (Aramaic, literally, "disintegrating" or "breaking up").

According to Daniel, it is "in the days of those kings" that the transcendent God will establish another regime that will never be destroyed and that will not be left to another people (v. 44). Indeed, that new power will crush and end all the others, but it itself will stand forever. This eternal regime is symbolized by a stone hewn not by human hands, a stone that would shatter the gold, silver, bronze, and iron and clay regimes (v. 45; compare v. 35).

Details in the account of the dream (vv. 34–35) and its interpretation (v. 45) supplement one another. One learns in verse 45 that the stone is derived from "the mountain" (not "a mountain"), perhaps suggesting that the reader is supposed to know which "mountain" is meant. The narrator is apparently drawing upon an idiom or a tradition that is familiar to those for whom the narrative was first intended. Moreover, the text refers to gold, silver, bronze, iron, and clay being "crushed" (literally, "pulverized") so finely that they become "like chaff of the summer threshing floor" and are carried away by wind until not a trace is left (v. 35). Yet, characterizing the destruction of metals in this way is patently strange. The description may suggest, again, an imagery that is borrowed from elsewhere. Indeed, the imagery is much more at home in the portrayal of the destruction of foreign nations in Isaiah 40–55. The lowly exiles will be so empowered by God, the poet of Isaiah 40–55 maintains, that they will pulverize mountains and make hills "like chaff," so that these mighty entities could be winnowed and carried away by wind (Isa. 41:15–16). In the same chapter, the poet envisions the coming of a victor from the East (Isa. 41:2), who most scholars properly assume to be Cyrus (mentioned by name in Isa. 44:28; 45:1). The point of that passage is that even the despised and lowly may, contrary to expectation, be empowered to humble the lofty and powerful. To the poet of Isaiah 40–55, that is possible because Israel-Jacob is none other than the Lord's chosen servant, "the seed of Abraham," before whom foreign potentates will become as nothing and perish (Isa. 41:11; compare Isa. 40:23–24). Hope for the exiles lies in their divine election, the fact that they are heirs to God's promise to Abraham. Hence, the poet encourages the exiles to remember the divine promise to Abraham: "Look to the rock (the Hebrew equivalent of the Aramaic word for "mountain" in Daniel) from which you were hewn, and to the quarry from which you were dug. Look to Abraham your father and to Sarah who bore you; for he was but one when I called him, but I blessed him and made him many" (Isa. 51:1–2). Surely this rock-mountain is the one to which Daniel now alludes, this mountain that is said to be "the mountain" from which the stone hewn not by hands would be derived. That stone in Nebuchadnezzar's dream is, therefore, the lowly and despised exiles, a remnant of "the mountain," so to speak. The stone is the elect people of God, whatever their sociopolitical conditions may be—indeed, whatever their context may be. Thus, just as the poet of Isaiah 40–55 promised that the Jewish exiles in Babylon would in some sense render the powerful nations as nothing, so Daniel affirms that the exiles will annihilate all the foreign powers.

Reflecting the pain of defeat and subjugation by foreign forces, the vision in Daniel points to a time when this entity will never again be destroyed or abandoned (Dan. 2:44). It will be, on the contrary, an enduring sovereignty. Just as the poet of Isaiah 40–55 drew on the divine promise to Abraham to multiply (Gen. 12:1–3), so the narrator of Daniel 2 envisions that the stone hewn "from the mountain" will grow again into a mountain so great that it will fill all the earth (v. 35). On the one hand, the imagery echoes the Isaianic vision of what will be "in the latter days" (literally "at the end of days"), when the nations of the world will come together to Mount Zion, an earthly locus where the reign of God is manifest (Isa. 2:1–4; compare Mic. 4:1; Ps. 22:28–29). On the other hand, the imagery is reminiscent of Isaiah's vision of the glory of God filling all the earth (Isa. 6:3; 11:9; compare Isa. 60:14).

## THE IMMEDIATE IMPACT OF THE REVELATION
## Daniel 2:46–49

The vision of the collapsing statue is certainly about the decisive triumph of God and the universality of divine reign. Daniel's account of the dream, however, remains vague about how and when in the future that reign will be made manifest. The story, though, does not end with the interpretation of the dream. Indeed, it climaxes with the obeisance of Nebuchadnezzar and his acknowledgment of God on the one hand (vv. 46–47), and the exaltation of Daniel and his friends on the other (vv. 48–49).

The similarities between the conclusion of Daniel 2 and the story of Joseph in Egypt have long been noted. Daniel is promoted after his successful interpretation of Nebuchadnezzar's dream, just as Joseph is promoted after successfully interpreting Pharaoh's dreams (Gen. 41:37–45). Just as Joseph receives authority over all the land of Egypt, so Daniel is put in charge of the whole province of Babylon. Yet, the stories differ in important ways. Pharaoh elevates Joseph so much that the latter is revered everywhere he goes, but Pharaoh also makes it clear that he remains superior to Joseph. In Nebuchadnezzar's case, however, he himself falls down on his face and prostrates himself before Daniel. He even instructs that a cereal offering and oblations be sacrificed to him. The language of worship here has proved to be an embarrassment to interpreters, given that the text says nothing of Daniel's reaction to the gesture. Some interpreters imagine that Daniel probably did refuse the honor, or that Nebuchadnezzar only tried to offer the sacrifices to Daniel but that the latter probably stopped him. Others frankly admit that Daniel's acquiescence is tantamount to acceptance of worship. Thus, for all his faithfulness and wisdom, Daniel is finally a human being with all his faults and foibles. The text is, in any case, silent about Daniel's response. The account simply depicts Nebuchadnezzar, who is called "the king of kings" (Dan. 2:36) now fallen, with his face upon the ground, prostrate before the lowly Jewish captive. The prediction of the collapse of the mighty statue of kingship by a mere stone is foreshadowed, and even set in motion, in this event, for the "head of gold" is now in fact on the ground. The gestures of worship convey the point of the narrator that the reign of God is manifest in Daniel, who, as the rhetorical allusions to the Joseph story imply, is also the seed of Abraham. Whereas in Isaiah 40–55, witnesses are unable to verify that the foreign gods are true (Isa. 43:9), Nebuchadnezzar, having heard the telling of what will happen before it happens, now confesses theological truth. "Truly, your God is God of gods and Lord of kings and a revealer of mysteries," he proclaims, "for you have been able to reveal this mystery!" (Dan. 2:47). As Daniel's early doxology anticipates, the wisdom and power of God are evident in the wisdom and power of the exile Daniel, the servant of God (vv. 20, 23). The reign of God is, in this way, already effected through this one who is "from the mountain." The promise that human power will be excelled by the enduring kingship of God is already coming to pass in this implausible way—through a human being, and a lowly one at that. The sacerdotal language of Nebuchadnezzar's obeisance before Daniel shocks the reader to this realization: the captive Daniel represents the reign of God!

The predicted growth of the stone is, likewise, also foreshadowed and its fulfillment set in motion in this event. Daniel predicted that the stone will grow to be "a great mountain" (v. 35). Now Nebuchadnezzar literally "made Daniel great," gave him many "great gifts," made him chief (literally "a *great* one") of the governors of all the province of Babylon (v. 48). Three times in one verse the text implies that the Jewish exile is becoming "great," the Aramaic word here being related to the Hebrew word used of the descendants of Abraham becoming "many" (Isa. 51:2). To be sure, that greatness is not yet to the extent predicted; the earth is not yet entirely filled. The greatness of the chosen servant of God is, for now, only over Nebuchadnezzar, over "all the province of Babylon" and over "all the sages of Babylon." Indeed, the exiles are still displaced and required to function under foreign rule; Daniel himself is still "at the king's gate," meaning he is at the beck and call of earthly power (v. 49), for the "king's gate" is where the king's retainers wait to be summoned to duty (see Esth. 2:19, 21; 3:2–3). Still, the prediction of the dream oracle has been set in motion in this preliminary way. Not only did Daniel become great. At his behest, three other Jews—referred to in verse 49 by their humiliating, nonsensical exilic names (contrast v. 17)—are now promoted with him, again fulfilling the promised growth of the stone from the mountain, which is, indeed, how the reign of God is made manifest on earth: worked out incrementally through the quiet faith of individuals, and in ways that the world does not expect or recognize.

# 3. The Fiery Furnace
## *Daniel 3:1–30*

1 King Nebuchadnezzar made a golden statue whose height was sixty cubits
and whose width was six cubits; he set it up on the plain of Dura in the
province of Babylon. 2 Then King Nebuchadnezzar sent for the satraps, the
prefects, and the governors, the counselors, the treasurers, the justices,
the magistrates, and all the officials of the provinces to assemble and come to
the dedication of the statue that King Nebuchadnezzar had set up. 3 So the
satraps, the prefects, and the governors, the counselors, the treasurers, the justices, the magistrates, and all the officials of the provinces, assembled for the
dedication of the statue that King Nebuchadnezzar had set up. When they
were standing before the statue that Nebuchadnezzar had set up, 4 the herald
proclaimed aloud, "You are commanded, O peoples, nations, and languages,
5 that when you hear the sound of the horn, pipe, lyre, trigon, harp, drum, and
entire musical ensemble, you are to fall down and worship the golden statue
that King Nebuchadnezzar has set up. 6 Whoever does not fall down and worship shall immediately be thrown into a furnace of blazing fire." 7 Therefore,
as soon as all the peoples heard the sound of the horn, pipe, lyre, trigon, harp,
drum, and entire musical ensemble, all the peoples, nations, and languages fell
down and worshiped the golden statue that King Nebuchadnezzar had set up.

8 Accordingly, at this time certain Chaldeans came forward and
denounced the Jews. 9 They said to King Nebuchadnezzar, "O king, live forever! 10 You, O king, have made a decree, that everyone who hears the
sound of the horn, pipe, lyre, trigon, harp, drum, and entire musical ensemble, shall fall down and worship the golden statue, 11 and whoever does not
fall down and worship shall be thrown into a furnace of blazing fire.
12 There are certain Jews whom you have appointed over the affairs of the
province of Babylon: Shadrach, Meshach, and Abednego. These pay no heed
to you, O king. They do not serve your gods and they do not worship the
golden statue that you have set up."

13 Then Nebuchadnezzar in furious rage commanded that Shadrach,
Meshach, and Abednego be brought in; so they brought those men before
the king. 14 Nebuchadnezzar said to them, "Is it true, O Shadrach, Meshach,

**and Abednego, that you do not serve my gods and you do not worship the golden statue that I have set up? 15 Now if you are ready when you hear the sound of the horn, pipe, lyre, trigon, harp, drum, and entire musical ensemble to fall down and worship the statue that I have made, well and good. But if you do not worship, you shall immediately be thrown into a furnace of blazing fire, and who is the god that will deliver you out of my hands?"**

**16 Shadrach, Meshach, and Abednego answered the king, "O Nebuchadnezzar, we have no need to present a defense to you in this matter. 17 If our God whom we serve is able to deliver us from the furnace of blazing fire and out of your hand, O king, let him deliver us. 18 But if not, be it known to you, O king, that we will not serve your gods and we will not worship the golden statue that you have set up."**

**19 Then Nebuchadnezzar was so filled with rage against Shadrach, Meshach, and Abednego that his face was distorted. He ordered the furnace heated up seven times more than was customary, 20 and ordered some of the strongest guards in his army to bind Shadrach, Meshach, and Abednego and to throw them into the furnace of blazing fire. 21 So the men were bound, still wearing their tunics, their trousers, their hats, and their other garments, and they were thrown into the furnace of blazing fire. 22 Because the king's command was urgent and the furnace was so overheated, the raging flames killed the men who lifted Shadrach, Meshach, and Abednego. 23 But the three men, Shadrach, Meshach, and Abednego, fell down, bound, into the furnace of blazing fire.**

**24 Then King Nebuchadnezzar was astonished and rose up quickly. He said to his counselors, "Was it not three men that we threw bound into the fire?" They answered the king, "True, O king." 25 He replied, "But I see four men unbound, walking in the middle of the fire, and they are not hurt; and the fourth has the appearance of a god." 26 Nebuchadnezzar then approached the door of the furnace of blazing fire and said, "Shadrach, Meshach, and Abednego, servants of the Most High God, come out! Come here!" So Shadrach, Meshach, and Abednego came out from the fire. 27 And the satraps, the prefects, the governors, and the king's counselors gathered together and saw that the fire had not had any power over the bodies of those men; the hair of their heads was not singed, their tunics were not harmed, and not even the smell of fire came from them. 28 Nebuchadnezzar said, "Blessed be the God of Shadrach, Meshach, and Abednego, who has sent his angel and delivered his servants who trusted in him. They disobeyed the king's command and yielded up their bodies rather than serve and worship any god except their own God. 29 Therefore I make a decree: Any people, nation, or language that utters blasphemy against the God of Shadrach, Meshach, and Abednego shall be torn limb from limb, and their houses laid in ruins; for there is no other god who is able to deliver in this way." 30 Then the king promoted Shadrach, Meshach, and Abednego in the province of Babylon.**

The opening of the literary unit (3:1–30) is jarring in light of the happy ending of chapter 2. Upon hearing the account of his dream and the interpretation of it, Nebuchadnezzar had fallen on his face and bowed down to Daniel (2:46), thus already setting in motion the fulfillment of the prediction that the reign of God would bring to naught human kingship. Yet the prediction had hardly been realized in full. The new story shows that the king had not in fact understood what he had heard, that he had accepted only part of Daniel's interpretation but not the rest of it, or, perhaps, that he willfully tried to reshape the vision to his own liking. Inasmuch as the account is introduced without any chronological notice (as in 2:1), reading it as a sequel to the preceding story seems natural, especially because this account also concerns a gigantic image. Indeed, interpreters of the passage long ago proposed that Nebuchadnezzar had probably been inspired by his own dream to build this image. In any case, he made it wholly of gold—not just a statue with only a head of gold, as he had seen in his dream, but an entire edifice of gold. The structure is not divided into parts, as the statue of his dream was, nor is it made of different materials, nor does the statue have feet of clay. The defiant will of the king is suggested by the number of times the text refers to the edifice as something that he "had set up." Nine times in verses 1 through 18 does the narrative report that Nebuchadnezzar has set the image up (vv. 1, 2, 3 [twice], 5, 7, 12, 14, 18). Moreover, even though he himself had previously fallen down and bowed down to Daniel (2:46), he would now have others fall down and bow down to the edifice that he has installed (vv. 5, 6, 11, 15). The initially unspoken challenge to God's will, dramatized in the construction of the image that is contrary to what has been revealed about his dream, later becomes explicit in the king's taunt and claim of power above any god: "who is the god that will deliver you out of my hands?" (v. 15). The king into whose hands God had given the exiles (so the Hebrew text of 1:2) now dares to challenge God—indeed, any god—to deliver his condemned subjects out of his hands.

The absence of Daniel in the story is difficult to explain. Indeed, this chapter is the only one in the book in which Daniel has no role whatsoever to play. Yet, the book of Daniel is not about one individual, but rather, describes the experience of faithful Jews under different circumstances. After all, the stone that would shatter the mighty statue represents not only one individual (see the commentary on chapter 2), but the powerless and lowly of different times and places.

## NEBUCHADNEZZAR'S SETUP
## Daniel 3:1–7

The story begins with Nebuchadnezzar's construction in the plain of Dura (an unknown location) of a giant "golden image," 60 cubits high and 6 cubits wide. Given that a cubit is the distance from the elbow to the tip of the middle finger of an adult male, a span of about 17.5 inches, the image would have been about 90 feet tall and 9 feet wide. The dimensions suggest an extraordinarily lanky edifice that is more like an obelisk than a well-proportioned statue. This odd shape has prompted some scholars to suggest that the edifice was not a statue per se, but a monolith that was sculpted only at the top or a tall pedestal with a statue mounted on it. Striking parallels to both models exist throughout the ancient Near East, as commentators have frequently noted. Unlike the image of the preceding chapter, however, the narrator provides no detail about the precise shape or the construction of this edifice. Indeed, apart from its dimension and its location, the reader is told nothing about the monument except that it was made of gold (vv. 1, 5, 7, 10, 12, 14, 18) and that Nebuchadnezzar had set it up (vv. 1, 2, 3 [twice], 5, 7, 12, 14, 18). One is not told the form of the edifice and never does the chapter state if it was an image of the king or a god, but the narrator repeatedly emphasizes that it was of gold and that Nebuchadnezzar had set it up.

Because the story comes immediately after the account of the statue of Nebuchadnezzar's dream in the preceding chapter, one may be inclined to think of the image in the dream, as many interpreters from ancient times have done. If so, Nebuchadnezzar is trying to concretize his dream and, perhaps, even to correct and improve on the image that he had seen. Despite his obsequious response to Daniel's interpretation of the dream (2:46–49), he seems to have heard only what he had wanted to hear. The edifice that he has made and set up has no parts made of different materials, no parts of inferior metal, no feet of clay. The entire statue was made of gold, not just the head that was supposed to represent him. If there is validity to the view that the structure was a monolith sculptured only at the top, Nebuchadnezzar may be interpreting the dream as he desired, with himself at the very peak of the entire golden edifice. Nebuchadnezzar is trying to reshape his vision!

The significance of the event to the king is suggested by the list of public officials summoned. The text mentions seven classes of "all the officials of the provinces," meaning that all who are in the government of the entire empire were summoned. The officials are listed in order of seniority: from the "satraps" (a Persian word for the provincial governors) to the "magistrates." The entire government, from the imperial high officials to the lowly local agents, is apparently summoned to attend the monument's "dedication," the same term used for the dedication of the altar (Num. 7:10–11, 84, 88; 2 Chr. 7:9), the temple (1 Kgs. 8:63; Ps. 30:1), and the rebuilt wall of Jerusalem (Neh. 12:27). The authority of the king is, indeed, indicated by the fact that all who were summoned immediately complied, and the narrator makes this point effectively by repeating the same tedious list in Daniel 3:2 and 3:3.

These public figures clearly represent the full extent and diversity of the empire, for the king's herald addresses them as "peoples, nations, and languages" (v. 4), a reference to the ethnic, political, and linguistic components of the empire. They are to respond with one accord to the signal of the various musical instruments (wind, string, and percussion instruments are all included) by falling and bowing down to the golden statue that Nebuchadnezzar has set up. And they do, as if mindlessly: every time they hear the cacophonous cue, they all bow down at once as if that bowing down were just a thoughtless reflex.

The narrator still does not say if the statue is specifically of a god or of the king. What is clear in the text is that the king's authority is at stake; failure to comply with his command would result in being thrown into a fiery furnace (v. 6). Perhaps what the image depicted precisely is irrelevant. The greater problem seems to be that the will of Nebuchadnezzar is set over against the will of Israel's God. The problem that the passage raises is allegiance to any other power than the God of Israel.

## THE ACCUSATION
## Daniel 3:8–12

Trouble for the Jews comes initially not from the king but from the Chaldeans, a term that may be used either in the ethnic sense for the Babylonians (see 5:30; 9:1; Jer. 24:5; 25:12; Ezek. 1:3) or in the professional sense for the Chaldean diviners (see Dan. 2:4–10; 3:8–12; 4:7; 5:7). Perhaps both are meant. Certainly, the Chaldeans are provoked not by professional jealousy alone but by the fact that the foreigners are receiving promotions in their own domain. Xenophobia is suggested by the terminology used: the narrator juxtaposes the Chaldeans (literally "the men, the Chaldeans") and the Jews (v. 8). While a specific charge is leveled against three Jews in particular—Shadrach, Meshach, and Abednego (v. 12)—the narrator suggests that the Jews in general are implicated. One gathers from the book of Esther, too, that the Jews were despised simply because they refused to assimilate completely to the cultures in which they found themselves. Mordecai refused to "bow down and do obeisance" before Haman, even as the king had commanded. And so some people plotted to eliminate all Jews because "their laws are different from those of every other people, and they do not keep the king's laws, so that it is not appropriate for the king to tolerate them" (Esth. 3:8). The offense was specifically committed by Mordecai, but all Jews were implicated. So, too, the Chaldeans now try to frame the Jews, not merely because of professional jealousy but because of their sheer hatred of these foreigners.

The Aramaic idiom translated in the NRSV as "denounced" (Dan. 3:8) is a vivid one: it means, literally, "to eat pieces of." The three men named are charged with sedition, specifically, for disobeying the edict of Nebuchadnezzar by not worshiping his gods and not bowing down before the image that he had set up.

## THE CONFRONTATION
## Daniel 3:13–18

The Chaldeans, thus, instigate the king to "furious rage" (v. 13). The last time that one read about the rage of the king, it was directed at the Chaldeans, who could not comply with the king's demand to tell him his dream and its interpretation (2:12) and that rage brought the threat of death. Now the Chaldeans manage to turn the anger of the king against the Jews, and the three accused are presently summoned to appear before him. The king asks if the accusation is true, but he does not wait for a reply to the question (v. 14). Instead, he establishes the criterion by which he would know if they were guilty: either they submit to the edict and bow down before the image or they would be thrown into the fiery furnace (v. 15). Clearly, however, the king's dare is not only directed at the three men but at God, for he asks, "who is the god that will deliver you out of my hands?" (v. 15). Nebuchadnezzar's challenge echoes the one issued centuries before by the Assyrians under Sennacherib who had besieged Jerusalem in the time of Hezekiah (Isa. 36:19–20; 37:11–12 // 2 Kgs. 18:33–35; 19:12–13). Sennacherib dared to set himself up as an alternative power to the God of Jerusalem. Not only did he challenge the Lord to deliver the citizens of Jerusalem out of his (Sennacherib's) hand, he also set himself up as someone who could deliver them out of their entrapment in the city to the abundance of a new promised land. Now Nebuchadnezzar, too, dares to insist that the Jews submit to his will and worship the image that he has set up, and he is arrogant enough to believe that no divine power can deliver the Jews from his power.

The response of the three men is a theological high point in the passage. The NRSV translation emphasizes the courage of the men. Accordingly, not only is Nebuchadnezzar addressed without his title, the three say defiantly that they would proffer no defense, presumably of their intended resistance, to him: "O Nebuchadnezzar, we have no need to present a defense to you in this matter" (v. 16). In the first place, the implicit discourtesy of their address is without parallel anywhere in the book, where the kings are always addressed by their titles. Indeed, in this very context, Nebuchadnezzar is properly addressed ("O king," vv. 17, 18). The text may, in fact, with a slight shift in punctuation, read "Shadrach, Meshach, and Abednego answered King Nebuchadnezzar, 'We have no need. . . .'" More importantly, the Aramaic actually says nothing about presenting a defense before the king. Instead of reference to a defense, the Aramaic text says simply that there is no need "to give back" or "to return" to the king on the matter. The point is that these men feel no compunction to give a comeback, as it were, regarding "this matter," namely, the theological challenge raised by Nebuchadnezzar: "who is the god who will deliver you out of my hand?" Therefore, the situation is not that they refuse to give a defense of their decision to the king, which if correct would indicate their courage. Rather, Shadrach, Meshach, and Abednego do not feel compelled to respond to the king's taunt at all. Courage is not really the issue, for a "comeback" is simply not theirs to give.

The meaning of their response in verse 16 is clarified in verses 17–18. Corresponding to the king's if–if not scenario in verse 15, they offer another point of view, an alternative if–if not scenario of their own in verses 17–18. The point-counterpoint structure evident in the two competing scenarios is much more clearly evident in the Aramaic than in the English translation. The king laid out his view of the situation: "*If* you are . . . but *if not* . . ." (v. 15). They, however, refocus the conversation: "*If* our God is . . . but *if not* . . ." (vv. 17–18). The same Aramaic particle indicating existence or presence ("is/are/exist") in verse 15 is repeated in verse 17. Thus, the three men shift the question from their being ("you are") to God's being ("God is")—from their being ready to fall down and worship Nebuchadnezzar's edifice to God's being able to deliver them. The issue is not whether or not they are, but whether or not God is!

All ancient and modern versions struggle with the proper rendering of verses 17–18, largely because of the conditional clauses ("if . . . if not") that may suggest doubt about God's existence or ability. The Greek translators, along with other ancient versions, disregard the conditionality of the Aramaic clause ("if . . .") and make the three men affirm the presence and power of God: "For there is a God whom we worship, capable of saving . . ." Other ancient interpreters take the word for "if" to mean "behold," but that grammatical particle can mean "behold" only in Hebrew, not Aramaic; the same word is translated as "if" in verses 15 and 18. Still, some modern translations find various ways to circumvent the implied conditionality of God's being and power. Thus the NIV, without any indication of emendation, reads: "If *we are thrown into the blazing furnace*, the God we serve *is* able to save us from it" (v. 17, emphasis added).

Similarly, RSV attempts to avoid the perceived theological problem by assuming that the Aramaic text was elliptical and so the translators supply words of clarification: "If *it be so*, our God whom we serve *is* able" (emphasis added). Such defensive moves are totally unwarranted and unnecessary when one reads the text in light of its context. The three men are not contemplating the question of divine presence or ability here; they are not wondering about God's power. Rather, the response is simply a rhetorical refocusing of Nebuchadnezzar's challenge away from themselves and their readiness to God's presence and power. The riposte to Nebuchadnezzar's taunt is not theirs to deliver (v. 16), because the issue to them is not whether or not they are ready to submit to the king's will, as Nebuchadnezzar implies (v. 15), but whether or not God is present and willing to save (vv. 17–18).

By structuring the dialogue in this point-counterpoint fashion, the narrator indicates that the decisive issue at hand is really not the courage of the Jews, although that aspect is part of the story. Rather, the critical question is the presence and power of God: inasmuch as a God exists who is able, it is entirely up to God to deliver, if that be the divine will. Nevertheless, even if the presence and power of God would not be made manifest in their deliverance, the three Jews state that they will not worship Nebuchadnezzar's gods or do obeisance before the golden image that he has set up. Indeed, the refocusing of the issue turns out to be an occasion for proclamation of their faith, an opportunity to instruct: "Be it known to you, O king. . . ." So the proclamation before the king provides an edifying lesson for the faithful of all times. There is no quid pro quo in faithful relation between God and humanity. On the one hand, faithful conduct is not conditional upon God's response, whatever that may be. Although the translators of the NRSV note that the final clause of verse 17 may be understood as indicative ("he will deliver us"), they prefer to take it to be injunctive ("let him deliver us" or "may he deliver us"). If the latter is correct, a prayer is implicit in the words of Shadrach, Meshach, and Abednego. Yet, their faith is not subject to God's willingness to respond. Their conduct is not conditional upon the answer to their prayer or their wish! They do not make a deal with God in the way that people sometimes do when they pledge that if God will do this or that for them, then they will believe or serve God. Rather, the three Jews decide that they will be faithful, whether or not God will save them. Simply put, their challenge is faithfulness to God as stipulated in the first commandment (Exod. 20:3–4; Deut. 5:7–9), which, together with all the other commandments, is predicated upon the saving acts of God already performed long ago (Exod. 20:2; Deut. 5:6). Faithfulness to that commandment is, therefore, a response to grace already experienced; divine deliverance can never be a condition to faithful conduct. Accordingly, one is to worship God alone and no other, regardless of how that God will or will not act.

Idolatry is here associated with political power; the text juxtaposes the worship of Nebuchadnezzar's gods and obeisance to the image that he has set up. Up to this point, the narrator has said over and over again that the image was Nebuchadnezzar's creation: he made it and set it up. What is at stake, then, is the idolatry of civil religion, the exaltation of political power in the name of religion. To Nebuchadnezzar, submission to his will is virtually the same thing as worshiping his gods, and the narrator seems particularly concerned about Nebuchadnezzar's demand for submission to *his* will and power. This idolatry is what Shadrach, Meshach, and Abednego refuse.

## THE CONSEQUENCE
## Daniel 3:19–23

Enraged by the resistance of the three, Nebuchadnezzar orders them to be thrown into the furnace, which apparently has an opening at the top (see v. 23) but also a door at the bottom (v. 26). Every precaution is taken to ensure that the three men cannot escape. The furnace is to be heated seven times beyond what is customary or necessary, seven being the symbolic number of completeness and extreme. The guards who are ordered to throw them in are among the most muscular, an unnecessary precaution. The three men are to be cast into the extreme heat bound and clothed with every flammable item of clothing, including even their headwear; they are to be executed in the formal attire in which they have come for the occasion. All these measures are taken no doubt to ensure that no one can deliver them from their deaths. Indeed, the fire is heated so much that its raging flames leap out of the furnace and immediately kill the executioners. The flames are that deadly even outside the furnace! But the three fall down into it, and, lest one forget the impossibility of their situation, the narrator asserts once again that they are bound and that the fire is blazing.

## IN THE MIDST OF THE FIRE
## Daniel 3:24–25

Nebuchadnezzar is startled by something that he, and apparently only he, sees. Although three individuals are thrown into the furnace bound, he sees four individuals unbound and walking about unharmed in the middle of the fire, the fourth being like "a son of god" (so the Aramaic text has it in Dan 3:25; NRSV has "a god"), an expression meaning a divine being (see also Gen. 6:2; Job 1:6; 2:1; Ps. 29:1). The Greek version, which is a greatly expanded text (including a prayer of one of the three men, a prose transitionary unit, and a hymn by the three men), elaborates on how, following the prayer, the angel of the Lord descends into the furnace to help them. That longer version is, however, probably a secondary attempt to elaborate on the terse report of Nebuchadnezzar. The Aramaic text, in fact, preserves the mystery and wonder of divine presence in the furnace. Contrary to the expanded version, it does not explain the presence of the divine being in the furnace, does not identify the being as an angel of the Lord, and does not say that the divine being comes down into the furnace. Rather, it merely affirms the appearance of one like a divine being "in the middle of the fire" (v. 25) and it asserts that the three who had been bound are now unbound and walking about unharmed with the mysterious being in the furnace. The expanded version describes how the angel of the Lord descends into the furnace, drives out the flames, and causes a cool breeze to blow through it. That interpretation perhaps misses the point of the story. The narrator does not say that the four individuals are walking in the furnace, but that they are walking amid the fire. Indeed, the text gives no indication that the three men are rescued *from* the fire. Rather, the story is that they are with a divine being *in the midst* of the fire. They encounter divine presence in the middle of the fire.

Here, as often in the Old Testament, fire is associated with the presence of God. On Mount Sinai, the presence of God was accompanied by, perhaps even made manifest by, the appearance of fire (Exod. 19:16, 19; 20:18, 21) and in Israel's hymnody fire is often associated with the manifestation of God (e.g., Pss. 18:8–16; 77:17–20). God spoke to people "from the midst of the fire" (Deut. 4:11–12, 15, 33, 36; Exod. 3:2). The people of Israel were led in the wanderings by the sight of a pillar of fire (e.g., Exod. 13:21; 14:24) and when they entered the promised land, they were to know that the Lord their God was going before them as a devouring fire (Deut. 9:3). So when Nebuchadnezzar had the three faithful Jews thrown "into the midst of the fire," as the Aramaic has it in Daniel 3:24, they were with the one who has the appearance of a divine being "in the midst of the fire" (v. 25).

## THE OUTCOME
## Daniel 3:26–30

Nebuchadnezzar summons the three men out of the furnace, addressing them as "servants of the Most High God" (v. 26), using the divine epithet that from ancient times had been used of the deity as the "God of gods and Lord of kings" (2:47). Thus, the narrator has Nebuchadnezzar acknowledging the superiority of the God of the Jews over all other powers in the universe, celestial and terrestrial (see Gen. 14:19–20; Num. 24:16; Deut. 32:8; Isa. 14:14). The king had set out to impose his will through the image that he had set up, an image that at once exalted his gods and himself. He had asked rhetorically what god there was that could deliver the three men from his power (v. 15), but now his eyes have seen, as it were, and he knows that it is "the Most High God," with whom he is dealing. He alone has caught a glimpse of the reality in the midst of the fire, but now others also witness the miracle of their encounter. The fire does not have power over the bodies of the three: their hair is not singed, their clothing is not burned, and there is not even the smell of fire on them. The specific reference to the power of fire is significant, especially in light of the fact that most of the words used of the officials are of Persian origin, for fire was venerated among the Persians and the fire ordeal was the ultimate judicial trial. Yet the narrator notes that they recognize that the fire has no power over the bodies of the three men. The Jews do not only survive the ordeal (compare also Isa. 43:2; Ps. 66:12), they even encounter divine presence in their fire ordeal. Thereupon, Nebuchadnezzar acknowledges that God has in fact intervened in this event, delivering those who have been faithful. The narrator even has Nebuchadnezzar issuing an edict forbidding anyone in his diverse imperial realm—all the ethnic, political, and linguistic components of the empire—to blaspheme the God of the Jews, for "there is no other god who is able to deliver in this way" (v. 29).

# 4. The Humbling of Nebuchadnezzar
## *Daniel 4:1–37*

1 **King Nebuchadnezzar to all peoples, nations, and languages that live**
**throughout the earth: May you have abundant prosperity!** 2 **The signs and**
**wonders that the Most High God has worked for me I am pleased to**
**recount.**

3 **How great are his signs,**
**how mighty his wonders!**
**His kingdom is an everlasting kingdom,**
**and his sovereignty is from generation to generation.**

4 **I, Nebuchadnezzar, was living at ease in my home and prospering in**
**my palace.** 5 **I saw a dream that frightened me; my fantasies in bed and the**
**visions of my head terrified me.** 6 **So I made a decree that all the wise men**
**of Babylon should be brought before me, in order that they might tell me**
**the interpretation of the dream.** 7 **Then the magicians, the enchanters, the**
**Chaldeans, and the diviners came in, and I told them the dream, but they**
**could not tell me its interpretation.** 8 **At last Daniel came in before me—he**
**who was named Belteshazzar after the name of my god, and who is**
**endowed with a spirit of the holy gods—and I told him the dream:** 9 **"O**
**Belteshazzar, chief of the magicians, I know that you are endowed with a**
**spirit of the holy gods and that no mystery is too difficult for you. Hear the**
**dream that I saw; tell me its interpretation.**

10 **Upon my bed this is what I saw;**
**there was a tree at the center of the earth,**
**and its height was great.**
11 **The tree grew great and strong,**
**its top reached to heaven,**
**and it was visible to the ends of the whole earth.**
12 **Its foliage was beautiful,**
**its fruit abundant,**
**and it provided food for all.**
**The animals of the field found shade under it,**
**the birds of the air nested in its branches,**

and from it all living beings were fed.
13 I continued looking, in the visions of my head as I lay in bed, and there
was a holy watcher, coming down from heaven. 14 He cried aloud and said:
'Cut down the tree and chop off its branches,
strip off its foliage and scatter its fruit.
Let the animals flee from beneath it
and the birds from its branches.
15 But leave its stump and roots in the ground,
with a band of iron and bronze,
in the tender grass of the field.
Let him be bathed with the dew of heaven,
and let his lot be with the animals of the field
in the grass of the earth.
16 Let his mind be changed from that of a human,
and let the mind of an animal be given to him.
And let seven times pass over him.
17 The sentence is rendered by decree of the watchers,
the decision is given by order of the holy ones,
in order that all who live may know
that the Most High is sovereign over the kingdom of mortals;
he gives it to whom he will
and sets over it the lowliest of human beings.'
18 This is the dream that I, King Nebuchadnezzar, saw. Now you,
Belteshazzar, declare the interpretation, since all the wise men of my kingdom are unable to tell me the interpretation. You are able, however, for you
are endowed with a spirit of the holy gods."

19 Then Daniel, who was called Belteshazzar, was severely distressed for
a while. His thoughts terrified him. The king said, "Belteshazzar, do not let
the dream or the interpretation terrify you." Belteshazzar answered, "My
lord, may the dream be for those who hate you, and its interpretation for
your enemies! 20 The tree that you saw, which grew great and strong, so that
its top reached to heaven and was visible to the end of the whole earth,
21 whose foliage was beautiful and its fruit abundant, and which provided
food for all, under which animals of the field lived, and in whose branches
the birds of the air had nests—22 it is you, O king! You have grown great and
strong. Your greatness has increased and reaches to heaven, and your sovereignty to the ends of the earth. 23 And whereas the king saw a holy
watcher coming down from heaven and saying, 'Cut down the tree and
destroy it, but leave its stump and roots in the ground, with a band of iron
and bronze, in the grass of the field; and let him be bathed with the dew of
heaven, and let his lot be with the animals of the field, until seven times
pass over him'—24 this is the interpretation, O king, and it is a decree of the
Most High that has come upon my lord the king: 25 You shall be driven away
from human society, and your dwelling shall be with the wild animals. You
shall be made to eat grass like oxen, you shall be bathed with the dew of

heaven, and seven times shall pass over you, until you have learned that the
Most High has sovereignty over the kingdom of mortals, and gives it to
whom he will. 26 As it was commanded to leave the stump and roots of the
tree, your kingdom shall be reestablished for you from the time that you
learn that Heaven is sovereign. 27 Therefore, O king, may my counsel be
acceptable to you: atone for your sins with righteousness, and your iniquities with mercy to the oppressed, so that your prosperity may be prolonged."

28 All this came upon King Nebuchadnezzar. 29 At the end of twelve
months he was walking on the roof of the royal palace of Babylon, 30 and
the king said, "Is this not magnificent Babylon, which I have built as a royal
capital by my mighty power and for my glorious majesty?" 31 While the
words were still in the king's mouth, a voice came from heaven: "O King
Nebuchadnezzar, to you it is declared: The kingdom has departed from you!
32 You shall be driven away from human society, and your dwelling shall be
with the animals of the field. You shall be made to eat grass like oxen, and
seven times shall pass over you, until you have learned that the Most High
has sovereignty over the kingdom of mortals and gives it to whom he will."
33 Immediately the sentence was fulfilled against Nebuchadnezzar. He was
driven away from human society, ate grass like oxen, and his body was
bathed with the dew of heaven, until his hair grew as long as eagles' feathers and his nails became like birds' claws.

34 When that period was over, I, Nebuchadnezzar, lifted my eyes to
heaven, and my reason returned to me.

I blessed the Most High,
    and praised and honored the one who lives forever.
For his sovereignty is an everlasting sovereignty,
    and his kingdom endures from generation to generation.
35 All the inhabitants of the earth are accounted as nothing,
    and he does what he wills with the host of heaven
    and the inhabitants of the earth.
There is no one who can stay his hand
    or say to him, "What are you doing?"

36 At that time my reason returned to me; and my majesty and splendor
were restored to me for the glory of my kingdom. My counselors and my
lords sought me out, I was reestablished over my kingdom, and still more
greatness was added to me. 37 Now I, Nebuchadnezzar, praise and extol
and honor the King of heaven,

for all his works are truth,
    and his ways are justice;
and he is able to bring low
    those who walk in pride.

Users of different English translations may be puzzled by the fact that some versions do not start at the same place as the NRSV. Rather, the first three verses in the NRSV are sometimes attached to the end of the preceding chapter, as they are in the Hebrew Bible. As a matter of fact, chapter and verse divisions in the Bible were not original; they were introduced into the text only from the thirteenth century C.E. onward. Therefore, editors of various modern versions always have to make judgments about whether or not to follow those divisions, and they make their decision largely on literary grounds.

The chapter division followed by the NRSV and many other versions is justified. The preceding literary unit ends with the promotion of the three Jews in Babylon (3:30), just as the story before it ends with the promotion of the Jews (2:49). Moreover, Nebuchadnezzar's confessional praise of God's sovereignty in 4:2–3 is neatly paralleled by the confessional praise of God's sovereignty at the end of the chapter (vv. 34–37). Indeed, by this framing, the key theological issue in this chapter is identified as the sovereignty of God over against human kingship, and for this reason the terms for sovereignty and kingship, the focus of the opening and closing doxologies (vv. 1–3, 34–37), are reiterated throughout the chapter (vv. 3, 17, 18, 22, 25, 26, 31, 32, 34, 36). The Aramaic words for "heaven" and "earth" are also repeated throughout (vv. 1, 10, 11, 12, 13, 15, 20, 21, 22, 23, 25, 26, 31, 33, 34, 35, 37). This chapter addresses the relationship between the earthly king and the heavenly king.

The account is presented as an open letter by Nebuchadnezzar addressed "to all peoples, nations, and languages that live throughout the earth" (v. 1). By the choice of this particular genre, the author implies that the content of this account is a matter for public consumption. Despite the emphasis on the lesson that Nebuchadnezzar himself had to learn (vv. 25–26, 32), the fact that the message is sent in the form of a royal encyclical suggests that what is reported here is not merely a private and personal matter. Rather, the lesson that Nebuchadnezzar learned is meant for "all . . . that live throughout the earth" (v. 1). Indeed, the text itself explicitly states the purpose of Nebuchadnezzar's experience: "in order that all who live may know that the Most High is sovereign over the kingdom of mortals; he gives it to whom he will and sets over it the lowliest of human beings" (v. 17).

## INTRODUCTION AND DOXOLOGY
## Daniel 4:1–3

The chapter begins with an epistolary formula that is standard in the Aramaic letters from the postexilic period, containing an address ("King Nebuchadnezzar to all peoples, nations, and languages that live throughout the earth") and a salutation ("May you have abundant peace!" [not "prosperity," as in the NRSV]). This letter is no ordinary letter, of course, but a royal missive. A letter from the Persian king to Ezra opens similarly: "Artaxerxes, king of kings, to the priest Ezra, scribe of the law of the God of heaven: Peace!" (Ezra 7:12). However, whereas the letter of Artaxerxes was addressed to a single individual, the letter of Nebuchadnezzar is addressed to a much wider audience: "to all peoples, nations, and languages that live throughout the earth." The allusion to all ethnic, political, and linguistic constituencies is not new in Daniel. We have already encountered the same expression several times in the preceding chapter (3:4, 7, 29). What is new here, however, is the expression "throughout all the earth." The expression is no doubt a hyperbole for the entire empire. Yet, "the earth" occurs seven other times in the chapter (vv. 10, 11, 15, 20, 22, 35 [twice]), four of which concern the impression of Nebuchadnezzar's power on earth (vv. 10, 11, 20, 22). These stand in contrast to the sixteen references to heaven in the chapter (vv. 11, 12, 13, 15, 20, 21, 22, 23 [twice], 25, 26, 31, 33, 34, 35, 37), most of which appear in connection with the domain and power of God. Clearly, at issue in the chapter is the relationship of earthly power and heavenly power—the power of Nebuchadnezzar versus the power of God. There is no denial of earthly might, only an insistence upon its subordination to the sovereignty and power of God in heaven. Here in the introduction to the chapter, then, one finds the earthly emperor issuing an imperial communiqué to the widest possible audience, pointing beyond himself to the superiority of the God of heaven.

The ostensible purpose of this royal communiqué, the letter states explicitly, is to recount the "signs and wonders that the Most High God" has performed (v. 2). This statement of purpose from the king who presides over the Babylonian captivity is most ironic, for the reference to divine performance of "signs and wonders" recalls the manifestation of God's power in the liberation of Israel from bondage (Exod. 7:3; Deut. 6:22; 7:19; Ps. 135:9). Moreover, the deity is called "the Most High God," an epithet of God as the supreme ruler of heaven and earth (see, for example, Gen. 14:19–20; Num. 24:16). Indeed, the imperial message begins with a doxology, a confessional praise of that supreme God, using terms that reverberate through the chapter: great, mighty, kingdom, sovereignty. Thus, this doxology at the beginning of the imperial proclamation provides a clue to the substance of the chapter, indicating that at issue in the story to come are the power and sovereignty of God. Divine kingship is eternal (Dan. 4:3)—not a temporal kingship, as human regimes inevitably must be, but a sovereignty that transcends the generations.

## THE DREAM RECOUNTED
## Daniel 4:4–18

Nebuchadnezzar begins by describing his condition when the dream came to him. He was "at ease" and "prospering" (v. 4). The first term suggests a carefree, indeed, a careless posture. The Aramaic word is related to the one used for blasphemy in 3:29 and for criminal negligence in 6:4 (see also Ezra 4:22; 6:9). So the text implies that Nebuchadnezzar was, at best, negligent. The second term, which is even more poignant, is used elsewhere of the luxuriance of plants, and so one may understand the text to suggest that Nebuchadnezzar was "luxuriating in his palace." Indeed, the word is used most often of verdant trees (e.g., Deut. 12:3; 1 Kgs. 14:23; Jer. 11:16; Hos. 14:9), once of a couch decorated with arboreal motifs (Song 1:16), and twice of people thriving like plants (Pss. 37:35; 52:8). The choice of this particular term is noteworthy, for it anticipates the depiction of Nebuchadnezzar later in the account as a luxuriant tree.

The king's experience is characterized variously as "a dream," "fantasies," and "visions" (Dan. 4:5). Whereas his previous dream had disturbed him and left him without sleep (2:1), this experience frightens and terrifies him (4:5). So, as before, he summons the experts—"all the wise men of Babylon"—to interpret the dream-vision-fantasy for him (v. 6). Unlike the previous occasion, when he demanded that the experts tell him both the content of his dream and its interpretation, Nebuchadnezzar now tells the consultants the dream's content. Still, they are not able to give him the interpretation (v. 7).

Despite the fact that Daniel had so marvelously interpreted the dream for Nebuchadnezzar before, he is not consulted until the end, only after the Chaldean sages have failed to deliver. This pattern accords with other stories of this sort, where the main character comes only at the end to save the day. So Daniel eventually appears and the king immediately recognizes him to be one endowed with a divine spirit (v. 8). The connection of Daniel's captive name, Belteshazzar, with the name of Nebuchadnezzar's god—that is, Bel (see Isa. 46:1)—suggests that from the king's perspective, Daniel's gift must have come from the Babylonian god: "he who was named Belteshazzar after the name of my god, and who is endowed with a spirit of the holy gods" (v. 8). The Aramaic expression interpreted by the NRSV to mean "a spirit of the holy gods" (presumed to be Nebuchadnezzar's perspective) may, however, also be understood as "a spirit of the holy God" (the narrator's perspective). In any case, Daniel is considered as one who has been divinely gifted, as Joseph in Egypt was (Gen. 41:38). Indeed, the linkage between Joseph and Daniel is closer in the original Hebrew in Genesis and the Aramaic in Daniel than is evident in the NRSV. Just as Joseph was said to have been a man "who a spirit of God was in him" (so the Hebrew of Gen. 41:38), Daniel is regarded as one "who a spirit of the holy God was in him" (so the Aramaic of Dan. 4:8).

Nebuchadnezzar's dream report consists of two parts: an optimistic scenario in verses 10–12 and a largely pessimistic one in verses 13–17. The first part focuses on a tree that is remarkable in its extraordinary greatness, its dominance on earth, and its beneficence. The Aramaic terms used for its greatness and strength (v. 11) mirror those used at the opening of the chapter in praise of the Most High God, whose marvelous deeds are praised as great and mighty (v. 3). Perhaps the reader of the chapter is supposed to understand that the greatness and strength of this tree are, in fact, God's wondrous doing on earth.

The tree is at the center of the earth (v. 10) and it is visible to the ends of the earth (v. 11). The tree is luxuriant and fruitful, providing shade for animals, a nesting place for birds, and food for all living creatures (v. 12). Although clearly an earthly tree, its top reaches heaven (compare Gen. 11:4; Isa. 14:13–14; Ezek. 31:3) and it provides for the birds of heaven (NRSV "birds of the air"); two references to earth (Dan. 4:11, 12) are matched by two references to heaven (vv. 11, 12). The tree appears to be of a cosmic nature.

The next scene makes it very clear, however, that the tree is an earthly one. What had seemed to be a cosmic tree is recognized to be merely a microcosm, for a "holy watcher" descends from heaven to order its destruction (v. 13). The "watcher" is said to be "holy" even as the deity whose spirit gifted Daniel to interpret dreams is said to be "holy" (v. 9). Still, the identity of this "watcher" is something of a mystery. This verse provides the only instance in the Old Testament that this particular term ("watcher") is used in Aramaic or in Hebrew. The root of the word is, however, found elsewhere and frequently refers to God's watchfulness of all that is happening in the world, especially of God's attention in the face of overwhelming evil in the world (Pss. 7:7; 44:23; 59:4; Isa. 51:9). As a psalmist puts it, the God who watches Israel will not slumber nor sleep (Ps. 121:4). In various Jewish writings from the Hellenistic and Roman periods, the "watchers" refer to various celestial beings.

The descent of the holy watcher from heaven underscores the earthly nature of the tree, despite the description of it as a tree with its top reaching the heavens. The heaven-to-earth movement is similar to the one we find in the account of the destruction of the Tower of Babel. Arrogant human beings tried to reach God by building a tower with "its top in heaven," but God descends to order its destruction (Gen. 11).

Significantly, the commands of the holy watcher are not issued to Nebuchadnezzar, for the imperative forms are all plural: "You (plural) cut down . . . chop off . . . strip off . . . scatter" (v. 13). The reader is probably to understand these imperatives to be directed at the divine council, all the celestial beings at the beck and call of God (see Isa. 40:1; 1 Kgs. 22:19–22). Poignantly, too, the plural forms recall the Tower of Babel story: "Come, let *us* go down, and confuse their language there" (Gen. 11:7, emphasis added).

The order for destruction is decisive, which is underscored by the threefold command: cut down, chop off, and strip off. At the same time, the annihilation is not to be complete, although it is unclear what precisely of the tree is to be left and what is to be done to that remnant. The NRSV suggests that "its stump and root" are left "with a band of iron and bronze" (v. 15) and the metallic band is presumed by some commentators to be a protective piece binding the stump. The conjunction "and" is not present in the Aramaic text, however, and the possessive suffix is with the second noun rather than the first—"its root" rather than "its stump." Indeed, the Aramaic probably means not "its stump and root" but something like "the tip of its root." The point here is that the tree is to be cut down so thoroughly that only the very tip of its root will remain, thus allowing only the faintest of hope for rejuvenation. Moreover, the metal constraints may apply not to the remnant of the tree, as the NRSV suggests, but to a tethered animal. In fact, the word for the band is used elsewhere of fetters and harnesses (Judg. 15:14; Eccl. 7:26; Ezra 7:26) and is never used in the sense of a protective band of any sort. One should, therefore, probably put a period at the end of verse 15a: "only the tip of its root do leave."

Befitting a dream, the sequence defies logic. One moment the subject is a tree (v. 15a), but the next moment it is a fettered animal (v. 15b), and then it is a human being with the mind of an animal (v. 16). Yet, as in a fantastic dream, portentous coherence prevails despite the rapid shifting of images. The tree that used to provide shade and food for animals of the field is now no longer able to provide. Instead, it has become a needy animal of the field, pitifully tethered and utterly dependent on others for its welfare. Significantly, provision comes not from any earthly source, but from heaven. Whereas animals had previously found shade under the tree that seemed at first blush to be a cosmic one, this animal is now amazingly drenched—the Aramaic means, literally, "dipped"—in dew from heaven. The similarity of the Aramaic words for "dew" (*ṭl*) and "shade" (*ṭll*) ironically underscores the difference in the scenarios in a way that makes sense only in dreams and fantasies. The tree that had been at the center of the earth and that provided for animals of the earth is now a tethered animal that receives its provisions from heaven: “its lot is with the animals in the grass of the earth” (v. 15).

In another illogical change of scene that typifies dreams, it becomes apparent in verse 16 that the subject turns out to be a human being after all. The heavenly voice orders that person’s mind (literally, “heart”) to be changed to that of an animal for “seven seasons”—probably meaning “seven years” (NRSV seven times). In Nebuchadnezzar’s dream fantasy, the tree changes into an animal that changes into a human being who changes, again, into an animal. Still, all three—the tree, the animal, and the human being—are really one. The tree that provided for other living things becomes an animal that needs to be provided for, and that needy animal turns out to be a human being.

All that is happening is said to be a sentence issued by the heavenly “watchers” who are also called “the holy ones” (v. 17), no doubt a reference here to members of the heavenly host (see Ps. 89:7; Zech. 14:5). In contrast to the strange sequence of images that seemed to change into one another, there is complete clarity in the objective of the celestial council’s verdict. The purpose of the judgment is that “all who live may know that the Most High is sovereign over the kingdom of mortals; he gives it to whom he will and sets over it the lowliest of human beings” (v. 17). The sentence issued from heaven is, in fact, a poignant counterpoint to the impression of the tree’s all-encompassing influence and power. The tree is described as visible to “all the earth” (NRSV “the whole earth”); it provided “food for *all*” and “from it *all* living beings were fed” (vv. 11–12). The intent of the heavenly verdict is that “*all* who live” may know who really is in charge (v. 17). As in the first dream (2:36–45), the implication here is that the powerful will be humbled and the text says that the Most High will set the lowliest of mortals over the kingdom of mortals. That sentence from heaven is immediately effected when, upon completing the account of his dream, Nebuchadnezzar turns to Daniel (whose lowliness is suggested by his captive name, Belteshazzar) to interpret his dream for him. The “lowliest of human beings”—in this case a captive—is thus set over “the kingdom of mortals,” which is made possible, as the king himself admits, because of the endowment of a holy, divine spirit (v. 18).

## THE DREAM INTERPRETED
## Daniel 4:19–27

Daniel was despondent and severely troubled by his thoughts, perhaps because of the fact that he, a captive, has to deliver a devastating interpretation of the dream to the king. One will not be surprised that Daniel interprets the cosmic tree to be Nebuchadnezzar, for the king has grown "great and strong" (v. 22) as the tree in the dream had grown "great and strong" (vv. 11, 20). Arboreal metaphors for human beings are found elsewhere in the Old Testament. They often convey the idea that a person's growth and even very existence are entirely subject to the will of God (see, especially, Isa. 10:33–11:1; Ezek. 17:22–24; 19:10–14). Thus, Israel is portrayed as a beneficent tree that owes its existence to God. Israel is able to bear fruit and provide shade and rest for all kinds of birds, but the end of it all is that "all the trees of the field shall know" that sovereignty of the Lord, the one who brings down trees and causes them to flourish (Ezek. 17:23–24). Tall trees are also used as metaphors for the arrogance of oppressors, who do not seem to realize that they do not exist on their own and that they must depend on the provisions of heaven for their existence (Ps. 37:34–35; Isa. 2:12–19; 14:4–20; Ezek. 31:1–9; Zech. 11:2). The arboreal metaphor in Ezekiel 31, in particular, parallels Nebuchadnezzar's dream in a number of ways. There, the Pharaoh of Egypt is likened to a tree so tall that it towers above all others and has its top among the clouds. It is a cosmic tree that has such great boughs that all the birds of the sky make their nests in them, the animals of the field give birth under its branches, and in its shade all great nations live. The great tree in Ezekiel symbolizes the arrogance of the king and, hence, would be cut down by the deity. So, too, the tree in Nebuchadnezzar's dream represents a human kingship that does not seem to recognize that its power is derived and its existence is contingent upon heavenly will. In particular, the tree is said to be "great" and "strong" (Dan. 4:10–11, 22), the very words used to depict God's marvelous deeds on earth (v. 3). It attains cosmic proportions—its top reaches heaven and it is seen at the very ends of the earth—but the tree will be destroyed by the holy watcher descending from heaven. The celestial decree is now explicated as the decree of the Most High himself (v. 24), whereas it has previously been attributed generally to the divine council, namely, the watchers and holy ones (v. 17).

According to Daniel's interpretation, the dream means that Nebuchadnezzar will be driven away from humanity and be made to live among the animals; the king will have to be fed grass like cattle and will be drenched with the dew from heaven. Some commentators have diagnosed Nebuchadnezzar's punishment as a psychiatric abnormality known as lycanthropy, an illness whose symptom includes delusion of being a wolf. Accordingly, God punishes Nebuchadnezzar by giving him a mental illness. The mind of an animal may, however, simply be a figure for a posture of total submission. In the Egyptian wisdom text known as *The Instruction of Ani*, a father rebuking a recalcitrant youngster for his resistance to learning draws examples from animals that learn to depend on their masters (see *COS* I, 114). Eventually, the youngster concedes and agrees to be "like all the beasts" and learn what they do (compare also Ps. 73:22). So the point in Daniel 4 is that the arrogant Nebuchadnezzar must somehow learn submission by taking on the mind-heart of a creature that is utterly dependent on grace for its very survival. The problem that the passage addresses is not rationality or the lack thereof. Rather it is the heart, the seat of human will. At issue is submission to the will of God versus human arrogance, an attitude of dependence over against an attitude of carelessness and conceit.

Nebuchadnezzar will be in this condition for a long time (seven years), until he has learned that the Most High has sovereignty over the kingdom of mortals. Yet, the imagery of the tip of the root suggests hope for the king, if ever so slight. Kingship will be restored to Nebuchadnezzar when he recognizes that "Heaven is sovereign" (v. 26), meaning no doubt that the God of heaven is sovereign (see 1 Macc. 3:18; 19:50; 2 Macc. 7:11). Human kingship must be subordinate to the absolute sovereignty of God. So Nebuchadnezzar is urged, literally, to "break off" (NRSV "atone for") his sins, that is, to turn from his sin to righteousness and from his guilt to mercy for the oppressed (v. 27). The Greek translators rendered the verb for "break off" as "redeem" and interpreted "righteousness" as referring to "almsgiving," thus sparking a debate during the Reformation between Protestant and Catholic interpreters about salvation by works. Daniel's counsel, however, is simply a call for Nebuchadnezzar to submit to the will of heaven for earthly governance (see Ps. 72:1–2; Isa. 11:3–4; Jer. 22:15–16). This view of government is in accordance with royal ideology throughout the ancient Near East, where legitimate rule is predicated upon "justice and righteousness" for the oppressed and lowly. Accordingly, rulers who are unwilling or incapable of maintaining social order in this sense are deposed. Nebuchadnezzar's hope for restoration rests on his willingness to turn away from his previous conduct, no doubt including his inattentiveness and arrogance (compare Dan. 4:4).

## THE DREAM FULFILLED
## Daniel 4:28–33

The text suddenly switches from the first-person style to the third-person narration at verse 28, and this third-person perspective will be maintained throughout the account of the fulfillment of the dream (vv. 28–33). The switch is entirely appropriate, for the king is supposed to have his mind changed to that of an animal. The switch implies, then, that the sentence was immediate. As soon as Daniel had finished giving his interpretation, the sentence was in effect.

Yet, Daniel's prediction was not immediately fulfilled. Apparently a full year went by, with no sign that Nebuchadnezzar had understood the dream. Nebuchadnezzar had made no effort to follow Daniel's counsel to "break off" his sins by righteousness and mercy. Instead, he ascends to the roof of the royal palace of Babylon and, perhaps surveying his building projects, is impressed by the power of his own kingship. The NRSV obscures somewhat the fact that the same words used in the dream to describe the arrogance of human power (vv. 10–11, 22) are repeated. He says, literally, "Is this not Babel the great, which I myself have built as the abode of my kingship by the strength of my power and for the glory of my majesty?" (v. 30).

Thereupon, a voice came from heaven, pronouncing the judgment that kingship is being removed from the king and that he will be driven away from humanity until he recognizes the sovereignty of divine kingship and its power over human kingship. This time the prediction is immediately fulfilled (vv. 31–33).

## CONCLUSION AND DOXOLOGY
## Daniel 4:34–37

The dream included an element of hope, symbolized by the very tip of the root of the tree (vv. 15, 26). Hence, the punishment of Nebuchadnezzar does not last forever. Rather, after a long time—seven seasons, according to verses 16, 25, 32—he "lifted up" his eyes to heaven and his "knowledge" (NRSV "reason") returned to him. This notice of the restoration is remarkable for its terseness. No other action on the part of Nebuchadnezzar is reported. The reader is not told if Nebuchadnezzar in his animalistic state did anything else or said anything to warrant his restoration. The distinct impression that one receives is that the mere upward gaze to heaven sufficed for God. Perhaps that heavenward gaze was an implicit acknowledgment of the creature's neediness and dependence on divine help, indeed, from the one who watches over Israel (Ps. 121). Perhaps the gaze meant recognition of the sovereignty of the one who is enthroned in the heavens and is merciful to the lowly (Psalm 123). The translators of the NRSV, assuming that Nebuchadnezzar had become insane, suggest that his "reason" is now given back to him. The word in Aramaic, however, simply means "knowledge." The noun here is related to the verb "learned" in verses 25 and 32: "until you have learned that the

Most High has sovereignty over the kingdom of mortals, and gives it to whom he will." "Knowledge" is also related to the verb "know" in verse 17: "in order that all who live may know that the Most High is sovereign over the kingdom of mortals." When Nebuchadnezzar lifted up his eyes to the heavens, this "knowledge" returned to him. And through his knowing, all who live would also know the sovereignty of the Most High in heaven. Hence his confessional praise of God in the form of a public discourse, through a message sent to all the inhabitants of the earth (vv. 1, 35). The human ruler is finally to be an agent of divine will, a vehicle through which the greatness and sovereignty of God are universally made known.

# 5. Belshazzar and the Handwriting on the Wall

## *Daniel 5:1–31*

**1 King Belshazzar made a great festival for a thousand of his lords, and he
was drinking wine in the presence of the thousand.**

**2 Under the influence of the wine, Belshazzar commanded that they
bring in the vessels of gold and silver that his father Nebuchadnezzar had
taken out of the temple in Jerusalem, so that the king and his lords, his
wives, and his concubines might drink from them. 3 So they brought in the
vessels of gold and silver that had been taken out of the temple, the house
of God in Jerusalem, and the king and his lords, his wives, and his concubines drank from them. 4 They drank the wine and praised the gods of gold
and silver, bronze, iron, wood, and stone.**

**5 Immediately the fingers of a human hand appeared and began writ-
ing on the plaster of the wall of the royal palace, next to the lampstand.
The king was watching the hand as it wrote. 6 Then the king's face turned
pale, and his thoughts terrified him. His limbs gave way, and his knees
knocked together. 7 The king cried aloud to bring in the enchanters, the
Chaldeans, and the diviners; and the king said to the wise men of
Babylon, "Whoever can read this writing and tell me its interpretation
shall be clothed in purple, have a chain of gold around his neck, and rank
third in the kingdom." 8 Then all the king's wise men came in, but they
could not read the writing or tell the king the interpretation. 9 Then King
Belshazzar became greatly terrified and his face turned pale, and his
lords were perplexed.**

**10 The queen, when she heard the discussion of the king and his lords,
came into the banqueting hall. The queen said, "O king, live forever! Do not
let your thoughts terrify you or your face grow pale. 11 There is a man in
your kingdom who is endowed with a spirit of the holy gods. In the days of
your father he was found to have enlightenment, understanding, and wisdom like the wisdom of the gods. Your father, King Nebuchadnezzar, made
him chief of the magicians, enchanters, Chaldeans, and diviners, 12 because
an excellent spirit, knowledge, and understanding to interpret dreams,
explain riddles, and solve problems were found in this Daniel, whom the**

king named Belteshazzar. Now let Daniel be called, and he will give the
interpretation."
13 Then Daniel was brought in before the king. The king said to Daniel,
"So you are Daniel, one of the exiles of Judah, whom my father the king
brought from Judah? 14 I have heard of you that a spirit of the gods is in you,
and that enlightenment, understanding, and excellent wisdom are found in
you. 15 Now the wise men, the enchanters, have been brought in before me
to read this writing and tell me its interpretation, but they were not able to
give the interpretation of the matter. 16 But I have heard that you can give
interpretations and solve problems. Now if you are able to read the writing
and tell me its interpretation, you shall be clothed in purple, have a chain
of gold around your neck, and rank third in the kingdom."
17 Then Daniel answered in the presence of the king, "Let your gifts be
for yourself, or give your rewards to someone else! Nevertheless I will read
the writing to the king and let him know the interpretation. 18 O king, the
Most High God gave your father Nebuchadnezzar kingship, greatness,
glory, and majesty. 19 And because of the greatness that he gave him, all
peoples, nations, and languages trembled and feared before him. He killed
those he wanted to kill, kept alive those he wanted to keep alive, honored
those he wanted to honor, and degraded those he wanted to degrade. 20 But
when his heart was lifted up and his spirit was hardened so that he acted
proudly, he was deposed from his kingly throne, and his glory was stripped
from him. 21 He was driven from human society, and his mind was made
like that of an animal. His dwelling was with the wild asses, he was fed
grass like oxen, and his body was bathed with the dew of heaven, until he
learned that the Most High God has sovereignty over the kingdom of mortals, and sets over it whomever he will. 22 And you, Belshazzar his son, have
not humbled your heart, even though you knew all this! 23 You have exalted
yourself against the Lord of heaven! The vessels of his temple have been
brought in before you, and you and your lords, your wives and your concubines have been drinking wine from them. You have praised the gods of
silver and gold, of bronze, iron, wood, and stone, which do not see or hear
or know; but the God in whose power is your very breath, and to whom
belong all your ways, you have not honored.
24 "So from his presence the hand was sent and this writing was
inscribed. 25 And this is the writing that was inscribed: MENE, MENE, TEKEL, and
PARSIN. 26 This is the interpretation of the matter: MENE, God has numbered
the days of your kingdom and brought it to an end; TEKEL, you have been
weighed on the scales and found wanting; 28 PERES, your kingdom is divided
and given to the Medes and Persians."
29 Then Belshazzar gave the command, and Daniel was clothed in purple, a chain of gold was put around his neck, and a proclamation was made
concerning him that he should rank third in the kingdom.
30 That very night Belshazzar, the Chaldean king, was killed. 31 And
Darius the Mede received the kingdom, being about sixty-two years old.

Chapter 5 begins abruptly. There is no chronological notice as in 1:1 and 2:1. There is no epistolary introduction as in 4:1. The chapter simply begins with a new character, King Belshazzar, giving a great banquet. The preceding unit ends with the restoration of Nebuchadnezzar and his praise of God as "the King of heaven" (4:34–37). Nothing is said about the rest of Nebuchadnezzar's reign, although chapter 5 clearly presumes the preceding story as background (see vv. 11–12, 18–21). The reader is not told about Nebuchadnezzar's death or anything at all about the succession immediately after his death. Indeed, the transition seems particularly abrupt in light of the fact that extant historical records indicate that Nebuchadnezzar (606–562 B.C.E.) was succeeded by his son Amel-Marduk (562–560), followed by Neriglissar (560–556), Labashi Marduk (a few months in 556), and Nabonidus (556–539), the father of Belshazzar. Thus, between the end of chapter 4 and the beginning of chapter 5 a chronological gap of almost a quarter of a century exists.

Cuneiform inscriptions record that Belshazzar was the eldest son of Nabonidus to whom the father had "entrusted the kingship" when he inexplicably left Babylon for the oasis of Teima in the Arabian desert, where he remained for almost a decade. Belshazzar governed the kingdom in his father's absence, although he is never called "king" in any of the documents from Babylon, and he never assumed leadership in the religious festivals, as the king was both privileged and required to do. As the Persians prepared to invade Babylon, Nabonidus returned to defend the city and belatedly to celebrate its religious festivals. But he, having alienated his own people by his years of neglect, was fighting for a lost cause. Babylon, being surrounded by two sets of double walls totaling some eighty-five feet in thickness and further defended by fortified towers throughout, was considered an impenetrable fortress, which perhaps accounts for the nonchalance in the city even when the invading force camped just outside. According to the Greek historians Herodotus and Xenophon, the leading citizens of Babylon were happily enjoying themselves at a banquet when the invaders surprised them. According to Xenophon, the Persians dug a trench around the city at night while the Babylonians were preoccupied with their nocturnal celebrations, temporarily diverted the Euphrates into the trench and entered the city unnoticed by going along the river bed. Swiftly the invaders moved to the palace and killed the drunken guards and eventually also the Babylonian king, whom the legend does not name but simply describes as a reckless and godless youngster.

The story in Daniel 5 is set in the context of the fall of the empire in 539, long after the death of Nebuchadnezzar in 562. Belshazzar could not have been the literal son of Nebuchadnezzar. One should keep in mind that in the Semitic languages, "father" is not limited to that of a biological or even adoptive parent. The term may be used simply of an ancestor or a progenitor. So Jabal is called the "father" of all who live in tents and have livestock, and Jubal is regarded as the "father" of all those who play musical instruments (Gen. 4:20–21). Elisha called Elijah "my father" (2 Kgs. 2:12), although there is no indication that the two were biologically related. Similarly, an unnamed king of Israel called Elisha "father" (2 Kgs. 6:21), as did King Joash (2 Kgs. 13:14), and the servants of Naaman also addressed Naaman as "father" (2 Kgs. 5:13). By the same token, the term "son" is used of a descendant, a successor, or simply a member of a group or class. So some members of the prophetic circles were called "sons of the prophets." In the cuneiform inscriptions, King Jehu is called "the son of Omri," even though he was not of the Omride dynasty and, in fact, slaughtered all the descendants of Omri to seize the throne. From the point of view of the narrator of Daniel 5, who is reflecting on the beginning and end of the Chaldean dynasty, Nebuchadnezzar was in some sense the father and Belshazzar was his son. And that father-son language is, in fact, reiterated through the chapter (Dan. 5:2, 11, 13, 18, 22). Perhaps to the narrator, Nebuchadnezzar and Belshazzar both belonged to the same family of arrogant Chaldean oppressors. The father-son language serves to link the two kings: the one who took the vessels from the temple in Jerusalem with the one who desacralized them; the one who ruled at the beginning of Judah's exile under the Chaldeans with the one who ruled at the end of that period. The trouble with Belshazzar, as this passage has it, is that he ought to have learned the lesson from his "father" Nebuchadnezzar (as told in chapter 4), but he has not (vv. 22–23).

According to the narrator, too, the Chaldean kingdom passed on to "Darius the Mede" (v. 31). None of the extant historical records, however, know of such a figure. Thus, some scholars believe that "Darius the Mede" is either a purely fictional character or that the narrator had drawn from confused sources about the reign of Darius I Hystaspes, who was a Persian and never identified as a Mede and who reigned after Cyrus, not before him. Others, however, contend that the name Darius, which in Old Persian means "He Who Holds Firm What Is Good," might have been a throne name. According to one variation of this view, Darius the Mede may be identified with Gaubaruwa (Greek Gobryas), the general of the Persian army who actually led the invasion of Babylon on that fateful night of the city's fall. Gaubaruwa was the governor of Gutium, a region that later historical works associated with the Medes. Installed as a vice-regent over Mesopotamia, the old general ruled virtually as king and appointed subgovernors in Babylon until his death only several months later. "Darius the Mede" was the throne-name of Gaubaruwa, these scholars speculate, but no record of it exists anywhere because his reign was much too brief. In any case, whoever this "Darius the Mede" was, he was the one to whom the power that had been in Chaldean hands was transferred, according to the narrator.

## BELSHAZZAR'S SACRILEGE
## Daniel 5:1–4

The opening scene is one of ostentatious opulence. Belshazzar is hosting an enormous banquet "for a thousand of his lords," and he is showing off, "drinking wine in the presence of the thousand" (v. 1). The mention of the women of his harem—his consorts and concubines (vv. 2–3)—also suggests debauchery, but that is not all. The reckless king sends for the temple vessels seized from the temple of God in Jerusalem in order that he and those he is trying to impress—his lords, his consorts, and his concubines—might drink from them. The text has it that the king acts in this foolhardy manner, literally, "in the taste of wine" or "with the taste of wine" (v. 2). The Aramaic probably does not mean that he is "under the influence of the wine" (NRSV), for that implies that he might have acted impulsively. Rather, the Aramaic may be taken to mean that he is deliberately ordering the vessels to be brought amid the revelry and making the desecration of those vessels an item on the evening's program. The vessels are to be brought out as part of the evening's entertainment, something to go with the tasting of wine. The problem, moreover, is not that the sacred vessels are now used in a secular manner, but that Belshazzar is showing off and that he and his company are praising their idols even as they are committing sacrilege and blasphemy against the God of the Jews. They drink wine from these sacred vessels of gold and silver (vv. 2–3), even as they praise their gods of gold and silver, bronze, iron, wood, and stone (v. 4). The sovereignty and power of the God of the exiles are, thus, blatantly called into question.

## HANDWRITING ON THE WALL
## Daniel 5:5–9

Amid the sacrilegious revelry, the fingers of a hand appear and begin writing on the plaster of the wall of the royal palace (v. 5). The NRSV has the fingers writing on the wall "next to the lampstand," yet the reference to the lampstand is not intended merely to locate the scene. Rather, the

Aramaic may be read in two ways. One may understand it to say that the hand is seen "because of the lampstand," meaning that the light of the lamp is illuminating the writing hand. Or, more likely, the Aramaic may be understood to mean that the hand is appearing "before the lampstand," that is, casting a shadow against the wall on which the king presently sees a hand writing something on the wall.

What the king sees is, literally in Aramaic, "the palm of the hand" (v. 5), that is, the back of the hand from the wrist to the tips of the fingers. The mysterious fingers that write recall the writing of the covenant tablets by "the finger of God" at Mount Sinai (Exod. 31:18; Deut. 9:10). They recall, too, the association by Pharaoh's magicians of the plague of gnats with "the finger of God" (Exod. 8:18). The finger of God in all these cases refer to the power of God, as it does also in the New Testament (Luke 11:20), and perhaps the singular (finger) suggests that these acts are all but a token of that divine power. What Belshazzar sees, however, is not a solitary finger but the fingers of an apparently disembodied hand. The text says only that the king watches as the hand writes, and the sight terrifies him. The implication is that he alone sees the hand writing on the wall, just as his predecessor Nebuchadnezzar alone saw the mysterious sight in the fiery furnace (Dan. 3:24–25). The inscription will later be visible to others, of course, but the sight of the fingers that write is apparently evident only to the king.

Belshazzar is terrified by his thoughts, but his fear cannot be internalized and kept private: his countenance changes, the Aramaic text suggests that "the knots of his hips loosened" (that is, either he collapses or he is losing control of his bowels), and his knees knock (v. 6). This portrayal of fear is as vivid and comical as any in the Bible. The pompous king's terror is indicated, too, by his scream for the consultants to be brought before him. Whereas his predecessor Nebuchadnezzar had regally "commanded" (2:2) and "made a decree" (4:6) when he was frightened by his dreams, Belshazzar screams (v. 7). But just as Nebuchadnezzar challenged his consultants both to tell him the dream and its interpretation (2:6), so Belshazzar now asks his soothsayers both to read the writing and to tell its interpretation (v. 7). If successful, they will be richly rewarded, he promises. They will be clothed in purple (compare the purple garb of Mordecai, Esth. 8:15) and, like Joseph who had successfully interpreted Pharaoh's dreams, the successful interpreter will be adorned with a golden necklace (Gen. 41:42) and become a triumvir (a "thirdling") in the kingdom (compare Gen. 41:40–44). The position of the triumvir mentioned here has been taken by some scholars to indicate awareness that Belshazzar was really the second-in-command in the kingdom, after his father Nabonidus, and so the successful interpreter (eventually Daniel) would be the third. Others imagine that the successful interpreter of the vision would be third in the kingdom, after the queen mother and Belshazzar. The "thirdling" is, however, attested in other contexts simply as some sort of high official.

The Chaldean soothsayers are, of course, neither able to read the writing nor to interpret it. Why they are unable to do so is not clear. Some imagine that the inscription was a cryptic anagram, that the letters were arranged in an unusual manner (perhaps the words were written vertically rather than horizontally), or that abbreviations were used, as they commonly were for weights. Others conjecture that the difficulty has to do with the fact that unvocalized Aramaic (only consonants would have been written) would have required some context to be read in any meaningful way. And, indeed, Daniel would later read the text one way (taking the words as nouns) and interpret it another way (taking the words as verbs).

## THE QUEEN MOTHER'S RECOMMENDATION Daniel 5:10–12

The "queen" who appears before the king is probably the queen mother rather than the queen consort. She is clearly not part of the carousing crowd of the king, his lords, and the women of his harem. Unlike a queen consort, who could not appear before the king at will (see Esth. 4:11), she apparently does so and addresses the king in an authoritative tone. Most importantly, she knows details from the reign of his "father" and informs her "son" about Daniel's endowment with the holy divine spirit (Dan. 5:11, compare 4:8, 18) and Daniel's promotion by Nebuchadnezzar (2:48; 4:9). She further commends Daniel as one with a reputation for unusual brilliance and possessing "wisdom like the wisdom of the gods" (v. 11), identifying him as a man who is able to interpret dreams, "explain riddles" and "to loosen knots" (v. 12, NRSV "solve problems"). The reference to Daniel's ability to "loosen knots" is ironic, since the king has already had "the knots of his hips loosened" (v. 6, NRSV "his limbs gave way"). There is obviously wordplay here.

In view of such a remarkable reputation, that Belshazzar had not summoned Daniel himself is puzzling. Commentators suggest that Daniel is by now already an old man and is, thus, forgotten and assumed to be a figure from the past, a has-been. It has, after all, been almost a quarter of a century after the death of Nebuchadnezzar, the king who had promoted Daniel. Just as the new pharaoh in Egypt "did not know Joseph" (Exod. 1:8), the new Chaldean king does not know Daniel. Other interpreters believe that Daniel is mentioned as a last resort for rhetorical reasons. As with Nebuchadnezzar's first and second dreams (Dan. 2:1–16; 4:8), Daniel is brought in only when the others have failed. Joseph in Egypt, too, appeared before Pharaoh when all the other experts proved unable to solve the mystery (Gen. 41:14–36). Nevertheless, in light of the queen mother's observation that Daniel has a reputation for his ability to "loosen knots," one wonders if the king, whose "knots" have already been "loosened" (v. 6), has not deliberately overlooked Daniel. Perhaps, like Ahab, who bypassed Micaiah the son of Imlah in favor of other prophets because Micaiah was not expected to say anything favorable in regards to him (1 Kgs. 22:5–18), Belshazzar has passed over Daniel in favor of other consultants. But now the queen mother, who has come barging into his party, places him in an awkward position. In front of his thousand nobles, his consorts, and his concubines, she goes on and on about this wonderful fellow whom Nebuchadnezzar had promoted, this brilliant person who has a reputation for all kinds of special gifts, including the ability to "loosen knots." She tells Belshazzar to let Daniel be brought forth to give his interpretation (v. 12). Belshazzar now has no choice but to summon Daniel.

## DANIEL READS AND INTERPRETS THE INSCRIPTION
## Daniel 5:13–28

Upon the public recommendation of the queen mother, Daniel is brought before the king, who clearly does not know him, except by reputation (v. 13). Despite the queen mother's "reminder" to him of Daniel's position, Belshazzar identifies him in the first instance not by his profession or his rank, but only as a Judean exile who had been taken into captivity by Nebuchadnezzar. Still, the king is apparently obliged to offer Daniel the incentives offered the consultants before him, although one cannot be sure about the precise tone of his challenge to Daniel. The king admits that he has heard of Daniel's ability to give interpretations and to "loosen knots" ("solve problems," v. 16). Daniel's response, without any salutation whatsoever, seems terribly ungracious to modern ears: "Let your gifts be for yourself, or give your rewards to someone else!" (v. 17). The comment also sounds somewhat disingenuous, for he had accepted rewards before (2:48) and at the end of this episode, he does accept the rewards after all (5:29). The rejection of gifts is important in the narrative, for it is necessary to establish that the content of a seer's message is in no way determined by any price tag. Thus, too, when Balaam was offered incentives to alter an oracle, he refused, insisting that no amount of gold or silver could make him do more or less than God had commanded (Num. 22:18). The prophet Elisha, who had brought about the miraculous healing of Naaman, also steadfastly refused the offer of gifts from him even after the miracle had been performed (2 Kgs. 5:16–17). In so doing, he maintained his credibility as a true prophet (see Amos 7:12; Mic. 3:5, 11). Thus, too, Daniel's outright refusal of rewards establishes his complete freedom from the pressures that might be put upon him. He would, indeed, deliver his message freely, with no strings attached.

Daniel begins his interpretation by recounting the story about God's punishment of Nebuchadnezzar for his arrogance (Dan. 5:8–21). The account essentially repeats details already given in chapter 4, except that Nebuchadnezzar "killed those he wanted to kill, kept alive those he wanted to keep alive, honored those he wanted to honor, and degraded those he wanted to degrade" (v. 19). That depiction of absolute freedom and power is typically used in the Old Testament of God alone (Deut. 32:39; 1 Sam. 2:6–8; Job 5:11; Ps. 75:7–8). The claim is that Nebuchadnezzar had dared to usurp the power that belonged to God alone; he had ventured to set himself up as a challenge to the sovereignty of God. Nebuchadnezzar was punished in order that all might *know* that the Most High is sovereign over the kingdom of mortals (see Dan. 4:17). Belshazzar has not learned that lesson from history, it seems, for he "knew all this" and yet has not humbled himself (5:22). On the contrary, he has dared to exalt himself against "the lord of heaven" by his idolatrous sacrilege (v. 23).

Daniel interprets the hand as something that has been sent from the presence of God (v. 24). The language here is reminiscent of the ancient Near Eastern notion of divine hypostasis, that is, the extension of divine presence through some entity that represents the deity. In ancient Near Eastern mythology, a god's name may go forth like a virtually independent entity to represent the deity's extended power. So, too, in the Old Testament the arm of the Lord is depicted as a sort of substitute divine presence, sent forth to fight on the deity's behalf (Isa. 51:9; 63:12; Ps. 89:10, 13). Therefore, that Daniel speaks of the hand being sent from the presence of God is ominous indeed.

According to the Aramaic text, Daniel reads the words as "*mene*, *mene*, *tekel*, and *parsin*" (v. 25). In some ancient versions, however, the first word is not repeated; only three words are found, not four, as in the Aramaic text. Because the interpretation focuses only on three terms, a reasonable assumption is that the version preserved in the Aramaic is secondary, being the result of an inadvertent scribal error, the scribe erroneously writing the word *mene* twice. Others reinterpret the first word as a verb, thus reading the inscription as "counted: *mene*, *tekel*, and *parsin*." The words of the inscription, taken by themselves, are most readily understood as references to monetary weights. The first word (*mene*) is the Aramaic equivalent of the Jewish talent, the *mina*, which was equivalent to sixty shekels. The word *tekel* is the Aramaic equivalent of Hebrew *shekel*. As for the last term, it means, "half-pieces." If the term "half-pieces" refers to "half-*minas*," as it does in some Akkadian texts, the "half-pieces" (equivalent in value to thirty *shekels*) would be of greater value than the *shekel*. If so, *parsin*'s final position in the trilogy may be explained not in terms of its value but because of the wordplay with the term for "Persians," the people who would bring about the end of Babylonian rule. The term is suggestive, too, for the "Persians" who came to replace the Babylonians were really two peoples—"the Persians and the Medes"—and so the "half-pieces" would correspond to the kingdom of iron that is "partly of iron and partly of clay" (2:33, 42). As the text has it, Daniel takes the root of each of the nouns and reinterprets them as verbs that refer to Belshazzar and his kingdom. Thus, the same consonants for the noun *mina* (*mene*) are reinterpreted as the verb "numbered," and Daniel explains that to mean that God has numbered the days of Belshazzar's kingdom. The word *shekel* (*tekel*), which is derived from the root meaning "to weigh," is reinterpreted to mean that Belshazzar has been weighed and found deficient. Similarly, the last item is read not as the plural noun "half-pieces" but as the singular form *peres*, which is then related to the root, *prs*, "to divide," meaning that the kingdom would be divided and given to the Persians and the Medes.

## CONCLUSION
## Daniel 5:29–31

Despite Daniel's negative interpretation of the writings, Belshazzar rewards him, even though Daniel previously rejected an offer of them (v. 29). In view of the unrelenting emphasis throughout the chapter on the arrogance of Belshazzar, his action here can hardly be viewed as beneficent. On the contrary, the narrative function of Belshazzar's response may be to show the hopelessness of his situation. There is no confession of guilt on his part, no sign of repentance, and no prayer for mercy. Rather, by rewarding Daniel, he implicitly acknowledges the correctness of the interpretation, but still he says and does nothing more. Unlike Nebuchadnezzar, his "father," Belshazzar expresses no regret whatsoever. He has, indeed, learned nothing from the experience of his "father." Hence, he is killed that very night (v. 30).

Thus, the events of the entire chapter all occur on a single night. Belshazzar is killed in the very night when he committed the sacrilege, received the ominous sign of the handwriting on the wall, was given the interpretation, and rewarded Daniel. At the beginning of the chapter, he called for the vessels of the Jerusalem temple that were brought to Babylon by Nebuchadnezzar, the Chaldean king who ushered in the captivity of the Judeans. Now Belshazzar is called "the Chaldean king," even as the narrator notes his death and the passing of his kingdom to Darius the Mede. No details are given about the death of Belshazzar. The narrator simply uses the passive voice to report that he "was killed." In context, one can only see Belshazzar's demise as an event according to the will of the sovereign God whom he dared to defy.

Furthermore, the narrator does not present the fall of the Chaldeans to the Persians in military terms. The passing of power from the Chaldeans to their successors is noted somewhat oddly as the reception of the kingdom by Darius the Mede. Again, the narrator does not say explicitly from whom the kingdom is "received." That Darius the Mede is already sixty-two years old is, however, observed—a curious but noteworthy datum, particularly if the term "half-pieces" in Daniel's interpretation refers to two half-shekels, for the weights would then add up to sixty-two! The narrator's point, subtly made, is that God's will is being worked out in history after all.

# 6. Daniel in the Lions' Pit
## *Daniel 6:1–28*

1 It pleased Darius to set over the kingdom one hundred twenty satraps,
stationed throughout the whole kingdom, 2 and over them three presidents,
including Daniel; to these the satraps gave account, so that the king might
suffer no loss. 3 Soon Daniel distinguished himself above all the other presidents and satraps because an excellent spirit was in him, and the king
planned to appoint him over the whole kingdom. 4 So the presidents and
the satraps tried to find grounds for complaint against Daniel in connection
with the kingdom. But they could find no grounds for complaint or any corruption, because he was faithful, and no negligence or corruption could be
found in him. 5 The men said, "We shall not find any ground for complaint
against this Daniel unless we find it in connection with the law of his God."

6 So the presidents and satraps conspired and came to the king and said
to him, "O King Darius, live forever! 7 All the presidents of the kingdom, the
prefects and the satraps, the counselors and the governors are agreed that
the king should establish an ordinance and enforce an interdict, that whoever prays to anyone, divine or human, for thirty days, except to you, O
king, shall be thrown into a den of lions. 8 Now, O king, establish the interdict and sign the document, so that it cannot be changed, according to the
law of the Medes and the Persians, which cannot be revoked." 9 Therefore
King Darius signed the document and interdict.

10 Although Daniel knew that the document had been signed, he continued to go to his house, which had windows in its upper room open
toward Jerusalem, and to get down on his knees three times a day to pray
to his God and praise him, just as he had done previously. 11 The conspirators came and found Daniel praying and seeking mercy before his God.
12 Then they approached the king and said concerning the interdict, "O
king! Did you not sign an interdict, that anyone who prays to anyone,
divine or human, within thirty days except to you, O king, shall be thrown
into a den of lions?" The king answered, "The thing stands fast, according
to the law of the Medes and Persians, which cannot be revoked." 13 Then
they responded to the king, "Daniel, one of the exiles from Judah, pays no

**attention to you, O king, or to the interdict you have signed, but he is say-
ing his prayers three times a day."**
**14 When the king heard the charge, he was very much distressed. He was
determined to save Daniel, and until the sun went down he made every
effort to rescue him. 15 Then the conspirators came to the king and said to
him, "Know, O king, that it is a law of the Medes and Persians that no interdict or ordinance that the king establishes can be changed."**
**16 Then the king gave the command, and Daniel was brought and thrown
into the den of lions. The king said to Daniel, "May your God, whom you
faithfully serve, deliver you!" 17 A stone was brought and laid on the mouth
of the den, and the king sealed it with his own signet and with the signet of
his lords, so that nothing might be changed concerning Daniel. 18 Then the
king went to his palace and spent the night fasting; no food was brought to
him, and sleep fled from him.**
**19 Then, at break of day, the king got up and hurried to the den of lions.
20 When he came near the den where Daniel was, he cried out anxiously to
Daniel, "O Daniel, servant of the living God, has your God whom you faithfully serve been able to deliver you from the lions?" 21 Daniel then said to
the king, "O king, live forever! 22 My God sent his angel and shut the lions'
mouths so that they would not hurt me, because I was found blameless
before him; and also before you, O king, I have done no wrong." 23 Then
the king was exceedingly glad and commanded that Daniel be taken up out
of the den. So Daniel was taken up out of the den, and no kind of harm was
found on him, because he had trusted in his God. 24 The king gave a command, and those who had accused Daniel were brought and thrown into
the den of lions— they, their children, and their wives. Before they reached
the bottom of the den the lions overpowered them and broke all their bones
in pieces.**
**25 Then King Darius wrote to all peoples and nations of every language
throughout the whole world: "May you have abundant prosperity! 26 I make
a decree, that in all my royal dominion people should tremble and fear
before the God of Daniel:**

**For he is the living God,**
**enduring forever.**
**His kingdom shall never be destroyed,**
**and his dominion has no end.**
**27 He delivers and rescues,**
**he works signs and wonders in heaven and on earth;**
**for he has saved Daniel**
**from the power of the lions."**

**28 So this Daniel prospered during the reign of Darius and the reign of
Cyrus the Persian.**

This story in chapter 6 parallels the one in chapter 3 in many ways. In each case, the integrity of the faith of the Jews is tested against the challenges of life in the dispersion. In each case, trouble for the Jews arises because of professional jealousy—one suspects also racism and xenophobia—on the part of their contemporaries, those who do not share their allegiance to their God. In each case, an imperial edict is passed that requires the exiles to compromise their religious convictions, and failure to comply with the edict means a death sentence: a fiery furnace in one story, a lions' pit in the other. In each case, the edict is met with passive resistance and the death sentence is ordered, but the faithful Jews encounter divine presence in the midst of their punishment and are miraculously delivered from death. Each story reaches a similar climax with the king's confession of the God of the Jews, the issuance of a new imperial decree favorable to Jewish faith, and the continued success of the Jews who survived the trial.

The stories are not merely duplicates of one another, however, for important elements distinguish them. To begin with, the first story concerns Shadrach, Meshach, and Abednego (with the noticeable absence of Daniel), whereas the second concerns Daniel alone. The stories also take place in two different eras—the first in the reign of Nebuchadnezzar of the Chaldean empire and the second in the reign of Darius of the Persian. In the first story, the imperial edict explicitly requires the Jews to bow down to an emblem of imperial power, but the friends of Daniel refused to do it. In the second story, people are forbidden to petition anyone other than the king, but Daniel does petition God. In the first case, civil disobedience takes place in public; in the second, it takes place in Daniel's own home.

The stories, thus, complement and supplement one another. Together they make the point that people of faith in different times and places are regularly challenged to live out their faith convictions despite the risks and dangers in their particular circumstances. The details may be different in each case, but for people who worship the God of the Jews, the same God delivers those who hold on to their integrity and their faith (see 3:28–29; 6:23, 27). These stories are not meant to be read as tales that assure one of God's deliverance in times of trial, for in each case the faithful are not delivered from their trials, and the response of the human heroes of these stories is never contingent upon any assurance of divine salvation. Indeed, biblical faith in general knows the reality of divine silence and the possibility of divine absence in the face of human suffering and injustice. Rather, these stories in the book of Daniel are not about what God will inevitably do whenever the faithful are threatened, but about what God can do whenever God so wills. In these cases, divine presence does break into the realm of the mundane, and that presence is encountered by the faithful in a fiery furnace and in a deadly pit. Life for those who believe in God is preserved despite the threat of death. Moreover, life is possible because of divine presence manifested through one who has the appearance of a divine being in the midst of the fire (3:25) or a being sent by God into the pit (6:22).

## JEALOUSY AND CONSPIRACY
## Daniel 6:1–9

The story begins with the new king and the new empire. Having "received the kingdom" upon the death of Belshazzar (5:31), Darius proceeds to appoint over his domain 120 "satraps," a term that in the Persian language means "protectors of the kingdom" or "protectors of kingship." The Greek historian Herodotus reports that Darius I (522–486 B.C.E.) reorganized the empire into 20 satrapies, while other sources suggest between 20 and 29 satrapies at that time. The figure of 120 satrapies is without parallel anywhere; the closest we come to it are the 127 provinces in the time of Xerxes (486–466 B.C.E.) mentioned in the book of Esther (Esth. 1:1; 8:9), and the Old Greek translation has that figure here. One should probably understand the term "satraps" here not in the strict sense used in the Persian imperial organization, however, but simply as regional administrators who are supposed to be "protectors of the kingdom/kingship." The term is already found in Daniel 3:2–3 of government officials under Nebuchadnezzar, before the Persians came to power.

Over these "protectors of the kingdom/kingship" Darius appoints three presidents (NRSV) or premiers (the word in Persian means "heads"), including Daniel. Like the 120 satraps, no record appears anywhere else of such a triumvirate within the Persian imperial organization. The notion of three premiers may, in fact, have been derived from the reference to Daniel's promotion as a triumvir, or thirdling (5:29).

As the NRSV has it, the whole organization is intended to ensure that "the king might suffer no loss" (v. 2). To judge by the usage of the same Aramaic verb ("suffer no loss" in the NRSV) elsewhere (see Ezra 4:13–15, 22), the political structure is an attempt to prevent deceit and graft, specifically the diversion of resources that are due the government. The implication is that these premiers are to watch their subordinates and, perhaps, also to watch one another to guard against disloyalty to the king. This type of organization is in accord with what we know of Persian bureaucracy, which included a carefully constructed hierarchy as well as an elaborate network of spies and other informants, all for the sake of protecting the welfare of the state, so that "the king might suffer no loss," as it were. Even the "protectors of the kingdom" have to be watched!

Daniel distinguishes himself above the others in the triumvirate because "an excellent spirit was in him" (v. 3), presumably meaning that he is endowed with the divine spirit (4:8, 18; 5:12). The presence of the divine spirit in Daniel meant that he was able to interpret dreams and solve problems. In the present context, the wording probably means that Daniel has proven himself to be an extraordinarily skillful and reliable government official. So Darius plans to promote him even further to be "over the whole kingdom," just as Joseph was promoted to be in charge of all of Egypt (Gen. 41:45).

The jealousy of Daniel's colleagues among the premiers and satraps provides the story's conflict. They are not able to find any grounds for complaints against him because he is loyal and without negligence or corruption. Unable to find fault with him in his professional conduct—"in connection with the kingdom" alone (v. 4)—they endeavor to catch him "in connection with the law of his God" (v. 5). The issue is laid out plainly. Daniel is unquestionably loyal to the state and reliable in his job. The question is how his devotion to his job might be compromised when it is pitted against commitment to his religion. Daniel's colleagues set the events on an inevitable collision course, pitting the law of the state against religious principles, secular success against religious integrity.

The NRSV uses two verbs ("conspired and came") for just one in the Aramaic (v. 6). The Aramaic verb implies action in concert (similarly the Hebrew of Pss. 55:14; 64:3; hence NRSV "conspire") and agitation (see Pss. 2:1; 83:3–4). The implication is that these government officials are conspiring to agitate. The NRSV reports that they come to the king, but the Aramaic is ambiguous, perhaps even deliberately so. The Aramaic preposition may, in fact, be taken to mean "upon" or "against." Therefore, one may understand them to be conspiring to bring unrest upon the king, that is, by agitating him against Daniel, which seems to be the surface meaning of the verse. One may, however, also understand the text to mean that they are agitating against the king, which is, perhaps, the subtext of the narrator, who has already raised the issue of loyalty to the king. These government officials are ostensibly trying to ensure loyalty to the king, but they themselves are, in fact, not such loyal subjects. Minimally, they are putting pressure on him to do their bidding. They are conspiratorial agitators.

Even though the reader is told only that the satraps and premiers are in cahoots, these conspirators claim before the king that "all the presidents of the kingdom, the prefects and the satraps, the counselors and the governors" have consulted with one another (v. 7), which is, of course, patently untrue, because Daniel is certainly not involved. The agitators give the impression of widespread consensus among all the government officials, a claim akin to the one that American politicians frequently make about what "the American people" as a whole want, even though the politicians may be expressing the view of only a few. Moreover, the conspirators presume to tell the king what he is to do. They tell him to pass a law forbidding the citizens to petition (NRSV "prays") anyone other than the king, they tell him to enforce that law, and they even prescribe for him the precise penalty for violation of such a law (vv. 7–8). Thus, they go far beyond the Chaldeans, who had earlier attempted to frame the Jews by tattling on them before Nebuchadnezzar (3:8–12). The Chaldeans merely reported the perceived problem to the king and left it to him to handle the case as he saw fit. By contrast, these officials now pressure the king to do what they want. Their plan is obviously a setup, however, and is also contradictory. On the one hand, the law they propose is supposed to be only for a period of thirty days. On the other hand, the law is said to be irrevocable. Still, preposterous and ridiculous as their recommendation may be, the king is manipulated into compliance. The king is duped. The trap is set both for Daniel and for the king.

## DANIEL IS CAUGHT ACTING NORMALLY
## Daniel 6:10–13

Daniel is aware that the document has been signed; the law has been officially established. Still he continues to go to his house for his daily prayers. The house has an upper room (compare Judg. 3:20; 1 Kgs. 17:19; 2 Kgs. 1:2; 4:10) that has windows that are open toward Jerusalem (Dan. 6:10), in which direction faithful Jews living in distant lands are to pray (see 1 Kgs. 8:30, 35, 38, 42, 44, 48). According to some ancient versions, when Daniel learns of the new law, he goes home and deliberately throws open the windows, thus flaunting his defiance. The Aramaic text does not make this point, however. Indeed, Daniel does not seem to go out of his way to challenge the law. In fact, he does not do anything new. Rather, he simply continues to do what he has always done. He does not deliberately show his defiance, but he does not try to hide the practice of faith either. He continues to go to his house (Dan. 6:10). His windows remain open as before. He prays as frequently as before. He does no more because of the new law, and he does no less.

Because Daniel's upper room has open windows, his would-be accusers need not go out of their way to catch him in the act of civil disobedience. They no doubt know that his habit is to pray kneeling down and facing Jerusalem three times a day (probably morning, noon, and evening; compare Ps. 55:17). Daniel has a particular place, particular times, and a particular posture of prayer. Jewish law makes no stipulation about the number of times that one must pray each day. A psalmist talks about praising God seven times a day (Ps. 119:164), while the Chronicler refers to Levites who pray in the morning and evening (1 Chr. 23:30). Other sources, too, speak of prayers at different times of the day, particularly at the beginning and the end of the day, but there is no indication anywhere of standard practice until centuries later. Neither is any posture in prayer required or recommended. People may stand in prayer (1 Sam. 1:26; 1 Kgs. 8:22; Ps. 106:30), but some kneel (1 Kgs. 8:54; 2 Chr. 6:13; Ezra 9:5) and others prostrate themselves (Num. 16:45; Josh. 7:6; 1 Kgs. 18:42). So Daniel may very easily avoid trouble from the authorities by simply changing his prayer place, his prayer routine, and his prayer posture. He can be faithful to God but be less obvious, less conspicuous about it. Perhaps he ought to pray when it is dark—in the early morning and in the late evening. Perhaps he ought to pray standing or sitting. Perhaps he ought to pray silently. Perhaps he ought to wait out the thirty days before resuming his routine. Easy alternatives and pragmatic options are available to him. Daniel could be more "private" about his faith. Yet, he does not alter his habit in the least, but continues doing what he has always done. He makes no changes whatsoever to accommodate the new law. His faith is at once private and public.

The conspirators catch Daniel praying to and praising God (Dan. 6:10), petitioning (NRSV "praying") and "seeking mercy" (v. 11), in contravention of the law against petitioning anyone other than the king (v. 7, NRSV "prays"). The offense of petitioning (which is what the law forbids) is part of a broader act of devotion: he prays, praises, petitions, and seeks mercy. The agitators seem to have analyzed the content of Daniel's devotional act in order to find evidence of his violation of the law; he has, indeed, petitioned God!

Unlike the Chaldean accusers of the Jews, who simply brought the case before Nebuchadnezzar, these agitators now pose a rhetorical question to the king (v. 12). "Did the king not establish the law forbidding petitions directed at anyone else but him?" they ask. So the king is trapped into confirming the law that he established apparently with little forethought of its consequences. Then only do the conspiratorial agitators set forth their accusation (v. 13). Daniel the Judean exile has been subversive, they claim, because he has disregarded the king's law by petitioning God three times a day, presuming to know the content of Daniel's prayers.

## THE KING'S QUANDARY
## Daniel 6:14–18

Darius is greatly distressed when he hears about the situation (v. 14), although one is not told specifically why he is so distressed. Perhaps he is troubled that Daniel, his favorite (according to v. 3), is now under a charge of sedition. Perhaps he is distressed as he now sees more clearly the trap that has been set for Daniel and for him as well; he realizes belatedly that he has been duped by his subordinates. Perhaps he simply dislikes conflicts and most certainly does not want to be set against the Judean exiles and their God. Whatever the reason, he is "determined to save Daniel" (v. 14).

We do not know what options are open to Darius, but he is clearly under constraints, for the narrator indicates that he has to make a concerted effort to rescue Daniel and that he does so only until sunset. Perhaps the law allows him only limited time to stay the execution. What is clear is that Darius is not above the law that he has made. What's more, the agitators, the Aramaic text indicates, throng upon or against him. They presume to instruct Darius that he is under the rule of the law, and they do so with apparent condescension: "Know, O king, that it is a law of the Medes and Persians that no interdict or ordinance that the king establishes can be changed" (v. 15).

Darius seems to have no choice but to order the execution. No investigation, no trial, no questioning of the accused, no defense offered by Daniel or on his behalf takes place. Perhaps some or all of these measures are implied in the narrator's notice about the efforts that Darius made before sunset. But Daniel is, of course, guilty as charged, for he did petition God. So Darius orders Daniel to be thrown into a pit of lions, although to Daniel, perhaps privately and quietly, the king raises the possibility of divine rescue. The precise intent of his comment to Daniel is, unfortunately, somewhat unclear. The NRSV takes the main verb to be injunctive, that is, a verb expressing a wish: "May your God . . . deliver you" (v. 16). Some commentators have noted, however, that the form in question can only be an indicative verb in biblical Aramaic, a verb indicating what will or must happen. The words of Darius may, therefore, be better translated: "Your God whom you fear constantly, he will/must rescue you." These words of Darius to Daniel are reminiscent of the reply of Shadrach, Meshach, and Abednego to Nebuchadnezzar when they were about to be thrown into the fiery furnace (3:17). Here in chapter 6, however, the possibility of divine deliverance is raised not by the victim himself, but by the one who orders the execution. Darius had "determined to save Daniel" (v. 14), but now he concedes that the saving is really up to God.

A stone is brought and placed over the mouth of the pit and sealed with the king's own seal and with the seal of the nobles, "so that nothing might be changed concerning Daniel" (v. 17). The double sealing of the pit indicates something of the distrust that exists between Darius and the officials who have manipulated him into this act. As the Old Greek translation of the story has it, the seals of the king and the nobles were made, "lest Daniel be snatched from them or the king draw him out of the pit." The double sealing ensures that neither side will be able to rig the outcome of Daniel's trial in the pit. The king (or the friends of Daniel) will not be able to rescue Daniel (perhaps by feeding the lions), and the nobles will not be able to kill him if the lions somehow do not. In terms of its rhetorical function, however, this notice of the sealing of the pit preempts alternative explanations for Daniel's liberation as anything but an act of God, a possibility that Darius himself has already broached.

## DELIVERANCE
## Daniel 6:19–24

The parting words of Darius to Daniel must have been uttered in all seriousness and sincerity, for the king does not simply presume the worst, as Nebuchadnezzar did when he cast the friends of Daniel into the fiery furnace (3:19–23). After an anxious and restless night (6:18), Darius hurries to the pit, apparently still thinking of the possibility of Daniel's survival (v. 19), and he calls out to Daniel (v. 20). He addresses Daniel as the servant of "the living God," a noteworthy designation that is found in ancient Canaanite literature in reference to Baal as the god of life and lord of all the earth. In the Bible, that divine designation is frequently used for the God of Israel as the true God (Jer. 10:10; 23:36) or as the God who manifests power in the face of threats posed by foreign nations against Israel (Deut. 5:26; Josh. 3:10; 1 Sam. 17:26; 2 Kgs. 19:4). Now, put in the mouth of a foreign king regarding the possibility of divine deliverance for a Jewish exile, the designation is tantamount to a confession, however tentative that may be.

Thereupon, Daniel, who is alive, answers from the pit, bidding the king longevity: "O king, live forever!" (Dan. 6:21), the only time in the book that the phrase "live forever" is spoken by a Jew in reference to the king. Coming immediately after the designation of the deity as "the living God," the phrase serves to link and to subsume the life of the king to the will of the God from whom life derives and on whom life depends.

Daniel proceeds to volunteer an explanation for his survival (v. 22). According to him, God sent an angel into the pit to shut the mouths of the lions because Daniel is pure before God and before the king. Even as a divine being was with Daniel's friends in the fiery furnace (3:25), now a celestial being is said to have been with Daniel in the lions' pit. As in chapter 3, the point here is not that God delivers one from danger, however, for Daniel's friends were not delivered from the furnace and Daniel is not delivered from the lions' pit. Rather, Daniel's friends encountered divine presence in the midst of the fire, for a divine being (literally "a son of God") was with them in the fire. So, too, Daniel is not spared the threat of death in the pit, but he experiences divine presence in the deadly pit itself. The story is full of ironies. To seal the fate of Daniel in the pit, the stone is laid on the mouth of the pit (v. 17), but Daniel is delivered because the mouths of the lions were miraculously shut (v. 22). The closing of mouths (of the deadly lions) neutralizes the intended consequence of the closing of the mouth of the pit. The story thus affirms that the living God is able to preserve life even when death seems certain.

Moreover, the story suggests that God knows what transpires on earth and God does respond whenever God wills. In this case, God has sent a divine intermediary to intervene so that the lions would do Daniel no harm (NRSV "hurt") because Daniel has done no harm (NRSV "done no wrong"). Despite Daniel's violation of the king's law, and despite the fact that human authorities did not attempt to find the truth of the matter, Daniel is found—the story implies that he is found so by God—to have integrity (NRSV "blameless"). The conspirators had framed the question in terms of legality, but the narrator has completely ignored that question, turning instead to the issues of integrity (v. 22) and trust in God (v. 23). The trust of which the narrator speaks in verse 23 refers to his integrity in verse 22, an integrity manifested in Daniel's steadfast adherence to his religious commitments despite the danger that they posed to his life (vv. 10–13). The point is not, therefore, that Daniel is delivered because he has trusted in the power of God to deliver him. Like his friends (compare 3:17), Daniel's commitment to God is not contingent upon God's will to save. Nor is there an implicit promise in the story that God will deliver all who trust God as Daniel does. The point is not that God will surely deliver but that God can when God wills. In this case, God does and does so marvelously.

So Daniel is brought up from the pit unharmed, while his accusers are thrown down into it together with their wives and children, with the lions attacking them and breaking their bones before they even reach the bottom (v. 24). Commentators, while noting that retribution for false witnesses is to be expected (see Deut. 19:16–19; Esth. 9:25; Ps. 140:9–11), are justifiably horrified by the excessive violence in this folkloristic flourish. One may wonder, too, about the likelihood that Daniel's accusers—all 122 of them (2 premiers and 120 satraps)—are thrown with their wives and children into a pit that is apparently small enough to be closed by a single stone. The detail, too, about the crushing of all their bones before they even reach the bottom of the pit seems like a hyperbole. Some ancient versions, indeed, try to make the story more believable by noting that only Daniel's two other presidential colleagues are meant here—only they are thrown into the pit. The intensity of this narrative detail may yet be meaningful; it is not merely a reflex of the narrator's all-too-human emotions about what the wicked really deserve. Rather, as Calvin has suggested, the point of this narrative detail is to anticipate any suggestion that Daniel might have been spared because the lions were not hungry or somehow unable to attack. No, they were so hungry that they immediately mauled the large crowd of people that were thrown into the pit—even before they reached the bottom! The ferocity of the lions only shows that Daniel's deliverance from them despite the long night with them could not be explained as anything but a divinely wrought miracle.

## THE KING'S ENCYCLICAL
## Daniel 6:25–28

Like Nebuchadnezzar (4:1–3), Darius now writes an open letter to "all peoples and nations of every language throughout the whole world" (6:25), publicizing the fact that he is reversing his earlier edict. By using the form of a public letter addressed to all peoples in the world, the narrator makes the point that at issue in the chapter is not a private experience of a Jew in exile but something that affects others as well. People who conspired against Daniel had set events on a collision course, pitting the law of the king against "the law of his God" (vv. 4–5), and it is asserted three times by the functionaries of the state (vv. 8, 12, 17) that the imperial law cannot be revoked. Yet, now the king himself publicizes to the world the reversal of his supposedly unchangeable edict, for God has brought about the change. Whereas people were forbidden to petition anyone other than the king, now the king himself decrees that all his subjects should "tremble and fear before the God of Daniel" (v. 26). The king himself publicly confesses the deity as "the living God" and affirms the infinite superiority of divine kingship over his own. In this way, the doxology of Darius points the reader beyond mundane powers to the sovereignty of a living God, who exists beyond the bounds of time ("enduring forever"). Unlike human kingdoms, with all their appearance of power, divine rule is one that will never be destroyed, for the divine ruler marvelously intervenes on earth to rescue and to save. The verb translated as "destroyed" in the NRSV (v. 26) is based on the same root as the word translated as "hurt" in verse 22 and "harm" in verse 23. Thus, Daniel's deliverance from destruction indicates that the kingdom of God shall never be destroyed, as Daniel's interpretation of Nebuchadnezzar's dream has already asserted. Indeed, as the stories in Daniel 1–6 constantly affirm, the power of the reign of God is manifest on earth through the lowly. Thus, saved from "the power of the lions" (v. 27), Daniel, the Jewish exile, whose career began during the days of the Chaldean kings, prospers through the reigns of Darius the Mede and Cyrus the Persian. The lowly exile outlasts the kings of those empires!

# 7. Monsters, Divine Judgment, and the Coming of a Humanlike One
## *Daniel 7:1–28*

1 **In the first year of King Belshazzar of Babylon, Daniel had a dream and
visions of his head as he lay in bed. Then he wrote down the dream:** 2 **I,
Daniel, saw in my vision by night the four winds of heaven stirring up the
great sea,** 3 **and four great beasts came up out of the sea, different from one
another.** 4 **The first was like a lion and had eagles' wings. Then, as I watched,
its wings were plucked off, and it was lifted up from the ground and made
to stand on two feet like a human being; and a human mind was given to
it.** 5 **Another beast appeared, a second one, that looked like a bear. It was
raised up on one side, had three tusks in its mouth among its teeth and was
told, "Arise, devour many bodies!"** 6 **After this, as I watched, another
appeared, like a leopard. The beast had four wings of a bird on its back and
four heads; and dominion was given to it.** 7 **After this I saw in the visions by
night a fourth beast, terrifying and dreadful and exceedingly strong. It had
great iron teeth and was devouring, breaking in pieces, and stamping what
was left with its feet. It was different from all the beasts that preceded it,
and it had ten horns.** 8 **I was considering the horns, when another horn
appeared, a little one coming up among them; to make room for it, three
of the earlier horns were plucked up by the roots. There were eyes like
human eyes in this horn, and a mouth speaking arrogantly.**

9 **As I watched,**
**thrones were set in place,**
**and an Ancient One took his throne,**
**his clothing was white as snow,**
**and the hair of his head like pure wool;**
**his throne was fiery flames,**
**and its wheels were burning fire.**
10 **A stream of fire issued**
**and flowed out from his presence.**
**A thousand thousands served him,**
**and ten thousand times ten thousand stood attending him.**
**The court sat in judgment,**
**and the books were opened.**

11 I watched then because of the noise of the arrogant words that the horn
was speaking. And as I watched, the beast was put to death, and its body
destroyed and given over to be burned with fire. 12 As for the rest of the
beasts, their dominion was taken away, but their lives were prolonged for a
season and a time. 13 As I watched in the night visions,

I saw one like a human being
 coming with the clouds of heaven.
And he came to the Ancient One
 and was presented before him.
14 To him was given dominion
 and glory and kingship,
that all peoples, nations, and languages
 should serve him.
His dominion is an everlasting dominion
 that shall not pass away,
and his kingship is one
 that shall never be destroyed.

15 As for me, Daniel, my spirit was troubled within me, and the visions
of my head terrified me. 16 I approached one of the attendants to ask him
the truth concerning all this. So he said that he would disclose to me the
interpretation of the matter: 17 "As for these four great beasts, four kings
shall arise out of the earth. 18 But the holy ones of the Most High shall
receive the kingdom and possess the kingdom forever—forever and ever."

19 Then I desired to know the truth concerning the fourth beast, which
was different from all the rest, exceedingly terrifying, with its teeth of iron
and claws of bronze, and which devoured and broke in pieces, and stamped
what was left with its feet; 20 and concerning the ten horns that were on its
head, and concerning the other horn, which came up and to make room for
which three of them fell out—the horn that had eyes and a mouth that
spoke arrogantly, and that seemed greater than the others. 21 As I looked,
this horn made war with the holy ones and was prevailing over them,
22 until the Ancient One came; then judgment was given for the holy ones
of the Most High, and the time arrived when the holy ones gained possession of the kingdom.

23 This is what he said: "As for the fourth beast,
there shall be a fourth kingdom on earth
 that shall be different from all the other kingdoms;
it shall devour the whole earth,
 and trample it down, and break it to pieces.
24 As for the ten horns,
out of this kingdom ten kings shall arise,
 and another shall arise after them.
This one shall be different from the former ones,
 and shall put down three kings.
25 He shall speak words against the Most High,

**shall wear out the holy ones of the Most High,**
**and shall attempt to change the sacred seasons and the law;**
**and they shall be given into his power**
**for a time, two times, and half a time.**
26 **Then the court shall sit in judgment,**
**and his dominion shall be taken away,**
**to be consumed and totally destroyed.**
27 **The kingship and dominion**
**and the greatness of the kingdoms under the whole heaven**
**shall be given to the people of the holy ones of the Most High;**
**their kingdom shall be an everlasting kingdom,**
**and all dominions shall serve and obey them."**

28 **Here the account ends. As for me, Daniel, my thoughts greatly terrified me, and my face turned pale; but I kept the matter in my mind.**

Often regarded as the most important chapter of the book, Daniel 7 is both transitional and pivotal. The chapter has links with the preceding six chapters in terms of its language and content. Daniel 7 is written in Aramaic (as is 2:4b–6:28, whereas chapters 8–12 are entirely in Hebrew), it concerns a dream, and it continues the theme of divine versus human sovereignties. There are in this unit, in fact, echoes of the dreams of Nebuchadnezzar in chapters 2 and 4 and the eerie vision of Belshazzar in chapter 5. The allusions appear to be intentional, so one cannot interpret Daniel 7 without the background of the first half of the book. Yet the chronological sequence present through Daniel 1–6 is broken, as the dream vision of Daniel begins with the first year of the reign of Belshazzar, whose death is already accounted for in chapter 5. The visions of the later chapters follow this date; they are in the third year of Belshazzar (8:1), the first year of Darius (9:1), the third year of Cyrus (10:1), and the first year of Darius (11:1). Thus, the first six chapters of the book primarily cover the reigns of Nebuchadnezzar, Belshazzar, and Darius, whereas the second six chapters concern visions in the reigns of Belshazzar, Darius, and Cyrus. Moreover, whereas the first six chapters are court narratives revolving around the encounters of Daniel and his friends in exile in a foreign land, beginning with chapter 7, the reader is presented with the visions revealed personally to Daniel concerning Jerusalem and the plight of the Jews there. Hence, whereas the stories in the first six chapters are told largely in the third person, from chapter 7 on, the accounts are reported in the first-person voice of Daniel (the only exception being 10:1). Indeed, a marked genre shift occurs from the didactic tales of chapters 1–6 to the apocalyptic visions of chapters 7–12.

Most scholars recognize some affinities between chapters 2 and 7. In each case, one finds reference to four kingships or kingdoms. Indeed, similarities are also present in terms of vocabulary. In each case, the fourth regime is said to be strong, iron is mentioned, and the fourth power is said to be capable of pulverizing and utterly destroying all those in its way. Still, clear differences exist between the two chapters as well. In chapter 2, only the first regime (the reign of Nebuchadnezzar) may be identified, while the other three do not appear to be consecutive kingdoms, because they are all crushed *together* (see 2:44). In chapter 7, however, the four kingdoms are clearly empires that arose consecutively. There is also little doubt that the vision in Daniel 7 climaxes with the oppressive reign of Antiochus IV Epiphanes in the second century B.C.E., whereas that is not the case in chapter 2. If, as many scholars contend, chapter 2 originated earlier than chapter 7, then one may posit that the latter represents an appropriation and reinterpretation of the earlier account. Here in Daniel 7, the dream vision and interpretation of chapter 2 are reconsidered in the light of more recent historical events, so that undeniable historical allusions appear throughout the passage. Nevertheless, one should resist the temptation to associate every aspect of the vision with historical realities, for such associations are more often than not impressionistic and cannot be substantiated. The text is, in any case, ultimately less interested in those details than about the ultimate triumph of God over cosmic evil.

The dream vision is framed by an introduction (v. 1) and a conclusion (v. 28). In between are descriptions of the dream vision in its various facets (vv. 2–14), followed by an interpretation by a celestial intermediary (vv. 15–27). The vision itself involves a depiction of four terrible beasts emerging from the sea (vv. 2–8), a heavenly court scene (vv. 9–10), the destruction of the beasts (vv. 11–12), and the enigmatic anticipation of a humanlike someone who comes "with the clouds of heaven" (vv. 13–14). The last matter, of course, has contributed most to the persistent fascination of Jewish and Christian interpreters alike with the passage, for this one who "comes with the clouds of heaven" has been variously understood to be a reference to the messiah, the Christ, the angel Michael, the angel Gabriel, the High Priest Onias III, Judas Maccabeus, Daniel himself, or simply a collective reference to the Jewish people.

## INTRODUCTION
## Daniel 7:1

The chapter begins with the first year of Belshazzar. One who reads the book sequentially already has encountered this king, who is portrayed as the son of Nebuchadnezzar and the last Babylonian ruler in Daniel 5. Strictly speaking, the last king of the Babylonian Empire was Nabonidus, who usurped the throne in 556 B.C.E. and was disposed of by the Persians in 539 B.C.E., but Nabonidus had inexplicably moved to the Arabian oasis-town of Teima, effectively handing over kingship to his son Belshazzar in the third year of his reign. The literary setting of Daniel 7 is, therefore, the beginning of the end of the Babylonian Empire. The reader is returned to the very beginning of that final reign, as history is previewed—really, reviewed—beyond that end to the very end of all evil power. More is at stake than the demise of Babylon.

In the first year of Belshazzar's reign, then, Daniel reportedly received his dream vision. Now the servant of God is not one who proclaims the Word of God to others, but one who receives it. Daniel does stand not over and against the wicked, he stands with them in being subject to divine will for all humanity. Indeed, the solution to the mystery of the dream visions will come not from a gifted earthly sage, which is how Daniel is portrayed in chapters 1–6, but from a celestial intermediary (see v. 18).

Importantly, the visions are recorded (v. 1). The commitment of such materials to writing is by no means unique. There are many instances of prophets recording their own visions for posterity (see Isa. 8:1, 16; 30:8; Jer. 30:2; 36:2; 51:60; Ezek. 43:11; Hab. 2:2). In apocalyptic writings, too, the visions of the seers are often deliberately written down (see Rev. 1:11, 19; 21:5). The original intention of such writing was probably to suggest the possibility of authentication of the predictions when they came to pass, the implication being that the events recorded are about the future (compare 8:26). Rhetorically, then, the very mention of the recording of the dream vision legitimates the account as divine revelation.

## FOUR BEASTS FROM THE GREAT SEA
## Daniel 7:2–8

"The four winds of heaven" that the text says Daniel saw (v. 2), mentioned two other times in the book (8:8; 11:4), no doubt are the winds from the north, east, south, and west (compare Jer. 49:36; Ezek. 37:9; Zech. 2:6; 6:5; Matt. 24:31; Mark 13:27). As for the expression "the great sea," it may refer to the Mediterranean Sea, as it does elsewhere in the Bible (Ezek. 47:10, 15, 19, 20). At the same time, however, it may be an allusion to the primordial ocean, known elsewhere as "the great deep" (see Gen. 7:11; Isa. 51:10; Amos 7:4)—the chaotic waters that have been stilled by the will of the divine warrior. The stirring of "the great sea" suggests, therefore, a return to primeval chaos, the state of the cosmos before order was established in creation. Indeed, the Hebrew root for the word "stirring" is the same one used in Job 38:8 of the turbulent sea that God is said to have contained (see also Job 40:23; Ezek. 32:2). To some extent, the vision here echoes a scene in the Babylonian creation epic known as the *Enuma Elish*, where one reads of Marduk, the patron deity of Babylon, subduing Tiamat (the great ocean personified as a sea monster) by summoning "the four winds" against her. According to the story, "the four winds [Marduk] stationed (so) that nothing of her might escape, the South Wind, North Wind, East Wind, West Wind" (*ANET*, 66). In consequence, primeval ocean was contained and order established in the cosmos. That worldview is echoed in the Bible as well, where winds are frequently portrayed as instruments used by God to bring order out of cosmic chaos (Job 26:12–13; compare Ps. 89:9–11). Indeed, in the description of the beginning of the world (Gen. 1:1–2), one reads of the divine wind hovering over "the deep," the Hebrew word there being a cognate of the name Tiamat in Akkadian. Like its neighbors in the ancient Near East, Israel viewed creation as the establishment of order out of chaos, and that order is maintained by the will of God in the face of the persistent threat of chaos. Here in Daniel 7, however, one finds a hint of the return of primeval chaos, as the very winds that are supposed to bring order out of chaos now stir up "the great sea." Nothing less than world order is at stake as creation seems to become undone.

Then, out of this turbulence, there emerge four terrifying monsters (v. 3) that are reminiscent of the sea monsters in ancient Near Eastern myths concerning the ordering of the cosmos, like the sea monster of Canaanite mythology, Lothan (biblical Leviathan), a slithering dragon with seven heads (see *ANET*, 137–38). In the Bible, too, there are references to various sea monsters subdued by God, including Leviathan (Job 41:1; Pss. 74:14; 104:26; Isa. 27:1), Rahab (Ps. 89:10; Isa. 51:9), and Tannin (Ps. 74:13; Isa. 27:1; 51:9). In Daniel 7, however, not just one monster appears but four different ones, matching the four winds of the heavens, their number perhaps indicating totality. Moreover, these predators are apparently hybrid and deformed. Their hybrid character no doubt suggests uncleanness to the original Jewish audience (see Lev. 11); their deformity perhaps indicates, as in Mesopotamian divination texts, ominous events on the horizon. Menacingly, these grotesque monsters now each emerge, one after the other, from the turbulent "great sea."

The first creature is a lion-like beast with wings like an eagle (Dan. 7:4). The creature is, thus, a sphinxlike creature reminiscent of the winged lions known from Assyrian and Babylonian iconography. The wings are being defeathered, however, and the beast is lifted up, so that it is standing on two feet like a human being, and it is given a human mind. This imagery reverses the scene of the judgment of Nebuchadnezzar in 4:10–33, where the Babylonian king is given the mind of animals and made to live among beasts and behave like them, his hair growing "long as eagles' feathers" (4:33). In Daniel 4, a human being (Nebuchadnezzar) is transformed into a beast and sent to be among beasts, and he ends up looking like an eagle. Here in Daniel 7, however, the eagle loses its wings and the beast is transformed into a human being. This terrible monster has come into the midst of humanity and it has assumed some semblance of human form. One who reads this passage with the story of chapter 4 in mind must surely ponder the role of God amid this apparent return to chaos. One wonders if God's decision to contain the arrogant Nebuchadnezzar has somehow been rescinded, just as cosmic chaos has been allowed to return (so 7:2). In any case, because Nebuchadnezzar is the first of the powers to be named in the parallel vision of Daniel 2, and because Nebuchadnezzar's experience is echoed in Daniel 4, commentators have for good reason concluded that this first beast is probably an allusion to the Babylonian Empire.

The second creature in Daniel's vision is said to be different from the first, resembling a bear, except that it is elevated on one side (v. 5). Many interpreters assume the Aramaic here to mean that the bear-like beast was getting up, standing on its hind legs and, thus, poised to attack. The text, though, may not be describing the rising of the bear but the disproportionate elevation of one part of the body—that is, the bear has one side of its body raised up. If so, the vision echoes Mesopotamian omen texts that portray deformed animals as signs of impending disasters, especially animals with one part of its body raised. In the case of Daniel's vision, however, the bearlike creature also has three ribs (the Aramaic never means "tusks," as the NRSV has it) "in its mouth among its teeth" (v. 5). One may, perhaps, compare a Mesopotamian omen text that records a malformed fetus holding its entrails in its mouth. In Daniel's vision, the malformed creature is told to arise and to devour voraciously. Just who is giving the command to devour is unclear and that uncertainty is itself disturbing. At all events, the imagery is that of an insatiable monster that has barely finished devouring—three ribs are still in its mouth—but which is able to eat voraciously again, even if it has to be told to do so. Nothing in the description clearly identifies this second beast. Yet, if one takes the first monster to refer to the Babylonian Empire and if one considers the chronological sequence assumed by the book, then the second creature must be the empire of Darius, who is identified as "the Mede." The second beast represents, then, the power of the Medes. Accordingly, the three ribs in the mouth of the beasts have been interpreted variously as an allusion to three rulers, three nations, or three peoples that the Medes vanquished.

The third monster is said to be like a leopard, although it, like the others before it, is a hybrid and grotesque creature, bearing four wings and four heads (v. 6). The four wings may suggest extraordinary speed, while the four heads imply ability to move readily in any direction. The multiple heads also echo the inaugural vision of Ezekiel, wherein the prophet saw sphinxlike creatures, each having four faces and four wings (Ezek. 1:6). What Ezekiel saw in that vision, though, was salutary. He saw a manifestation of the awesome presence of God; the sphinx-like creatures with four heads and four wings bore the throne that symbolized the absolute rule of God. In Daniel's vision, by contrast, dominion is said to have been given to the monster with four wings and four heads (v. 6), as if God has ceded dominion to this terrible beast. Thus, just as creation is apparently undone (v. 2) and just as the decision of God to punish wicked power is rescinded (v. 4), dominion is given up in favor of another dangerous predator (v. 6). According to the sequence presumed by the book, Darius the Mede was succeeded by Cyrus the Persian (6:28). So one may understand the third beast to represent the Persian Empire.

The first three creatures are compared, then, to the lion, the bear, and the leopard, although they are all hybrid and grotesque. Interestingly, the same three beasts are mentioned in Hosea 13:7–8, where the Lord is said to be ready to attack like a lion, a leopard, and a bear. In Daniel, however, the threat is clearly not from the Lord. Rather, these dangerous forces must be subdued for the well-being of the universe. In Daniel 7, too, as in Hosea 13, yet another beast is present (compare the unspecified "wild animal" in Hos. 13:8), one that is not likened to any other. This creature is rhetorically set apart from the others and, in fact, represents the culmination of the vision of chaotic terror: "After this, I saw in the visions by night a fourth beast" (Dan. 7:7). More frightening and dangerous than all the others, this monster is said to be exceedingly strong, having great teeth of iron that devoured its victims, crushing them in pieces, and stamping out with its feet whatever was left. The characterization of the fourth beast here curiously uses the vocabulary depicting the fourth regime and its fate in the vision of the statue in chapter 2: "a . . . kingdom, strong as iron; just as iron crushes and smashes everything, it shall crush and shatter all these" (2:40). There the Aramaic verb used for "crushing" appears to be an allusion to the prophetic prediction of the pulverizing of the nations by the exiles (Isa. 41:15–16). In Daniel 2, the narrator implies that the prediction of Isaiah 41 will come to pass after all, for the lowly exile will crush mighty empires. That vision was already being realized, if only in a preliminary fashion, in the exaltation of the lowly exile, Daniel, over the mighty King Nebuchadnezzar (Dan. 2:46–48). Yet, as Daniel 7 now suggests, the kingship of God is still not fully realized. On the contrary, dominion on earth seems to have been ceded by the deity (v. 6), and evil earthly power devours and crushes.

This fourth beast is clearly different from the others that preceded it. Unlike the other three monsters, the fourth is not compared to other known creatures. It is not "like a lion," "like a bear," or "like a leopard." That difference is, perhaps, the most important: this creature simply commands no comparison, no analogue whatsoever. That characteristic makes it all the more terrifying; the beast is a new kind of terror—something for which there is no known analogy, no antecedent. Moreover, whereas passive forms are used to describe the other three monsters, active verbs are used for this one. Thus, the first beast had its feathers "plucked off," was "lifted up," "made to stand" on its feet, and "given" a human mind (v. 4). The second monster was "raised up on one side" and "told" to devour voraciously (v. 5). The third had dominion "given" to it (v. 6). These first three creatures are described with passive verbs—four verbs, two verbs, and one verb, respectively. By the time we read about the fourth predator, there is no more passivity; only active verbs are used to describe the beast: "devouring," "breaking in pieces," and "stamping." These pernicious creatures seem to have become increasingly bold in their activity and in asserting their independence from the source of all dominion and power.

The fourth monster is described as having ten horns, "horns" being a frequent metaphor in the Old Testament for power and kingship. Whether the number "ten" is meant to be symbolic for the totality of power, or allusions are being made to historical reality, as many commentators would have it, is not clear. Among those who hold the second view, some suppose that the horns refer to ten rulers of states within the empire. Others, however, point to other apocalyptic texts that refer to a sequence of ten generations of kings. Some argue that the ten horns refer to ten Hellenistic rulers before Antiochus IV Epiphanes (175–164 B.C.E.). Still, the identity of the three horns that are uprooted is disputed, although the suggestion that they refer to Seleucus IV and his sons Demetrius (who was sent to take the place of Antiochus IV as a hostage in Rome) and the infant Antiochus (with whom Antiochus IV served as co-regent for a short period) seems most plausible.

In any case, the text does not say how those "three horns" are removed or by whom, only that they are. Clearly, however, the appearance of the "little horn" is the climax of the scene, and this horn has "eyes like human eyes" and "a mouth speaking arrogantly" (v. 8). The threat, in other words, is monstrously dangerous, but is one wrought by a human being.

This little horn is probably an allusion to Antiochus IV Epiphanes, who came to power when Seleucus IV was murdered, one of his sons was sent to take the place of Antiochus in Rome, and the other son eventually also eliminated. Certainly Antiochus IV, who dared to claim for himself the name *Theos Epiphanes* ("God Manifest") fits the characterization of one whose mouth speaks arrogantly (see 1 Macc. 1:41–50).

## DIVINE RESPONSE
## Daniel 7:9–14

The scene of the monsters emerging from the chaotic "great sea" (vv. 2–8) is followed by a vision of a divine court (vv. 9–10). The vision of the heavenly court is, appropriately, presented in poetic lines, evidenced by parallelisms: "thrones were set in place" // "took his throne," "white as snow" // "like pure wool," "fiery flames" // "burning fire," "a thousand thousands served him" // "ten thousand times ten thousand stood attending to him." The switch from prose to describe the chaos of the world to poetry to depict the heavenly scene may be made for rhetorical effect, reflecting a shift from the prosaic realities of earthly experience to the sublime encounter of a heavenly court. In any case, the threat posed by the terrible monsters on earth is so severe, it seems, that a decision in the divine court is needed to deal with it. In Canaanite mythology as well, the threat of chaos in the world reaches the divine assembly that was presided over by the high god, El, a gray-haired figure who is known in various Ugaritic texts as "eternal king" and "father of years." Before the enthroned gods of this divine council, the emissaries of the deified sea monster, symbolizing cosmic chaos, come to claim dominion and demand the surrender of Baal, the god of life (see *ANET*, 129–42). So in Daniel's vision, too, dominion over the cosmos is at stake as the world seems to turn topsy-turvy. Creation seems to be unraveling, as terrible sea monsters are unleashed. God's decision seems to have been reversed, as wicked powers have apparently seized control that is supposed to belong to the supreme deity alone.

The mythic background of the vision is suggested by the plurality of thrones that are set up in the heavenly council, although Israelite theology would allow for only one to be enthroned—"thrones were set in place, and an Ancient One took his throne" (v. 9)—and that enthroned deity is depicted in terms that echo the Canaanite mythological portrayal of the high god, El, as an "Ancient One" (literally, "the ancient of days"). This Ancient One is said to have a garment that is white as snow, presumably an indication of his glorious splendor, his otherness (compare

10:5–6; Ps. 104:1–3; Matt. 28:3; Mark 9:2). He has hair like lamb's wool, no doubt meaning it is white, an indication of the deity's old age, just like El, "the father of years" in Canaanite mythology. His throne, however, is not an immobile one like the throne of the Canaanite high god. Rather, it comes with fiery wheels that are reminiscent of Ezekiel's inaugural vision of the presence of God (Ezek. 1). As in Ezekiel's vision, this mobile throne suggests the dynamic nature of divine presence. The deity is not simply seated in remote heaven, uninterested or unable to attend to specific local needs. Thus, amid the threat of cosmic chaos, Daniel (whose name means "my judge is El") sees a vision of God enthroned as judge in the heavenly court. The point of the vision seems clear enough. Forces of evil on earth may appear to have dominion on earth, but the fate of the world is determined in another realm by a God who is wholly transcendent and yet ever ready to intervene in human history.

As in other depictions of divine manifestations (see, e.g., Ps. 97:1–3), fire accompanies the divine presence (Dan. 7:10). An entourage of "a thousand thousands" and "ten thousand times ten thousand" comes along, no doubt an allusion to the celestial hosts that attend to and fight alongside the divine warrior (see Num. 10:36; Deut. 33:2; Ps. 68:17). Still, no protracted battle takes place between the forces of good and evil; the forces of good are not arrayed against the forces of evil. What one finds, instead, is a judgment scene in the divine court. The documents that are laid open presumably record the conduct of those whose lives are judged (see Pss. 40:7; 56:8; Mal. 3:16) or they set forth their destinies (Exod. 32:32–33; Pss. 69:28; 139:16; Rev. 17:8; 20:15). The sovereignty of God as the supreme ruler is in this way poignantly asserted. The fate of the world depends not on the result of a battle among the gods, as Canaanite mythology would have it, but by the unilateral judgment of God alone.

Reflecting on the earthly condition again, the narrator in Daniel 7 returns to prosaic language (vv. 11–12). On account of its arrogance, the fourth monster from the sea will be destroyed. Other biblical texts speak of the slaying and piercing of the sea monsters by the sword (Isa. 27:1; 51:9–10) or the crushing of their heads (Ps. 74:12–13). The fourth monster in Daniel's vision will have its body destroyed and burnt with fire, just as deified Mot in Canaanite mythology is completely annihilated and its body burnt with fire (*ANET,* 140). As for the other predators, their dominion will be taken away. One is reminded here that dominion on earth is a divine prerogative; mortals possess it not on account of their own right and power but only as a gift from God that may readily be rescinded. The God who gives dominion (Dan. 7:6) is free to take it away (v. 12). Yet, the judgment of these creatures is qualified. The text speaks enigmatically of an extension of life granted to them by God "for a season and a time" (v. 12). The point, perhaps, is that while the most dangerous beast is immediately and completely annihilated, threats to world order may still persist for a while. Evil remains a persistent threat to wholeness in the universe.

In the traditional myth of the slaying of the chaos monster, the ancient god El sits enthroned as a king, presiding over the divine council and pronouncing judgment. He does not rise to fight the chaos monsters personally. Instead, the youthful god, the storm-god Baal, known in ancient Canaanite texts as "the rider of the clouds," rises to the challenge. The language of the deity coming on a cloud still finds reminiscences in the Bible (Deut. 33:26; Pss. 18:10; 68:4, 33; 104:3; Isa. 19:1). Specifically, in the Bible, the Lord is typically portrayed as coming upon a cloud to help people in distress. In Daniel's vision, too, a champion would come "with the clouds of heaven" (Dan. 7:13) before the Ancient One, the divine Sovereign.

This champion who comes with the clouds of heaven is said to be "one like a human being" (v. 13). The Aramaic expression translated in the NRSV as "a human being" has traditionally been rendered as "the Son of man," making the expression anticipatory of Jesus' enigmatic self-designation in the New Testament. Hence, this one who comes is frequently understood as a messianic figure—for Christians, the Christ. The Aramaic term in Daniel 7 is, however, an indefinite one; it is certainly not yet an epithet, as in the New Testament and in various rabbinic writings. In fact, the definite expression (with the definite article) never occurs in the Old Testament. Thus, while it may be argued that the gospel writers in the New Testament interpreted the mission of Jesus in terms of Daniel's vision (see, especially, Mark 13:26), to say that the vision in Daniel is strictly about "*the* Son of man" is untenable. The expression here, like its equivalents in Hebrew and other Semitic languages, simply refers to a human being, any human being. Indeed, in early Aramaic, the expression is used to refer to "a certain person" and, hence, meaning simply "someone." Significantly, the expression is often used to convey the sense of a mere mortal—someone who unexpectedly receives God's special attention and care (Pss. 8:5; 144:3; Job 25:6). Such a mortal, it is said, certainly cannot save (Ps. 146:3), yet this champion who comes with the clouds of heaven appears just like such a one. Against all the terrible predators comes one just like that, who will, indeed, save; the one who appears incapable of saving will, in fact, save! Just as Baal in Canaanite mythology is finally given dominion and kingship, so, too, this champion in Daniel's vision will be given "dominion and glory and kingship" so that "all peoples, nations, and languages should serve him" (Dan. 7:14). What is to be given to this one is what God has hitherto given to human rulers like Nebuchadnezzar (2:37; 5:18–19), a reflex of God's own eternal kingdom and power and glory (4:3; 6:26). The one who comes with the clouds of heaven as a mere mortal will, indeed, be so endowed.

This savory one who comes with the clouds of heaven stands in stark contrast with the unsavory ones that emerge from the primordial deep, the turbulent "great sea." The former is poignantly *like* a mortal, even as the pernicious beasts are *like* a lion, *like* a bear, and *like* a leopard. Moreover, in contrast to the dominion of the monsters from the sea, which will be for limited periods in history, the dominion of the one coming with the heavenly clouds will be forever. Their dominion is ephemeral, but his is eternal. His dominion shall not pass away, like the dominion of other earthly powers (2:21; 4:31; 5:20), notably the evil empires (see 7:12). His reign "shall never be destroyed" (v. 14).

The notion of an indestructible power echoes the vision of the four regimes in Daniel 2, where the text affirms that God will establish a regime that "shall never be destroyed" (2:44). Represented in that vision by the stone cut not by human hands, that eternal regime is expected to crush all others, even as it "shall stand forever." The mysterious figure who comes with the clouds of heaven in Daniel 7 thus corresponds to stone that is cut not by human hands in Daniel 2, and both represent divine response to the threat of domination by pernicious earthly powers. Just as Daniel has previously asserted that God is the one who gives "the kingdom, the power, the might, and the glory" (2:37), so, too, one understands that God now gives "dominion and glory and kingship" (7:14).

## INTERPRETATION
## Daniel 7:15–27

Like Nebuchadnezzar, whose spirit was troubled by his dreams (2:1, 3), Daniel's spirit is troubled; as the visions in Nebuchadnezzar's mind terrify him (4:5), so the visions of Daniel's mind terrify him (v. 15). Whereas Daniel previously served as the interpreter of dreams and visions, however, he is now like Nebuchadnezzar insofar as he is a recipient of the vision and in need of help to make some sense of it. Here Daniel is not the disinterested interpreter providing a clear solution to others; he is the empathetic visionary—one who shares the terror of the world that is being judged. He—and the reader with him—needs some explication of the dream, in desperate need of the Word of God. Hence, Daniel approaches one of the "attendants"—presumably one of the members of the divine council who attend to the celestial king—and thereby receives the interpretation while still in the midst of his dream vision.

Given the vision of the four regimes in Daniel 2, one should hardly be surprised by the interpretation of the four terrible beasts arising "out of the sea" as four kingdoms arising "out of the earth" (v. 17). Here, as elsewhere in the Old Testament (see Isa. 17:12–14), myth is historicized. Mythological symbols are given earthly equivalents. Thus, one gathers that the battle against the chaotic forces of evil is not a distant reality, but a very present one. Indeed, the chaotic sea corresponds to the historical world, the chaotic world in which mortals have their being. As the terrible sea monsters of the creation stories threatened cosmic order, so, too, evil earthly kings threaten earthly order. All who know the ancient myths realize what the outcome of those battles has always been: the divine warrior will ultimately triumph. In Canaanite mythology, the victory over the forces of chaos resulted in the enthronement of Baal, "the rider of clouds," who is given dominion and kingship over all the earth. One should expect, therefore, that the mysterious one who comes "with the clouds of heaven" will be given the trophy of eternal rule. So verse 14 asserts that "dominion and glory and kingship" would be his forever, which is, however, not precisely how the interpretation goes in verse 18. Instead, kingship is said to be given to "the holy ones of the Most High." The one who comes with the clouds of heaven, who is "like a human being," turns out to be not a single individual, as in Canaanite mythology, but a plurality of beings, namely, "the holy ones of the Most High." The divine champion of Canaanite lore is now apparently reinterpreted and democratized. Thus, interpreters who argue that the one who comes with the clouds of heaven like a mere mortal is a collective figure, a symbol of God's faithful on earth, are not mistaken. The view that the one who comes with the clouds is a messianic individual—for Christians, ultimately a reference to "the Son of man" who comes to save the world—has poetic truth. The one is the many; the many are the one. The two views are, indeed, not mutually exclusive.

In Canaanite mythology, as frequently in the Old Testament (see, for instance, Deut. 33:2; Job 5:1; 15:15; Ps. 89:5–7; Zech. 14:5), the designation "holy ones" refers to the heavenly hosts that surround the deity. In Daniel 4:17, in fact, "the holy ones" are members of the divine council that issue a verdict against Nebuchadnezzar. Yet, as the interpretation of Daniel's vision further unfolds, the designation "holy ones of the Most High" clearly refers not to angelic beings alone, but also to God's faithful people on earth. Indeed, the expression seems to refer at once to God's angelic hosts (the holy ones who serve God in heaven) and God's terrestrial hosts (the holy ones who serve God on earth). The faithful people of God on earth are a microcosm, an earthly image of the holy ones in heaven (7:21, 22, 25, 27). The "holy ones" are, thus, also called by the narrator "*the people* of the holy ones" (v. 27, emphasis added). In this way, then, the figure of the "rider of clouds" that is well-known in Canaanite mythology is radically demythologized, as it were; the mythological champion in the cosmic battle with chaos is democratized and, if only in part, historicized as the faithful people of God. To put it another way, the struggle of the faithful in the face of seemingly overwhelming evil is articulated in terms of the cosmic battle for good. The holy ones on earth do not fight alone, for they mirror a reality that transcends the earthly. Nothing less than world order is at stake, and "the holy ones of the Most High"—both the celestial and the terrestrial—are together the champions fighting on the side of all that is good.

The interpretation of the heavenly intermediary then turns to the fourth beast, the most fearsome one (v. 23). This beast is of the greatest interest to the narrator, presumably because it is the predator that menaces the world in the time of the narrator and the original audience. So Daniel, still in the midst of his dream vision, wants to know the truth concerning this creature. The narrator reiterates the description already given in verse 7, adding only that it has "claws of bronze" (v. 19). The significance of this additional datum is unclear, however. The four beasts have already been interpreted as four kings (v. 17), but now the ten horns that grew on the head of the fourth beast are said to refer to ten kings coming from the fourth kingdom (v. 24). The ten kings have been interpreted as ten successive kings of the Hellenistic Empire from Alexander the Great to Seleucus IV, and the three horns that were removed to make room for the little horn are supposed to be this Seleucus and his two sons. Accordingly, the new horn sprouting after them must be Antiochus IV Epiphanes, who, scholars believe, "made war with the holy ones and was prevailing over them" (v. 21) and who made them weary (v. 25). Hence, the reference to the eyes of the little horn is seen as an allusion to his covetousness as regards the throne, and the mention of the mouth speaking arrogantly is believed to point to the infamous blasphemy of his self-designation as "God Manifest."

Moreover, the reference to the attempt to change "the sacred seasons and the law" (v. 25) is thought to allude to the replacement of the solar calendar with the lunar one, the consequent disruption of the observation of religious festivals and the abolition of certain Jewish religious rites (1 Macc. 1:41–61). The word translated in the NRSV as "sacred seasons" in verse 25 is the same one rendered simply as "seasons" in 2:21, while "law" is elsewhere translated as "decree." In Daniel 2, Nebuchadnezzar had also assumed that he had authority over time, for he would not permit the

Chaldeans to "gain time" (2:8) and to wait till "time changes" (2:9, NRSV "things take a turn"), knowing that he had made the "decree" (2:8). The point is made, however, that God, not human rulers, is the one who "changes times and seasons" (2:21). Yet, now it seems that human power is once again attempting to, literally, change the seasons and the decree (7:25). This power, presumably Antiochus IV Epiphanes, is harassing "the holy ones of the Most High" and they will apparently be "given into his power" (v. 25), even as the Jews in the sixth century B.C.E. were given for a time into the hand of Nebuchadnezzar, indeed, by God (1:2).

As for the duration of the subjugation under this new oppressor, it will be "for a time, two times, and half a time" (v. 25). The Aramaic has, literally, "until a time, and times, and a portion of time." The expression is enigmatic. A common interpretation takes the phrases to refer to a period of three and a half years and to be somehow related to the historical calculations in 8:14; 9:2; and 12:11–12. To think, though, that "a time and times, and a portion of time" means "a year, two years, and half a year" is somewhat of a stretch. The coordination with historical events in the reign of Antiochus IV Epiphanes does not work out precisely in any case. What is more important to observe here is the recurrence of the word for "time" and its contrast with the references to eternity in verse 27. The point is the temporal nature of oppressive rule, which may be for a period, any number of periods, or just part of a period. No matter, the rule will only be temporary. As such, it is subject to the eternal God, the One who "changes times and seasons" (2:21).

The book of Daniel opens with a reference to God's deliverance (giving) of the Jews into the hand of Nebuchadnezzar (1:2), and now Daniel is told of the deliverance of the "holy ones of the Most High" into the hand of the new oppressor up to a period, periods, or part of a period. Whether "a period" would mean the reign of a particular ruler, or the domination of an empire, or some other definition of an era is not clear. Regardless of how one looks at the issue, the point seems clear that human oppression would be only up to (so the Aramaic in v. 25) a period, multiple periods, or just an incomplete period. Whether long or short, for a single period or several periods, the duration will inevitably be temporal—necessarily bound by time. The heavenly court will sit in judgment and determine that human dominion will be made to pass away and it will be decisively destroyed, literally, "up to the end" (v. 26, NRSV "totally"). The earthly reality will be reversed as the regimes under the heavens, with all their dominion and greatness, will be given to "the people of holy ones of the Most High." Whereas the holy ones of the Most High had been given to earthly power (v. 25), the earthly regimes will eventually be given to the people of the holy ones (v. 27). Moreover, in contrast to the dominion of earthly powers that would be only temporary (whether for a period, multiple periods, or just part of a period), the rule of the people of the holy ones will not be bound by time, but will be "an everlasting kingdom" (v. 27). The eternal reign, elsewhere said to be of God, is attributed to the people of the holy ones of the Most High. As in Daniel 2, then, the oppressed people of God are expected to become triumphant through this rule that transcends time—beyond a period, periods, or part of a period.

## CONCLUSION
## Daniel 7:28

As the account ends, Daniel's reaction is surprisingly not one of relief. Inasmuch as the vision ends with a prediction of the triumph of those on God's side, one might expect Daniel to react more positively. Yet, he does not. Already in verse 15, while apparently still in his dream state, his spirit is said to be disturbed and he is terrified by the visions. Now that the vision has been reported and interpreted, he is still "greatly terrified" by his thoughts, his countenance changed, and he "kept the matter" in his mind. In some ways, his reaction is comparable to those of Nebuchadnezzar and Belshazzar following their dream and vision experiences (2:1; 4:5; 5:6, 9). In those cases, however, the recipient of the divine communication is the expected object of God's predicted punitive action; fear is entirely expected. By contrast, Daniel has envisioned here the destruction of certain wicked powers of the world, monstrous oppressors whose demise should bring relief to anyone who stands with God. He himself does not appear to be the direct object of divine judgment. One may speculate that Daniel's fear has to do with the enormity of the evil threat, the implication that suffering is inevitable, since the holy ones of the Most High would be delivered into the hand of the terrible oppressor in the person of "the little horn." The terror may have arisen, too, because of the lack of a clear indication of when oppression might end: it may last a period or many periods, or it may last only a part of a period. The uncertainty of when the end might come may itself be cause for deep concern. Indeed, the promise of triumph is conveyed through the confusing imagery of someone who comes from heaven with the cloud and yet is "like" a human being.

Moreover, how one who comes from heaven like a human being is related to the holy ones of the Most High is also not clear, and some mystery exists as to the heavenly or earthly origin of the holy ones. Indeed, when all is said and done, much remains mysterious and confusing. Even so, that is where Daniel ends up and, perhaps, that is where the reader is supposed to be at this point in the book. Daniel, however, kept the matter in his heart. Because the vision is written down and made public, the point surely cannot be that he has kept it to himself. Rather, the point is probably that he did not lose sight of it; he kept on pondering it—mysterious and enigmatic as it is. Perhaps the reader is expected to keep on pondering the vision as well.

# 8. The Ram, the Goat, and the Interpretation of Gabriel
## *Daniel 8:1–27*

**1 In the third year of the reign of King Belshazzar a vision appeared to me,
Daniel, after the one that had appeared to me at first. 2 In the vision I was
looking and saw myself in Susa the capital, in the province of Elam, and I
was by the river Ulai. 3 I looked up and saw a ram standing beside the river.
It had two horns. Both horns were long, but one was longer than the other,
and the longer one came up second. 4 I saw the ram charging westward and
northward and southward. All beasts were powerless to withstand it, and
no one could rescue from its power; it did as it pleased and became strong.**

**5 As I was watching, a male goat appeared from the west, coming across
the face of the whole earth without touching the ground. The goat had a
horn between its eyes. 6 It came toward the ram with the two horns that I
had seen standing beside the river, and it ran at it with savage force. 7 I saw
it approaching the ram. It was enraged against it and struck the ram, breaking its two horns. The ram did not have power to withstand it; it threw the
ram down to the ground and trampled upon it, and there was no one who
could rescue the ram from its power. 8 Then the male goat grew exceedingly
great; but at the height of its power, the great horn was broken, and in its
place there came up four prominent horns toward the four winds of
heaven.**

**9 Out of one of them came another horn, a little one, which grew
exceedingly great toward the south, toward the east, and toward the beautiful land. 10 It grew as high as the host of heaven. It threw down to the
earth some of the host and some of the stars, and trampled on them. 11 Even
against the prince of the host it acted arrogantly; it took the regular burnt
offering away from him and overthrew the place of his sanctuary.
12 Because of wickedness, the host was given over to it together with the
regular burnt offering; it cast truth to the ground, and kept prospering in
what it did. 13 Then I heard a holy one speaking, and another holy one said
to the one that spoke, "For how long is this vision concerning the regular
burnt offering, the transgression that makes desolate, and the giving over of
the sanctuary and host to be trampled?" 14 And he answered him, "For two**

**thousand three hundred evenings and mornings; then the sanctuary shall be restored to its rightful state."**

**15 When I, Daniel, had seen the vision, I tried to understand it. Then**
**someone appeared standing before me, having the appearance of a man,**
**16 and I heard a human voice by the Ulai, calling, "Gabriel, help this man**
**understand the vision." 17 So he came near where I stood; and when he**
**came, I became frightened and fell prostrate. But he said to me,**
**"Understand, O mortal, that the vision is for the time of the end."**

**18 As he was speaking to me, I fell into a trance, face to the ground; then**
**he touched me and set me on my feet. 19 He said, "Listen, and I will tell you**
**what will take place later in the period of wrath; for it refers to the**
**appointed time of the end. 20 As for the ram that you saw with the two**
**horns, these are the kings of Media and Persia. 21 The male goat is the king**
**of Greece, and the great horn between its eyes is the first king. 22 As for the**
**horn that was broken, in place of which four others arose, four kingdoms**
**shall arise from his nation, but not with his power.**

**23 At the end of their rule,**
**when the transgressions have reached their full measure,**
**a king of bold countenance shall arise,**
**skilled in intrigue.**
**24 He shall grow strong in power,**
**shall cause fearful destruction,**
**and shall succeed in what he does.**
**He shall destroy the powerful**
**and the people of the holy ones.**
**25 By his cunning**
**he shall make deceit prosper under his hand,**
**and in his own mind he shall be great.**
**Without warning he shall destroy many**
**and shall even rise up against the Prince of princes.**
**But he shall be broken, and not by human hands.**

**26 The vision of the evenings and the mornings that has been told is true. As**
**for you, seal up the vision, for it refers to many days from now."**

**27 So I, Daniel, was overcome and lay sick for some days; then I arose**
**and went about the king's business. But I was dismayed by the vision and**
**did not understand it.**

With chapter 8, the book of Daniel reverts to Hebrew, a shift that is now corroborated by manuscripts from Qumran. While the shift from Hebrew to Aramaic in 2:4 seems to have been prompted by the speech of the Chaldean interpreters speaking in their own language, no reason is obvious for the reversion to Hebrew at precisely this juncture. Readers can only speculate.

The vision of chapter 7 is posed as one of cosmic significance, with four unsavory monsters emerging from the sea made turbulent by four winds. The presence of the terrible beasts suggests the undoing of creation, the surrendering of divine sovereignty to demonic powers, and the disruption of world order. That vision concerns world empires and the cosmic consequences of their evil. In Daniel 8, however, the four grotesque chaos monsters are replaced by two domestic animals, indeed, two animals that are clean according to ritual laws: the ram and the goat. In general, the vision of Daniel 8 seems to be connected more concretely with historical events than the vision of Daniel 7. With its allusions to the attack on Jerusalem, the desecration of the temple, and the violation of the cult (8:11–12), the vision and its interpretation clearly concern the experience of the Jewish people at a particularly traumatic time in their history—their experience of repression under Antiochus Epiphanes. Perhaps the very subject matter, namely, the survival of the Jewish people and their faith in the face of such humiliation, inspired the linguistic shift from Aramaic, still the *lingua franca* of the Eastern Mediterranean world, to the rejuvenated national language of the Jewish people. To be sure, scholars have long judged the Hebrew of Daniel 8–12 to be inelegant, unidiomatic, and even downright poor; the language is certainly not the literary Hebrew that one finds in other late biblical Hebrew texts, such as Ezra-Nehemiah. That difference has prompted some to argue that the Hebrew text of Daniel 8–12 was originally written in Aramaic and translated into Hebrew or that the text was written in Hebrew but had been poorly transmitted. The author certainly appears to be more at home with Aramaic than with Hebrew, yet that may merely reflect a nationalistic reclamation of the narrator's native tongue after years of exile and existence under foreign rule.

The vision of this chapter is dated to the third year of Belshazzar's reign, thus, two years "after the one that had appeared to me at first" (v. 1), namely, two years after the vision of chapter 7. The relationship of chapter 8 to chapter 7 is suggested, too, by the similar structure evident in both passages. Each passage is framed by an introduction with a chronological notice (7:1; 8:1–2) and a conclusion with an account of the seer's reaction (7:28; 8:27). Within that framework, one finds first a recounting of the vision (7:2–14; 8:3–14), followed by an explanation by a celestial interpreter (7:15–27; 8:15–26). Thematic links are present as well: the culmination of the threat by way of the little horn, the attack upon "the people of the holy ones," and an interpretation provided by a celestial intermediary.

Nevertheless, the two chapters also differ starkly in certain respects. Whereas the four powers represented by the four monsters of chaos are not named in Daniel 7, the ram and the goat in Daniel 8 are explicitly identified with the Medo-Persian and Greek empires, respectively.

Whereas the identities of the ten horns as well as the three that are removed in favor of "the little horn" are obscure in Daniel 7, little doubt exists about the identities of "great horn" of the he-goat or the four horns that arose after the great horn is broken off: they refer, respectively, to Alexander the Great and the four rulers who divided up his empire when he suddenly died in 323 B.C.E. Whereas the offense of the "little horn" is previously characterized somewhat vaguely in terms of his arrogance of speech and an attempt to change the times and law (7:25), allusions are now made specifically to the desecration of the temple and the suspension of its festivals by Antiochus, events that occurred in 167 B.C.E. Whereas 7:25 speaks ambiguously of "a time, two times, and half a time" when the little horn will be in power, the text now speaks unambiguously of "two thousand and three hundred evenings and mornings" before the sanctuary would be restored (v. 14). Whereas the interpretation of Daniel's previous dream vision is left to an unidentified celestial intermediary (7:16), the vision in Daniel 8 is interpreted by a particular angel by the name of Gabriel. In short, Daniel 7 is cosmic and implicit, while Daniel 8 is nationalistic and explicit. The difference is such that one might think of the latter as a fleshing out of the former. The vision of Daniel 8 may, indeed, be viewed as a sort of "contextualization" of the dream vision in chapter 7, which is itself a reworking of the account of Nebuchadnezzar's dream vision in chapter 2.

## INTRODUCTION
## Daniel 8:1–2

The chapter begins with a chronological notice, placing the vision in "the third year of the reign of King Belshazzar" (v. 1). Two years have supposedly passed since the vision of chapter 7, which is dated to the first year of that reign (7:1). Apart from the date, the text also links this vision with the previous one, for the vision in chapter 8 is described as "after the one that had appeared to me at first." Perhaps the reader is expected to wonder if the predictions in the previous vision have been fulfilled in any way. Now the chapter will show at least one way in which they might be.

Apart from placing this vision after the vision of chapter 7, the significance of the date, if any, is unclear. If one assumes that the date is in reference to Belshazzar's co-regency with Nabonidus while the latter was in Arabia, then Belshazzar's first year would have been about 553 B.C.E. Accordingly, the third year would be 550 B.C.E. or thereabouts. At about that time, Cyrus first achieved political independence from the Medes and embarked upon a course of conquest that would lead eventually to the establishment of his empire. If this dating is correct, therefore, "the third year of the reign of King Belshazzar" would signify the imminent end of the Chaldeans and the beginning of the empire of the Medes and the Persians.

This vision takes one to Susa (8:2), the long-time capital of the Median "province of Elam," a region between Babylon and Persia, in the present-day Iranian region of Khuzistan, about 150 miles north of the Persian Gulf. The city was destroyed by Asshurbanipal of Assyria in 646 B.C.E. Although the city was restored around the year 625 B.C.E., it languished for years before eventually gaining prominence as a winter residence of Darius I in 521 B.C.E. Hence Susa came to be known as the imperial city par excellence (see Neh. 1:1; Esth. 1:2). Because the vision is dated to the reign of Belshazzar and is explicitly said to be "in the province of Elam," however, one should think not of the glorious imperial city of the Persian rulers but of the dilapidated provincial fortress of the Babylonians.

Despite an old tradition that Daniel lived in Susa for some time and was even buried there (where to this day a tomb is associated with "the Prophet Daniel"), the text does not say that he was physically present in that city, only that he saw himself there in the vision. The emphasis is on what he envisaged, for in the Hebrew text of verses 1–2, the verb "see" appears five times and the word "vision" occurs three times. The seer was somehow transported to that location in his vision, just as Ezekiel was taken in his vision to Jerusalem (Ezek. 8:3) and to the exiles in Chaldea (Ezek. 11:24), and just as the seer in the book of Revelation was spirited, so to speak, into the wilderness in his vision (Rev. 17:3). At the same time, the account is also reminiscent of Ezekiel's inaugural vision, which he received when he was by the river Chebar (Ezek. 1:1), near a dilapidated quarter of Nippur called Tel-Abib (Ezek. 3:15). As Ezekiel was by the river Chebar, so Daniel was by the river Ulai (Dan 8:2).

Ulai is the Akkadian name of the waterway on a bank of which Susa was built. Asshurbanipal once boasted that he had turned it into a river of blood and he depicted the capture of the city on a relief in his capital. So one thinks, again, of the end of the dynasty of which Belshazzzar was the last king. The river was known in the classical sources as Eulaeus. Significantly, under the Seleucids, among whom Antiochus Epiphanes was the most infamous dynast, Susa was reestablished as a Greek polis and renamed Seleucia-on-the Eulaeus, and it became a renowned center of Hellenism, the culture that Antiochus vigorously promoted to, even imposed on, the Jews. Daniel's audience no doubt would have recognized it as such.

## THE RAM AND THE GOAT
## Daniel 8:3–8

The initial words of the Hebrew text in verse 3 are curiously reminiscent of Genesis 22:13, where Abraham, after being told to refrain from slaughtering his own son Isaac, literally, lifted up his eyes and saw a ram. Daniel, too, according to the Hebrew text, lifted up his eyes and saw a ram. Perhaps the reader is supposed to gather from the allusion, if indeed an allusion was intended, that the descendants of Abraham are not the ones whose survival is at risk "in the third year of the reign of King Belshazzar" (v. 1), but "another ram" that the Lord will now provide. This ram has two long horns of uneven lengths, with the longer one coming after the shorter one (v. 3). One learns later in the passage that the ram symbolizes the empire of the Medes and the Persians and the two horns represent the two kings (v. 20), perhaps meaning specifically "Darius the Mede" and Cyrus the Persian. The shorter horn that comes first is, accordingly, the Median kingdom, which came first, while the longer one that arises after it is the stronger and longer-lasting Persian regime. The Persians often used the ram motif in their architecture. Indeed, in ancient astrological speculations, Persia was represented by the sign of the ram, Aries. So the ram is used here appropriately to symbolize the Persians.

The ram is seen charging unstoppably westward, northward, and southward (v. 4). A few textual witnesses add "east" to the three directions, and some modern commentators favor correcting the Hebrew text by adding this reading. Later scribes more likely added the fourth direction for completeness, thus matching other references to all four directions or four corners of the world. In fact, the allusion here is probably to the conquests of Cyrus, who, for the biblical writers in Palestine, was one coming from the east (compare Isa. 41:2). The directions recall various Persian incursions—west into Asia Minor and as far as Greece, north into Scythia, and south into Egypt.

Another animal appears to Daniel while he is still considering what he saw (v. 5). The seer apparently receives no relief in his vision. Even as he is still trying to make sense of the first symbol, he is confronted with another one: a he-goat. This goat that comes from the west, one is told in the interpretation in verse 21, represents Greece. The zodiac that placed Persians under Aries, the ram, also has the Seleucids—the Greek rulers who ruled Syria-Palestine after the death of Alexander—under Capricorn, the horned goat.

The goat charges across the face of the whole earth "without touching the ground," probably meaning that it moves with tremendous speed, which is likely an allusion to the swift advance of the army of Alexander the Great. In short order, the army of Alexander besieged Tyre (333 B.C.E.), invaded Palestine and Egypt (332 B.C.E.), and defeated the Persian ruler, Darius III Codommanus in the decisive battle of Gaugamela in 331 B.C.E., capturing the palace on the first of October. The extent of the goat's advance—expressed as "across the face of the whole earth"—echoes the notice in 1 Maccabees 1:3 that Alexander advanced "to the ends of the earth." Alexander was depicted on various coins wearing a horned helmet and he came to be known in later traditions by an Arabic epithet meaning "the one with two horns." Yet, given that the two horns on the ram are explained as representing Media and Persia, this goat that represents Greece is now said to have a single horn between its eyes. Some commentators, citing Mesopotamian iconographic practices, suggest that the single horn is a result of the artist depicting the animal from the side so that only one horn is visible. In any case, this goat with one horn attacks the ram with two horns. As a result, the two horns are broken, cast to the ground and trampled upon, with none to rescue them (v. 7).

Ironically, at the height of its power, the conspicuous horn on the goat is broken and in its place come four horns toward "the four winds of heaven," that is, the four cardinal points on the compass (v. 8). The sudden breaking of this great horn is doubtlessly an allusion to the death of Alexander in 323 B.C.E. As for the four horns appearing in place of the broken great horn, they must refer to the dividing of the empire among the Diadochi ("successors"). Philip, a half-brother of Alexander, controlled Macedonia, Antigonus dominated Asia Minor, Seleucus I Nicanor took Syria and Babylon, and Ptolemy I ruled Egypt. Those four regions represented the four cardinal points of the compass—"the four winds of heaven"—the west, the north, the east, and the south, respectively.

## THE LITTLE HORN
## Daniel 8:9–12

Then yet another horn appeared, "a little one." The reader has already encountered a "little horn" in chapter 7, where it appears to be an allusion to Antiochus Epiphanes. Now this little horn is said to come from one of the four horns that grew after the prominent one was broken off, meaning probably that he comes from the Seleucid domain. Why this horn is called "little" is unclear. Perhaps the adjective is meant as a contrast to "the great horn" (v. 8), namely, Alexander the Great. In comparison to the founder of the Greek Empire, Antiochus is but an insignificant figure, a local tyrant. Possibly, too, the designation is a derogation derived from the fact that Antiochus was the youngest among his brothers and, as such, had at best questionable claims to the throne.

Still, despite his being little, this horn "grew exceedingly great" (v. 9). He advances toward the south, toward the east, and toward "the beautiful land." The Hebrew text, in fact, has "the Beauty" instead of "the beautiful land," but most modern translations assume that what is found here is an abbreviation of a fuller expression found in 11:16, 41. That assumption is plausible, because Israel is elsewhere characterized as a beautiful land (see Ps. 106:24; Jer. 3:19; Ezek. 20:6, 15; Zech. 7:14). In all probability, though, "the Beauty" in this context is a reference to Mount Zion (Jerusalem), where the sanctuary of the Lord was located. So in 11:45, one reads of "the beautiful holy mountain" (compare 1 Macc. 2:12). God's "holy mountain," Mount Zion is elsewhere said to be "beautiful in elevation" (Ps. 48:1–2). Mount Zion is also known as "the perfection of beauty" (Ps. 50:2; Lam. 2:15). Indeed, the related expression in Daniel 11:16, 41 defines the land in terms of "the Beauty," for Judea is called, literally, "the land of the Beauty" (that is, the land in which beautiful Mount Zion is). Antiochus dares to advance upon Mount Zion and the sanctuary of the Lord.

The arrogant act is expressed in mythological terms. The horn is said to have grown up to the host of heaven, causing some stars to fall and be trampled upon (v. 10). The language here is reminiscent of various ancient Near Eastern myths concerning a rebellion in the heavenly realm against the supreme deity of the universe. Thus, among the Canaanite myths, for instance, one tells of an attempt by Athtar, the Morning Star (that is, Venus), to ascend the heights of Mount Zaphon to seize the throne that rightfully belongs to Baal. That usurper, however, was not up to the task; he was too little, so to speak (*ANET*, 140). A reflex of this ancient myth is found in Isaiah 14:12–15, which depicts the fall of an astral deity referred to as "Day Star, son of Dawn." The arrogant challenger in that case ventured to ascend the heights of heaven, "above the stars of God" and on to "the mount of assembly" in the farthest reaches of Zaphon, the sacred mountain that in Canaanite lore was home to the gods. He who dared to compare himself to the Most High would, however, be cast down to Sheol. Myth is historicized in this Isaianic poem, a taunt song uttered against "the king of Babylon" (Isa. 14:4), here probably an allusion to King Sennacherib, who led his army in a siege of Jerusalem in the late eighth century B.C.E. That invader who encroached upon Jerusalem and surrounded it is, thus, compared to the arrogant rebel of myth—the inadequate rebel who dared to imagine himself ascending the holy mountain, rising even above the stars. Interestingly, the rulers of the nations in this taunt song are called, literally, "the goats of the earth" (Isa. 14:9, NRSV "leaders of the earth"). In ways that are reminiscent of the myth preserved in Isaiah 14, then, Daniel now envisages the "little horn" ascending to the host of heaven, meaning the stars that symbolize the divine council.

In Canaanite mythology, as well as in the Old Testament, stars are portrayed as members of the heavenly host, the divine council and allies of the Most High (Judg. 5:20; Isa. 5:9–11; 24:21). Now this "little horn" has even reached the heavens and some of the heavenly host have been made to fall and are trampled (Dan. 8:10). A later apocalyptic text speaks of a monstrous dragon with seven heads (as in Canaanite lore) and ten horns (as in Dan. 7) sweeping down a third of the stars of heaven and causing them to fall down to earth (Rev. 12:3–4). In Israelite theology, God is the one who presides over the divine council and who alone determines that errant members of the heavenly council be cast out from heaven, just like the fallen astral deities of myth (see Ps. 82). Yet, now the arrogant "little horn" presumes to take up that task: he casts out some of the host from heaven. Indeed, Antiochus dares to deal with the members of this host as the goat (Greece) dealt with the ram (the Medes and the Persians); he casts them to the ground and tramples upon them (Dan. 8:10; compare v. 7).

As the Hebrew text has it, "he grew great up to the commander of the host" (v. 11a, NRSV "prince of the host"). The word for "commander" in the book of Daniel is always used in reference to divine beings (8:25; 10:13, 20, 21; 12:1). The epithet is, in fact, a martial one. It recalls the "commander of the army of the LORD," whom Joshua had encountered as he led his people in holy warfare (Josh. 5:13–15). In the case of Joshua, the commander of the Lord's terrestrial host, the earthly army of God's faithful, encounters his celestial counterpart, the commander of the Lord's heavenly host. Who precisely the narrator in Daniel 8 has in mind remains something of a mystery, although the text would later refer to "the commander of commanders" in verse 25 (NRSV "the Prince of princes"). Since what is at stake here is an attack on "the place of his sanctuary," however, "the commander of host" is most likely to be understood as a manifestation of God in person, the one who is known elsewhere in the Bible as "the Lord of hosts." Still, the passage is concerned not with what goes on in heaven only. Rather, the text proceeds immediately to speak of atrocities perpetrated on earth. Despite some difficulties in the Hebrew of verse 11, the arrogant challenger to God's supremacy clearly seems to be taking away regular burnt offerings and desecrating the temple. The allusion is probably to the offenses committed by Antiochus. In 167 B.C.E., he stormed the city with a large army, plundered it, and established a garrison of foreign troops and renegade Jews on the mount known as the city of David. He defiled the sanctuary, terminated the regular festivals, and imposed foreign customs in the city (1 Macc. 1:29–61). So arrogant was he, in fact, that he was later remembered as one who "thought that he could touch the stars of heaven" (2 Macc. 9:10). Indeed, Antiochus in that period had commissioned coins to be minted, each depicting his own head with a star next to it. To the narrator, such arrogant acts affect not only the earth; they touch even the heavens and affect God personally. The consequences of the sacrilege are not limited to the earth. Atrocities committed against the people of God are atrocities perpetrated against the heavenly host and, indeed, against God. Violence against human beings may well be violence against the divine.

The Hebrew of verse 12 is uncertain. One should be careful not to assume that the text is referring to "*the* host" in verses 10, 11 (the heavenly host), for the word in verse 12 is indefinite; it refers to a host or an army. Indeed, an earthly army is likely the focus. Accordingly, one may interpret the Hebrew to mean that an army (the army of Antiochus?) is given or permitted "upon the regular offering in transgression." Moreover, the passive verb "given" or "permitted" is a circumlocution for divine agency. The implication is that God is the one who gives or permits the results. Here, as elsewhere in the book, the actions of kings—even the most wicked tyrants—are subsumed under God's sovereignty. The book of Daniel began by affirming that God gave Judah into the power of Nebuchadnezzar (1:1). Even though the Babylonian king was exercising his oppressive rule on earth, ultimately his rule was possible only because God had granted him that possibility. So now the text asserts that the attack on Jerusalem is possible only because God has given it. Even the desecration of the cult was something that was possible only because of the sovereign power of God. Indeed, the word that the NRSV renders as "wickedness" in verse 12 is the same one used of the desecration of the sanctuary in verse 13. That desecration, as horrible as it was, was not a result of the powerlessness of God nor the power of the outsider's army. That God had lost control is not the intended meaning. Indeed, God, according to divine freedom and purpose, has allowed the tragic event to occur. The army of Antiochus was thus able even to desecrate the temple and to "cast truth to the ground"—a probable allusion to his desecration of the Torah by the troops of Antiochus (1 Macc. 1:56).

## AN ANGELIC CONVERSATION
## Daniel 8:13–14

Daniel hears the voice of "a holy one" (compare 4:13, 23) speaking and then another. The plurality of voices of celestial beings is reminiscent of the divine council scene in Isaiah 6, where one angelic creature calls out to another. Daniel overhears the celestial conversation, apparently catching only the end of it. As in the Isaianic vision, the holy ones wonder about the duration of what is seen, asking "how long?" (Dan. 8:13, compare Isa. 6:11). Whereas in Isaiah 6 the prophet asks "how long," in Daniel 8 one of the holy ones does so. The Hebrew text is exceedingly awkward at this point, however. Most modern commentators believe the text to be corrupt and offer various proposals to emend it. One may imagine, however, that for the writer the problem of divine consent to allow the temple to be desecrated and its feasts suspended must have been so terrifying that even a member of the divine council could only stammer in response to the prospect. Hence, the question is posed with many ellipses, literally, "Until when . . . the vision . . . the regular offering . . . and the transgression . . . devastating . . . delivering . . . and the sanctuary . . . an army . . . trampling?" (author's translation). Still, despite the syntactical incoherence, the concern of the holy one comes through well enough. At issue is no doubt the duration of the vision-scene: how long will it all last? Though the stammering question is posed by one celestial being to another, the conversation does not remain in the heavenly realm. The answer is given not to one of the holy ones (so the NRSV has "and he answered him," following the ancient Greek versions instead of the Hebrew). Rather, as the Hebrew text has it, the answer is given to the seer of the vision, Daniel himself.

Moreover, in contrast to the sputtering question concerning the duration, the answer is crisp and to the point: "Two thousand three hundred evenings and mornings; then the sanctuary shall be restored to its rightful state" (v. 14). The idiom "evening and morning" designates a full day, as it does in Genesis 1:5–31. So the figure refers to the actual number of days when regular sacrifices were made: twenty-three hundred days, that is, a period of under seven years. If one assumes that the allusion in Daniel 8:13 is to the rededication of the temple and the restoration of sacrifices in 164 B.C.E., then the twenty-three hundred days must have begun around 171 B.C.E., the year when the legitimate high priest Onias III was murdered at the instigation of the renegade Menelaus, a henchman of Antiochus Epiphanes and a plunderer of the temple (2 Macc. 4:23–50). In this view, the desecration of the temple in 167 B.C.E. is but the culmination of atrocities that had begun years earlier, when Onias III was assassinated, and those atrocities lasted until the temple was rededicated in 164 B.C.E. The latter date is important, for the legitimacy of the temple was then restored and sacrifices were offered once again (1 Macc. 4:53). One may read the Hebrew at the end of Daniel 8:14 in that way: "Then the sanctuary will be legitimate (again)." Whatever the precise historical significance, however, the point of the text seems clear. The situation will not last forever; there will be an end to it all.

## THE INTERPRETATION
## Daniel 8:15–26

Despite the opportunity to overhear the deliberations in the divine council, the meaning of the vision is not at all obvious to Daniel. He still seeks an understanding of it. He who has been the skillful interpreter of dreams and visions still needs his own vision explained. Then, by the river Ulai, he sees someone standing before him, according to the Hebrew text, "like the appearance of a man" (v. 15). The language is reminiscent of Ezekiel's vision by the river Chebar of a virtual reality of divine presence a "likeness . . . that seemed like a human form" (Ezek. 1:26). The figure that is like a human being in Ezekiel's vision is, however, sitting enthroned like El, the supreme deity of the divine council, whereas Daniel's humanlike figure is standing before him. What Daniel sees, then, is apparently one of the members of the heavenly host.

The seer also hears a voice (Dan. 8:16). Most commentators naturally believe that a divine voice is meant, and one may note that Ezekiel in his inaugural vision by the river Chebar also heard a voice speaking, understood to be the voice of God (Ezek. 1:28). One thinks, too, of the unidentified voice in the divine council, calling for the consolation of God's people (Isa. 40:1) or the voice calling for the wilderness to be readied for the divine warrior's return for holy warfare (Isa. 40:3). If so, the voice of the supreme deity of the divine council is the one authorizing the interpretation to be given to Daniel. Yet, none of these passages so plainly identifies the voice as "a human voice." Taking the text here at face value, one may understand the voice as a plea from humanity—from a mortal, any mortal—for the mystery to be revealed. For the sake of humanity, the vision cannot remain a complete mystery, so the unidentified voice by the river Ulai calls for the mystery of the vision to be explicated.

The addressee of the plea, probably the being who stands before Daniel "like the appearance of a man," is named Gabriel. The Hebrew text is most tantalizing at this point, for the figure whose appearance is like a "man" (Hebrew *gāber*) is named *gabrî'ēl*, which taken at face value, means "my man is God." For the first time in the Bible, an angelic being is explicitly named. This same angel will appear again in Daniel 9:20–27, and he will later be identified in Luke-Acts as "the angel of the Lord" (Luke 1:11, 19, 26; compare also Luke 2:9; Acts 5:19; 8:26; 12:7). In later Jewish traditions, Gabriel and Michael (who is mentioned in Dan. 10:13,

21; 12:1) are named together with Raphael and Uriel as four angels that surround the throne of God. Here in Daniel's vision, Gabriel is asked to help Daniel understand the sight, the Hebrew word here being the same for "appearance" in verse 15. Ironically, then, Gabriel ("my man is God") who is "like the appearance of a *gāber*" is asked to explain the appearance to Daniel. Like the inaugural vision of Ezekiel, something obviously profound and mysterious seems to be taking place, yet the details are elusive, which is perhaps to be expected. Daniel is not, after all, encountering a human being, but a heavenly reality, a mysterious presence. Hence, when Daniel is approached, he understandably panics and falls prostrate (v. 17)—the standard reaction in the Old Testament of people encountering the presence of God. Thus, too, Joshua fell prostrate on the ground when he encountered the "commander of the army of the LORD" (Josh. 5:14). Like that "commander of the army of the LORD" who appeared as a man standing before Joshua (Josh. 5:13), Gabriel, whose appearance is like a man, stands before Daniel.

The seer is presently addressed as "mortal," the same way that the deity typically addressed the prophet Ezekiel. The designation also echoes the vision in Daniel 7:13 of the one who comes with the clouds of heaven "like a human being." The name of the heavenly interpreter (Gabriel, "my man is God") and the designation of the earthly seer ("mortal") are both tantalizing. They provide a hint as to how God's response to the terrible threat posed by evil power would come. God's solution would be mediated through divine presence in human form (compare 7:13); the solution would also come through a desperate and uncomprehending mortal. Even as the threat of evil power is posed on earth as in heaven, so God's response comes by way of God's host in heaven and on earth. At issue in this vision is, as the Hebrew text has it literally, "a time of an end" (v. 17). The point is not the end of history, the end of time per se, but a time of an end to the apparent dominance of evil power.

Daniel's reaction to the announcement may be surprising to modern readers: he falls into a deep sleep at this critical juncture, even as the heavenly interpreter is speaking! The motif is not unique, however. Abram, too, fell into a deep sleep in the midst of his vision (Gen. 15:12). The seer in the book of Revelation collapsed "as though dead" when he encountered the deity (Rev. 1:17). Perhaps such encounters are so tremendous that they cannot be received in full human consciousness. One must be in a deep sleep, a trance. So Daniel, who has apparently been awake for his vision until now, falls into deep sleep, still in a posture of complete submission and awe, his face to the ground (see Ezek. 1:28; compare Lev. 9:24; 1 Kgs. 18:39; 2 Chr. 7:3).

Then the angel touches him and sets him on his feet. The celestial touch is reminiscent of Isaiah's vision of the divine council, for a seraph touches the prophet on his mouth with a coal (Isa. 6:7). The prophet Jeremiah, too, is touched by the Lord on his mouth (Jer. 1:9). In both cases, the celestial touch on the mouth is meant to empower the prophet to speak the Word of God. A more pertinent parallel is 1 Kings 19, where the prophet Elijah is asleep when an angel touches him and tells him to get up (1 Kgs. 19:5). Comparable, too, is the experience of the prophet Ezekiel who, upon encountering divine presence like the appearance of a human being, falls on his face to the ground, only to be set on his feet by a heavenly voice (Ezek. 1:28–2:1). Similarly, upon encountering divine presence, the seer in the book of Revelation collapses "as though dead," but is touched by the deity and encouraged (Rev. 1:17). So Daniel, though totally passive, is able to receive the message.

The meaning of the enigmatic expression "for a time of an end" in Daniel 8:17 is then explicated. The translation in the NRSV suggests that it has to do with "what will take place later in the period of wrath" (v. 19). The Hebrew text, though, shows other interpretations. In fact, what the NRSV renders as "later in the period of wrath" means, literally, "at the end of the wrath." But whose wrath is meant and at whom is it directed? Many commentators believe that the wrath of the aggressor is meant, that is, the wrath of Antiochus, which does make sense in the immediate context. Yet the Hebrew word that is translated as "wrath" is, with only one possible exception (Hos. 7:16, a corrupt text!), always used of divine affliction. The term is often used of divine punishment of God's people at the hand of outsiders, such as the affliction of Judah by Assyria (Isa. 10:5, 25). As such, the punishment is always of limited duration. Hence is posed the question, "How long?" Although Ezekiel would speak of a "day of wrath" (Ezek. 22:24, 31; NRSV "indignation"), other texts usually do not specify the duration of the experience. Thus, in Isaiah 26:20, people are asked to hide for a while until God's "wrath" passes, the word here being used, as in Daniel 8:19, for an unspecified period. Lamentations 2:6 is especially relevant for the interpretation of Daniel's vision, for the wrath of God in that context has to do with God's role in the destruction of Zion and its temple, the end of religious festivals and the Sabbath, divine rejection of the altar and the sanctuary, and the spurning of Israelite kingship and priesthood. Thus, too, one may understand the wrath in Daniel's vision to refer to the period of tribulation at the hand of unbelievers, something akin to the humiliation of the destruction of Jerusalem and the termination of its festivals in the sixth century B.C.E. (compare Dan. 1:2). The important point scored in this talk of the wrath of God is that God is still in charge, not human powers, despite signs to the contrary. In spite of the arrogance of human challenge to God's authority, the events occurred only because God had allowed them. At the same time, however, the narrator reckons that the people who are subject to the indignities and sufferings in this case are not entirely blameless. For the biblical writers, without a doubt the suffering such as those of the exile was a result of God's will acting in response to the faithlessness of God's own people.

For modern interpreters, the notion of political repression as divine retribution for the victims is troubling. Yet such a view of suffering does have an indisputable place in biblical theology. The doctrine is instructive inasmuch as it blatantly raises the question of human responsibility in the face of tragedy. Without such a theological reminder of that possibility, one may be too quick to deny human culpability; blaming the situation on an unjust and uncaring God or questioning the very presence of God may be all too convenient. Indeed, sometimes tragedies do happen to people because they have been careless, irresponsible, faithless, or plain wicked. Indeed, the notion of divine retribution reminds one that God is not at all oblivious to the possibility of humanity's role. For all our discomfort with the idea, at times suffering may, indeed, be meaningful and instructive, perhaps even bringing about positive outcomes. Along with this view of divine retribution, however, other traditions within scripture recognize that such a view of suffering is not adequate. The wisdom tradition, for one, affirms that human deeds may well have their consequences, whether or not one chooses to speak of divine causality. Even within that tradition itself, one finds a skeptical strain evident in Job and Ecclesiastes that sometimes suffering on earth occurs for which there is no logical explanation. Be that as it may, the text in Daniel 8 provides no justification, no rationale for the wrath of God in this case—only a bold assertion that the events are a result thereof, and that silence leaves interpreters more than a little uncomfortable.

The detailed interpretation of the vision, however, occasions no surprise. The ram with two horns of unequal lengths is explicitly identified with the empire of the Medes and the Persians (v. 20). The goat represents the Greek kingdom, while the great horn that arose is its "first king" (v. 21), namely, Alexander the Great. The four horns appearing after that (v. 22) are the four kingdoms that arose when Alexander died suddenly. Unfortunately, the clarity dissipates after these initial identifications.

The denouement of the interpretation—concerning the rise and fall of the one who dares to challenge divine hegemony (compare vv. 9–12)—is presented rhythmically. The reason for the shift from prose to verse is unclear. Perhaps what we have here is an imitation of a prophetic oracle, proclaiming the inevitable demise of the aggressor. The text speaks of "the end of their rule" (v. 23), the expression being an echo of the earlier expression, "the end of the wrath" (v. 19). Hence, one may now interpret "the wrath" as the period under the rule of the kings of the Medo-Persian and Hellenistic empires. In light of the allusion to the period as one of divine wrath, one may think of the transgression as a reference to the sins of the people that brought about the culminating atrocities. Yet, the same word rendered as "transgressions" in the NRSV, which assumes a slight repointing of the Hebrew, already appears in verse 12 (translated in the NRSV as "wickedness") and verse 13, both in reference to the rebellious acts of the "little horn." Furthermore, the idea of transgressions running their course is more appropriate for foreign nations than for the Jewish people. Whereas God disciplines and corrects the Israelites whenever they transgress, the punishment of outsiders is a matter of vengeance, something that comes in due time—when their sins have reached their full measure (compare 2 Esdr. 4:36–37; 1 Thess. 2:16). Thus, Genesis 15:16 speaks of the sins of the Amorites not being complete, that is, not yet due for a full divine response. Similarly, the apocryphal work called the Wisdom of Solomon reflects on the Egyptians accumulating their offenses during the time of the exodus "in order that they might fill up the punishment that their torments still lacked" (Wis. 19:4). Most importantly, a document from the time of Antiochus IV reflects God's different responses to the unfaithful in Israel as opposed to the other nations:

> In fact, it is a sign of great kindness not to let the impious alone for long, but to punish them immediately. For in the case of the other nations the Lord waits patiently to punish them until they have reached the full measure of their sins; but he does not deal in this way with us, in order that he may not take vengeance on us afterward when our sins have reached their height. Therefore he never withdraws his mercy from us. Although he disciplines us with calamities, he does not forsake his own people. (2 Macc. 6:13–16)

Thus, whereas the suffering of God's people may be a consequence of the wrath of God, there is nevertheless an "end of the wrath." The silence of God in the face of the oppressor's triumph is not a sign of the loss of nerve on God's part. On the one hand, silence is an exercise of divine wrath that is disciplinary and instructive for God's people, which is how the faithful should view their present plight. The Seleucids are, at best, mere instruments of the Lord's intentional pedagogy, in the same way that Assyria and Babylon were at various points in history also unconscious agents of divine will. On the other hand, God may be waiting for the right moment to take decisive action against the foreigners who dare to challenge God's authority.

The transgressions of the outsiders against Israel reach their climax with the rise of "a king of bold countenance" who is also "skilled in intrigue" (v. 23). Whether these descriptions are specific allusions to the characteristics of Antiochus or they are formulaic descriptions of any foreign ruler is difficult to say; while these traits may well describe Antiochus, they are also general enough to be applied to other oppressive rulers. At all events, this ruler will increase in power, wreak devastating destruction, and "destroy the powerful and the people of the holy ones" (v. 24).

Some commentators take "the powerful" in verse 24 to be the political rivals of Antiochus—the other horns that had to be removed to make room for him (7:8, 20, 24), yet the juxtaposition of such with "the people of the holy ones" would be most odd if that were the case. The word translated as "the powerful" is often used of multitudes, in which case it means "numerous," "massive," or "populous" (Deut. 4:38; 7:1; 9:1; 11:23; etc.). As such, "the powerful" is frequently juxtaposed with the word "many." That the text should also speak of the destruction of "many" in verse 25 is suggestive. Even as "he shall destroy numerous" (Dan. 8:24), "he shall destroy many" (v. 25). Joel 2:11 portrays the Lord as leading his host, which is described as "many" (NRSV "vast") and "numerous" (NRSV "numberless"). This parallel is especially tantalizing, since "the holy ones" in Daniel and elsewhere may refer to the celestial host as well as its earthly counterpart. Israel is elsewhere also described as both "many" and "numerous." Thus, in the exodus story, the reader is told that Israel's enemies are bent on destroying them because they have become many and numerous (Exod. 1:9; see also the parallel verb forms in Exod. 1:6). Hence, one may understand Daniel 8:24 to be a reference to the attack of the Lord's hosts, both the celestial host and the terrestrial one, namely, "the people of the holy ones." This interpretation is consistent with the vision in verses 10–12, where one reads of the attack against the host, with the result that some of that host are made to fall. Moreover, as in verse 11, the arrogant challenger dares even to go up against the deity. Whereas verse 11 speaks of attack against "the prince of the host" (or "the commander of the army"), the text now identifies (v. 25) the deity as "the Prince of princes," the quintessential leader of hosts. God is unquestionably and personally involved in these events. The atrocities committed by Antiochus on earth do not merely have earthly consequences, but they reach the heavens and draw in the supreme ruler of hosts. Thus, the interpretation promises that "he [Antiochus] shall be broken, and not by hands" (v. 25). This promise echoes Daniel's own interpretation of

Nebuchadnezzar's dream of the statue in chapter 2, where it is said that earthly power will be crushed by a stone hewn from the mountain, but "not by human hands" (2:34, 45). The defeat of evil power will be by the will of God alone through those who represent the reign of God, that is, the faithful.

Gabriel's interpretation ends with an affirmation of reliability of the vision and an instruction for Daniel to "seal up the vision" (see also 12:4, 9), for it concerns not the present moment but "many days from now." The assertion that the vision has to do with the distant future stands in stark contrast with the view recorded in Ezekiel 12:27–28. The contemporaries of Ezekiel were wont to disregard the prophet's visions, thinking that they had to do with the distant future and not the present. To that charge, the prophet insisted that the fulfillment of his visions would, in fact, be imminent. Indeed, proclamation ought not to be concerned only with the distant future—as it were, "in the bye and bye"—but with contemporary lives. Theology must have relevance for the present, which, in fact, is the point of the statement in verse 26. The closing was intended not only as a stamp of authority but also an assertion that the vision finally concerns not the events of its historical setting, namely, the sixth century B.C.E., but a long time thereafter, namely, for the reader in the time of Antiochus, in their generation. Modern readers may, likewise, take the cue that the meaning of the passage is not locked in the past—not in the time in which the vision is set (the sixth century B.C.E.), nor even in the time in which it is presented (the second century B.C.E.)—but for days to come, including one's own.

## CONCLUSION
## Daniel 8:27

As in chapter 7, the vision of Daniel provides no relief for the seer. The Hebrew text is difficult in part, but the general sense of it seems clear enough. Daniel's reaction is something like what he experienced at the end of the vision in the preceding chapter (7:28). In this case, he becomes sick for days. Nevertheless, he soon arises and continues his civil duties, although still troubled by the vision and, despite the interpretation provided from on high, still not understanding it. Indeed, much in the vision and its interpretation continues to puzzle and trouble all who learn of them. To be instructed that human actions of earth can have consequences beyond the mundane world—that violence on earth can somehow be violence against heaven—is frightening and sobering. Accepting that horrible suffering at the hand of wicked powers can somehow be, at least in part, a consequence of divine indignation for human wrongs is difficult. To be told that the atrocities on earth will end, but that the appointed end is still far away, is disconcerting. When all is said and done, one still cannot be sure about the answer to the question asked in heaven on behalf of humanity: "How long?"

# 9. Daniel's Prayer and the Predicted End of Desolation
## *Daniel 9:1–27*

1 **In the first year of Darius son of Ahasuerus, by birth a Mede, who**
**became king over the realm of the Chaldeans—2 in the first year of his**
**reign, I, Daniel, perceived in the books the number of years that, accord-**
**ing to the word of the LORD to the prophet Jeremiah, must be fulfilled for**
**the devastation of Jerusalem, namely, seventy years.**

3 **Then I turned to the Lord God, to seek an answer by prayer and sup-**
**plication with fasting and sackcloth and ashes. 4 I prayed to the LORD my**
**God and made confession, saying,**

**"Ah, Lord, great and awesome God, keeping covenant and steadfast love**
**with those who love you and keep your commandments, 5 we have sinned**
**and done wrong, acted wickedly and rebelled, turning aside from your**
**commandments and ordinances. 6 We have not listened to your servants the**
**prophets, who spoke in your name to our kings, our princes, and our ances-**
**tors, and to all the people of the land.**

7 **"Righteousness is on your side, O Lord, but open shame, as at this day,**
**falls on us, the people of Judah, the inhabitants of Jerusalem, and all Israel,**
**those who are near and those who are far away, in all the lands to which**
**you have driven them, because of the treachery that they have committed**
**against you. 8 Open shame, O LORD, falls on us, our kings, our officials, and**
**our ancestors, because we have sinned against you. 9 To the Lord our God**
**belong mercy and forgiveness, for we have rebelled against him, 10 and have**
**not obeyed the voice of the LORD our God by following his laws, which he**
**set before us by his servants the prophets.**

11 **"All Israel has transgressed your law and turned aside, refusing to obey**
**your voice. So the curse and the oath written in the law of Moses, the ser-**
**vant of God, have been poured out upon us, because we have sinned**
**against you. 12 He has confirmed his words, which he spoke against us and**
**against our rulers, by bringing upon us a calamity so great that what has**
**been done against Jerusalem has never before been done under the whole**
**heaven. 13 Just as it is written in the law of Moses, all this calamity has come**
**upon us. We did not entreat the favor of the LORD our God, turning from**

**our iniquities and reflecting on his fidelity. 14 So the LORD kept watch over this calamity until he brought it upon us. Indeed, the LORD our God is right in all that he has done; for we have disobeyed his voice.**

**15 "And now, O Lord our God, who brought your people out of the land of Egypt with a mighty hand and made your name renowned even to this day—we have sinned, we have done wickedly. 16 O Lord, in view of all your righteous acts, let your anger and wrath, we pray, turn away from your city Jerusalem, your holy mountain; because of our sins and the iniquities of our ancestors, Jerusalem and your people have become a disgrace among all our neighbors. 17 Now therefore, O our God, listen to the prayer of your servant and to his supplication, and for your own sake, Lord, let your face shine upon your desolated sanctuary. 18 Incline your ear, O my God, and hear. Open your eyes and look at our desolation and the city that bears your name. We do not present our supplication before you on the ground of our righteousness, but on the ground of your great mercies. 19 O Lord, hear; O Lord, forgive; O Lord, listen and act and do not delay! For your own sake, O my God, because your city and your people bear your name!"**

**20 While I was speaking, and was praying and confessing my sin and the sin of my people Israel, and presenting my supplication before the LORD my God on behalf of the holy mountain of my God—21 while I was speaking in prayer, the man Gabriel, whom I had seen before in a vision, came to me in swift flight at the time of the evening sacrifice. 22 He came and said to me, "Daniel, I have now come out to give you wisdom and understanding. 23 At the beginning of your supplications a word went out, and I have come to declare it, for you are greatly beloved. So consider the word and understand the vision:**

**24 "Seventy weeks are decreed for your people and your holy city: to finish the transgression, to put an end to sin, and to atone for iniquity, to bring in everlasting righteousness, to seal both vision and prophet, and to anoint a most holy place. 25 Know therefore and understand: from the time that the word went out to restore and rebuild Jerusalem until the time of an anointed prince, there shall be seven weeks; and for sixty-two weeks it shall be built again with streets and moat, but in a troubled time. 26 After the sixty-two weeks, an anointed one shall be cut off and shall have nothing, and the troops of the prince who is to come shall destroy the city and the sanctuary. Its end shall come with a flood, and to the end there shall be war. Desolations are decreed. 27 He shall make a strong covenant with many for one week, and for half of the week he shall make sacrifice and offering cease; and in their place shall be an abomination that desolates, until the decreed end is poured out upon the desolator."**

Daniel 9 stands out from among the other parts of the book for at least three reasons. In the first place, its point of departure is neither a direct encounter of a threat posed by an oppressive regime (as in chaps. 1, 3, and 6) nor a dream or vision by one of the principal characters in the book (as in chaps. 2, 4, 5, 7, 8, and 10–12). Rather, the story begins with reflections on what is "in the books," a reference to certain prophecies of the prophet Jeremiah. Moreover, the chapter includes a long prayer of confession and supplication (vv. 4–19) that is unlike anything encountered so far. To many interpreters, who assume that the main issue is that Jeremiah's prediction of restoration after a seventy-year exile has not been fulfilled, the prayer seems entirely out of place. One should expect here a petition for clarification of the prophecy or a prayer of illumination to help one cope with the dissonance of failed prophecy, they argue, not a prayer of confession and supplication. A suggestion often made is that one might skip the prayer entirely and move directly from verse 3 to verse 20 and not miss a beat. Indeed, the narrative would read better without the prayer, some interpreters maintain. Furthermore, the language of the prayer (vv. 4b–19) is at odds with the rest of the chapter. Unlike the inelegant Hebrew of the rest of Daniel 8–12, which is replete with Aramaisms, the prayer is written in good Hebrew prose and contains no Aramaisms at all. Hence, some have proposed that the prayer has been added secondarily to the chapter.

While stylistic disparity does exist between the prayer and the rest of the chapter, the prayer being linguistically more conservative, that disparity may indicate only the archaism characteristic of liturgical material, as opposed to the language of a contemporary report (the narrative framework). Similarly, the prayers of Nehemiah, when compared with the Hebrew prose in which they are embedded, manifest relatively conservative linguistic features. The author quite conceivably might have drawn substantially on existing prayers or even adapted an older prayer for this context. Indeed, whatever the origin of the prayer, several noteworthy links are present between the prayer and the rest of the chapter. For instance, Jerusalem is mentioned nowhere else in the book, but appears both in the prayer (vv. 7, 12, 16) and in the introduction (v. 2). By the same token, the word "supplication" appears only in this chapter, both in the prayer (vv. 17, 18) and in the narrative framework (vv. 3, 20, 23). References to desolation in verses 17–18 are reiterated in verse 27, the admission of iniquities in verses 13 and 16 is matched by the promise of atonement of iniquities in verse 24, and the allusion in verse 11 to an oath being "poured out" is met by the decree in verse 27 of an end to be "poured out."

An argument can be made that the prayer of confession is integral to the chapter, for Daniel "perceived" (NRSV) the words of Jeremiah (v. 2). Indeed, the prayer is the very sign that Daniel had understood Jeremiah, for the prophet, following the promise of restoration after the seventy years (Jer. 29:10), had urged earnest prayer: "When you search for me, you will find me; if you seek me with all your heart, I will let you find me . . . and I will bring you back to the place from which I sent you into exile" (Jer. 29:13–14). The promise of restoration is, indeed, contingent upon the right response to God, a response that Daniel takes up in the prayer. The chapter, thus, cannot be properly understood apart from the prayer of confession and supplication.

The result of the prayer is the appearance of Gabriel (Dan. 7:20–23), who had already appeared to Daniel previously, in the vision of chapter 8. Thus, chapter 9 presupposes chapter 8, which in turn presupposes chapter 7. The angel provides an interpretation not of Daniel's own vision but of Jeremiah's prophecy (vv. 24–27), although the details of that interpretation are frustratingly confusing. Jeremiah's "seventy years" is reinterpreted to mean seventy periods of sevens, that is, seventy "weeks" of years. And the entire period of 490 years is divided into three segments of (1) seven sevens, that is, 49 years; (2) sixty-two sevens, that is, 434 years; and (3) one final period of 7 years. The numerology, together with tantalizing references to an "anointed prince" who is to come at the end of the first 49 years (v. 25) and another "anointed one" who would appear after the end of the next 434 years (v. 26), have made this passage one of the most controversial in the history of the interpretation of the book. On the one hand, traditional Christian exegetes, who take the numbers literally and believe the second "anointed one" to be a prediction about Christ, tend to begin their calculation from the time of Nehemiah in the mid-fifth century, for then the 490 years would lead one to the time of Christ. Most modern historical critics, on the other hand—wanting the arithmetic to lead to the time of Antiochus IV Epiphanes in the early second century—prefer to begin their calculation from the time of Jeremiah's prophecy in 605 B.C.E. or from the Babylonian exiles of 597 or 586 B.C.E. Moreover, in addition to the sum total of the years, interpreters have had to contend with the specific segments of time and the allusions associated with each period. In any case, the numbers never quite match the dates of the historical events. As a result, neither the traditionalists nor the historical critics have been able to arrive at any consensus in their approaches. Gabriel's interpretation in verses 24–27 remains one of the most enigmatic passages of the book.

The chapter begins, like others in the book, with an introduction indicating the date of the event (vv. 1–2). This opening is followed by the introduction to the prayer (v. 3) and the prayer itself (vv. 4–19) and then an account of Gabriel's appearance and his interpretation of Jeremiah's prophecies (vv. 20–27).

## INTRODUCTION
## Daniel 9:1–2

The chapter begins, as so often in the book of Daniel (1:1; 2:1; 7:1; 8:1; 10:1), with a chronological notice: the first year of Darius the Mede (vv. 1–2). Nothing is said about King Belshazzar of the previous chapter, but the implication is that he is a figure of the past, for Darius, according to the Hebrew text, "has been made king over the kingdom of the Chaldeans" (v. 1). The text does not say that Darius "became king," as the NRSV would have it, but that he "has been made king," the passive verb here being a circumlocution for divine agency; the implication is that Darius has been made king by divine action. The Babylonian Empire is finished and history moves on by the will of God.

Whereas Darius was previously introduced simply as "the Mede" (5:31), he is now said to be the "son of Ahasuerus." The father of Darius the Mede cannot be the Ahasuerus (Xerxes) that we know from elsewhere in the Bible, where he is recognized not as the father but as the son of Darius (Esth. 1:1; 2:16–17; compare Ezra 4:6). If the name reflects historical reality or tradition, Ahasuerus must refer to someone else.

The date is noteworthy, especially if its repetition in the Hebrew text is correct (Dan. 9:1–2). The prophet Jeremiah had predicted that the Babylonians would be defeated and replaced by "the kings of the Medes, with their governors and deputies, and every land under their dominion" (Jer. 51:28). For the narrator of Daniel, that prophecy has apparently come true with this Darius, who is of Median stock and who, indeed, is "son" of the other Mede who, in the time of Jeremiah, had helped bring about the downfall of the predecessors of the Babylonians. Jeremiah had, however, also predicted the end of devastation and the beginning of restoration after seventy years (Jer. 25:11–12; 29:10), but now that the Babylonian Empire has ended, there appears to be at least another reign that the exiles have to endure. So it is appropriate at the beginning of the reign of Darius the Mede to reflect on the prophecies of Jeremiah concerning Jerusalem's "devastation" (Dan. 9:2)—the same word used by Jeremiah in his prophecy concerning the seventy years of exile (Jer. 25:11).

In the first year of Darius, Daniel "perceived in the books the number of years that, according to the word of the LORD to the prophet Jeremiah, must be fulfilled for the devastation of Jerusalem, namely, seventy years." This NRSV language implies that there was already a corpus of authoritative books—"the books"—at the time when the passage was composed. The Hebrew word for "books," however, simply means "documents." Hence, the documentary sources here may refer not to any notion of "scripture" per se, but to the letters that Jeremiah had sent to the exiles of Babylon, one of which is, in fact, explicitly called a document (Jer. 29:1, 3, 29). Indeed, in one of these "documents" Jeremiah wrote to the exiles about the end of seventy years of Babylonian rule (Jer. 29:10). Surely Daniel 9 is alluding to such documents.

How one should take the seventy years in Jeremiah is not entirely clear. From elsewhere in the Bible and extant historical sources, we know that the Babylonians had brought about two exiles of the Judeans, the first in 597 B.C.E. and the second in 586 B.C.E. If one takes the seventy years literally and begins with the first exile (597 B.C.E.), the end of that period would be 527 B.C.E. If one begins with the more devastating destruction of Jerusalem in 586 B.C.E., one ends up with 516 B.C.E., about the time when the temple was rebuilt—which is, indeed, the date assumed by some postexilic biblical interpreters of Jeremiah's prophecy: the rebuilding of the temple, some seventy years after the exile began, was viewed as the fulfillment of Jeremiah's prediction (2 Chr. 36:21; Zech. 1:12). Both dates are problematic, however, because the Babylonian Empire technically ended with the taking of Babylon by Cyrus in 539 B.C.E. If one accepts the chronology assumed by the book of Daniel itself, beginning with the exile in the third year of King Jehoiakim's reign (see 1:1–2)—that is, 606 B.C.E.—one ends up with 536 B.C.E., which is perhaps close enough to the date of the end of the Babylonians. Yet, Jeremiah did not likely mean the seventy years literally. The figure is probably representative of a normal human life span (so Ps. 90:10; Isa. 23:15). Thus, one may understand the prophet to be telling his contemporaries that the exile would last an entire lifetime. The prophet's point is that exiles themselves may not live to see Palestine again, so they should remain where they are and make the best of their situation. Whatever the case, Daniel now considers this datum that has confounded other postexilic writers.

The issue here, however, is not the mathematical conundrum of determining what date in history the prediction of Jeremiah should forecast. Rather, to judge by the prayer that follows, the problem is a theological one: what is the meaning of the exile, why does it last, and when will it really end? Simply put, the prophecy of Jeremiah had not been fulfilled in any meaningful way for the audience of the book of Daniel during the reign of Antiochus Epiphanes. Indeed, the exile seems not to have ended for them at all after all these years. The narrator of Daniel thus begins with this cognitive dissonance brought about by the apparent failure of prophecy. His particular challenge is to reconsider, reinterpret, and reappropriate that authoritative tradition so that it may once again be heard as the Word of God for a new generation. Here the biblical narrator as theologian is not a slave to tradition but a lively participant in it; the theologian is an interpreter engaging the tradition and bringing it up to date.

## DANIEL'S PRAYER
## Daniel 9:3–19

In a previous account of life under the reign of Darius, the narrator has already alluded to Daniel's habit of prayer (Dan. 6), where one learns that Daniel's custom was to pray three times a day, a routine that he continued even after Darius had issued an edict against it. In fact, on account of his prayers Daniel was framed by his jealous colleagues and cast into the lions' pit, only to be rescued by the power of God. Now, again, one finds Daniel in prayer, in the first year of the reign of the king who sought to prevent him from doing so. Perhaps this prayer was one that landed Daniel in trouble in the reign of Darius the Mede.

Daniel turns to God in a prayer of confession and supplication, that is, as the Hebrew suggests, an appeal for mercy (v. 3). The Hebrew text has it, too, that Daniel set his "face unto the Lord God," alluding here perhaps to the practice of facing Jerusalem when one prays (see 6:10, but also 1 Kgs. 8:35; 1 Esdr. 4:58). The Hebrew text does not indicate the direct object of Daniel's quest, however, although the NRSV, assuming that at issue is the enigma of the seventy years in Jeremiah, takes it that Daniel was turning to God "to seek an answer." More likely he was seeking God in earnest prayer, which he does with fasting, an act requiring complete dedication and focus, and with sackcloth and ashes, symbols of profound sorrow. While these gestures and symbols may be associated with penitence, they are not confined to that. Such rituals are, more broadly, associated with people in desperate straits, people in need of divine mercy. In Psalm 35, for instance, the psalmist fasts and puts on sackcloth in order to pray for the sick (Ps. 35:11–14). In that case, fasting and sackcloth are associated with fervent prayer and, perhaps, with grief for those in pain. In Lamentations 2:10, sackcloth and ashes are symbols of mourning over the destruction of Jerusalem. Elsewhere in the Bible, fasting, sackcloth, and ashes may also be marks of humility and desperation (Isa. 58:5; Jonah 3:6). Thus, the Jews, facing annihilation at the hand of their Persian oppressors, fasted, donned sackcloth, and put ashes upon their heads (Esth. 4:1–3). The Jews in Nehemiah's time, too, fasted, wore sackcloth, and put on ashes as part of their preparation for prayer and confession (Neh. 9:1–2). So one may understand Daniel's acts as part of his preparation for coming before the deity; the fasting, sackcloth, and ashes are manifestations of his earnestness. He seeks the Lord, just as Jeremiah had instructed, using the same Hebrew verb that is found here: "When you seek me (NRSV 'search for me'), then you will find" (Jer. 29:13).

Daniel's words, quoted in 9:4–19, are introduced as both a prayer and a confession (v. 4), which tells us something of what is at stake for the narrator. The main issue is not the confusion over the reliability of Jeremiah's prophecy of the seventy years, as the NRSV implies; Daniel is seeking not "an answer" but God, as Jeremiah had prescribed. Indeed, if confusion over Jeremiah's prophecy were the main problem, one should expect a prayer for illumination here. But no, Daniel understood Jeremiah properly, for the prophet had spoken of devastation and exile as God's punishment for sins, and hence the response that follows Daniel's perception of the documents (v. 2) is a prayer of confession and supplication. The Hebrew verb used for making a confession occurs also in Ezra 10:1 and Nehemiah 9:2, both introducing confessional prayers expressing contrition for communal sins. That same verb is used for the intercessory prayer of the high priest for the sins of his people (Lev. 16:21). That verb appears, too, in Leviticus 26:40 in reference to the proper response of the faithful in the face of the devastation of the land brought about by the sins of the generations, which is precisely the kind of prayer called for in the face of Jeremiah's prophecy. Although the prophet had promised the restoration of the exiles after seventy years, the fulfillment of that promise was contingent upon a faithful response; the people are to seek God earnestly through prayer (Jer. 29:10–14). Hence, Daniel properly turns his face to seek God in a prayer of confession and supplication.

In contrast to the narrative framework, the language of the confessional prayer itself is relatively conservative, as public prayers are wont to be. Unlike the framework, the prayer presents good, classical Hebrew prose. Daniel's prayer is also very similar in form and content to other prayers in the Old Testament, notably Solomon's prayer at the dedication of the temple (1 Kgs. 8:23–53); the communal prayer in the face of the destruction of the temple (Ps. 79); the penitential prayer of Ezra, which he prays with fasting and symbolic gestures of penitence (Ezra 9:6–15); and the prayers of Nehemiah (Neh. 1:5–11; 9:6–37), which is also accompanied by fasting, sackcloth, and ashes (Neh. 9:1). Thus, in terms of its overall structure and phraseology, the confessional prayer in Daniel replicates prayers found elsewhere in the Bible. In fact, the archaism of the language and the affinities with other prayers together indicate that what we have here is not a spontaneous prayer but a set prayer—a liturgical prayer, as it were—analogous to traditional prayers that faithful people have committed to memory for generations. This prayer has been prayed by others or, at least, it is patterned after prayers that others have prayed before. The communal nature of this confessional prayer is indicated, too, not only by the "we/us" language but by the very fact that this prayer is the shared prayer of a community that transcends any particular generation. The iniquities confessed are not only of the present generation, but those of generations past as well (see v. 16).

While many people today may prefer spontaneous prayers, perhaps regarding them as more authentic and sincere, liturgical prayers certainly have an important role to play in the life of a community of faith. On many occasions, particularly when finding just the right words to express one's needs is difficult, comfort can be found in traditional prayers on which one may rely, profound prayers that one has taken to heart and committed to memory. Such is "the Lord's Prayer" that most Christians know by heart. Hence, at many critical moments, times of dire need, times when people may be too terrified or otherwise distressed to formulate their own words of prayer, people often find themselves able to express their needs by reciting traditional prayers. In such prayers, one stands in solidarity with everyone in the community of faith through time and space—those present now and those who have gone before, those who are here and those who are elsewhere.

Daniel's prayer begins with an invocation praising "the great and awesome God" (v. 4), which is a standard characterization of God (so Deut. 7:21; Neh. 1:5; 4:14; 9:32). In earlier materials, the phrase is used of God in the context of God's ability to save, especially in connection with the exodus (so Deut. 6:22; 7:21; 2 Sam. 7:23), and it is used of God as the supreme deity of the divine council (so Pss. 47:2; 89:7). Thus, the prayer begins by assuming God's power to deliver and God's sovereignty over the whole universe. The "great and awesome God" is at once an immanent God who saves and a transcendent God who rules the cosmos. The prayer juxtaposes that acknowledgment of God's character with traditional language about God's involvement with humanity: God is one who is "keeping covenant and steadfast love" (Dan. 9:4). Thus, the great and awesome God is also one who deigns to be a partner with people in a covenant. The phraseology here echoes Deuteronomy 7:9 and Nehemiah 1:5. It is attested also on a tiny silver amulet discovered outside Jerusalem, dated to the early sixth century B.C.E., an inscription that contains an abbreviated version of the priestly benediction in Numbers 6:24–26. The God who is powerful enough to deliver and who is sovereign in the divine council is, thus, also God the faithful covenant partner. That paradox of God's power and sovereignty on the one hand, and God's faithfulness as a covenant partner on the other, forms the basis for prayer.

Then the text moves from the characterization of God to the characterization of God's people. Even though Daniel alone is praying, his confessional prayer is a corporate one. He prays a communal prayer. Thus, when he ruminates about his prayer, he refers to the deity as "my God" (so 9:4, 18, 19), but when he addresses the deity within the prayer itself, he refers to "our God" (vv. 9, 10, 13, 14, 15, 17). Throughout the prayer, too, he expresses solidarity with others in the community of faith by using the first-person-plural forms ("we"/"us"), confessing culpability with those in his community. The admission of corporate guilt comes almost like a litany, with the reiteration of the first-person-plural subject in the Hebrew: (1) we have sinned, (2) we have done wrong, (3) we have acted wickedly, (4) we have rebelled, and (5) we have not listened (vv. 5–6). These terms are reiterated throughout the prayer (see vv. 9, 10, 11, 13, 14, 15, 16) and they are corroborated by other expressions of guilt: "shame" (vv. 7, 8), "treachery" (v. 7), "transgressed [the] law and turned aside" (v. 11), "iniquities" (vv. 13, 16).

In stark contrast to the manifold guilt of the people stands the covenant faithfulness of God. On the one hand, then, the prayer reiterates in verse 7 that God is in the right in the covenant relationship, the language there being a forensic one, which one may translate, "Rightness, O my Lord, is yours!" (NRSV "Righteousness is on your side"). On the other hand, the failings of the people are readily admitted: "But ours is the shame of face" (v. 7, NRSV "open shame . . . falls on us"). That contrast between the rightness of God and the wrongness of humans is found also in Exodus 9:27, where the pharaoh of Egypt is forced to admit, "This time I have sinned; the LORD is right, and I and my people are in the wrong." Yet, the iniquitous community in Daniel is not the oppressive outsider like the pharaoh. Rather the community is specified as "the people of Judah, the inhabitants of Jerusalem, and all Israel, those who are near and those who are far away" (Dan. 9:7), that is, all the covenant people, whether they are in Palestine or have been exiled to a foreign country, as the recipients of Jeremiah's "documents" were. In any case, it is admitted that God would be entirely justified to bring affliction upon that sinful people. Hope, if any, can come only on account of God's steadfast love (v. 4), mercy (vv. 9, 18), will to forgive (vv. 9, 19), fidelity (v. 13), and righteousness (vv. 7, 14, 16). Yet, God's righteousness does not condemn unrighteous sinners forever. On the contrary, God's righteousness is manifested in mercy (vv. 16, 19). The righteousness of God, thus, reflects God's will to do what is right for humanity, whatever the cost may be (compare Rom. 3:21–26).

The prayer of confession reflects the perspective of "the Deuteronomistic History"—that is, the literary corpus that includes the core of Deuteronomy and the books of the former prophets through the end of 2

Kings—narratives that reflect the language and ideology of Deuteronomy. That history in its final form was addressed to the exiles of the sixth century B.C.E. to justify God's role in the devastating destruction of Jerusalem and the consequent exile of the Judeans, in accordance with the covenant curses stipulated by Moses in Deuteronomy. At the same time, however, that extended narrative also offers a word of hope to all who would return to God through a genuine repentance of their ways. For the Deuteronomistic Historian (the author of that history extending from the core of Deuteronomy to 2 Kings), the problem with Israel lay in the persistence of their disobedience; God kept trying to reach the people through the prophets, but they and their leaders have been recalcitrant. The problem lay not in the ancestors alone, but in the present generation as well. The end result of their history of sin, then, was complete and unmitigated doom. Daniel's prayer, in a similar manner, alludes to God's call issued through the prophets, a message that the leaders of Israel—their kings, their princes, and their ancestors—indeed, "all the people" stubbornly refused to heed. Thus, the covenant curses set forth by Moses in the Torah (see Lev. 26:14–22; Deut. 28:15–68; 29:18–28) would be brought upon the people inasmuch as they have violated their pact with God.

Daniel's prayer thus recontextualizes Deuteronomistic theology, as it were, so that it applies not only to the distraught exiles of the sixth century, as Solomon's prayer in 1 Kings 8 did, but also to the Jews of the time of Antiochus Epiphanes, in the second century. The theology is for those who are far away, in distant lands, but equally for those who are near, presumably in Palestine. The first-person application is, therefore, particularly poignant: the prayer is not about those in the past, but about "us"—those to whom the book of Daniel is addressed. In this way, then, the narrator is able to maintain the historical stage in which the book is set—namely, the sixth century B.C.E.—while addressing the concerns of people who lived long after that time.

The prayer, though addressed to God, is meant also to be instructive to the reader, as suggested by the switch from the second-person direct address of God ("you") in 9:4–8 to the third-person references to God in verses 9–10. The text reads as if the narrator has turned aside in the middle of the prayer to provide a commentary for the reader, thereby drawing the reader into the prayer of confession. Then the prayer is resumed and God is addressed directly again in verse 11, but the very next verses (vv. 12–14) revert to third-person language yet again. Now the reader is told that God has confirmed the divine oath made against the people and their leaders by bringing about unprecedented calamity upon Jerusalem. The oath is "poured out" upon sinners (v. 11). Given the historical setting of the prayer, one thinks immediately of the destruction of Jerusalem at the hands of the Babylonians in the sixth century B.C.E., yet the description of unprecedented destruction—"a calamity so great that what has been done against Jerusalem has never before been done under the whole heaven" (v. 12)—is certainly appropriate as a characterization of the devastation under Antiochus IV Epiphanes in 167 B.C.E. (see 1 Macc. 1:29–40; 2:7–13).

The prayer returns to a direct appeal to God (Dan. 9:15–19) that begins with an allusion to the exodus from Egypt: God is addressed as one who brought God's people out of Egypt "with a mighty hand" (v. 15). The point is that the deity who delivered people from oppression long ago can surely do so again. At issue now is the destruction of Jerusalem, called God's "holy mountain" (v. 16), and the desolation of the sanctuary (v. 17). The reference to the temple in verse 17 as "your desolated sanctuary" is perhaps a deliberate allusion to Antiochus's rededication of the Jerusalem temple to Zeus Olympius, who was known as Baal Shamem (see 2 Macc. 6:2). The holy sanctuary has become desolated, *šāmēm*, indeed, replaced by one named *ba'l šāmēm!*

The appeal to God is not, however, on the basis of the wickedness of the foreign aggressor, who has been depicted as one who presumes to ascend the mount of God, challenging even the host of heaven (see Dan. 8:10). Given the allusions already made to the exodus event, associating the present arrogant oppressor with the pharaoh of Egypt would have been easy enough, but that analogy is not pursued. Rather, the prayer readily acknowledges the sins of the people past and present: "we have sinned, we have done wickedly" (9:15); "our sins and the iniquities of our ancestors" (v. 16). No, the basis of the plea is not the righteousness of the people of God, but the righteousness of God alone (v. 16), for God's own sake alone (v. 17). Nothing is said about the legitimacy of the community's case, the rightness of their cause. The appeal is made simply on the assumption of divine righteousness, mercy, and will to forgive (vv. 18–19). God is passionately implored—to heed, to forgive, to pay attention, and to act without delay (v. 19)—for nothing other than God's own sake and for the city and the people that bear God's name, meaning that their very existence is a testimony to the nature and character of God (v. 19). The basis for hope, therefore, lies not in anything that mortals do but on the will of God to save, regardless of what human beings may have done.

## AN ANGELIC INTERPRETATION Daniel 9:20–27

The response to Daniel comes swiftly; indeed, the text is emphatic that it comes even while he is still praying and confessing (vv. 20–21). The response comes through "the man Gabriel," whom Daniel immediately recognizes as the one he had previously encountered in a vision (see 8:17–18). That angelic being, who had already appeared before Daniel to help him interpret his vision, now brings Daniel wisdom and understanding, presumably to reinterpret Jeremiah's prophecy. Indeed, Jeremiah's prophecy seems to convey more than is apparent. A first understanding evokes a due response of prayer and confession, but the prophecy offers more. Daniel has more things to consider and further understand. According to the angel, a word was sent forth even when Daniel was only beginning his prayer; now that word, which is no doubt the Word of God, is made known to Daniel because he is "greatly beloved" (v. 23). God's nature seems to be responsive to human pleas even before they are fully articulated (see Isa. 65:24; Matt. 6:8), simply because of God's love and dire human needs.

Gabriel's interpretation suggests that the seventy years in Jeremiah's prophecy may be understood to mean seventy "weeks" (Dan. 9:24). Because the Hebrew word for "week" may be taken more generally to mean a period of seven (days or months or years) and because Jeremiah spoke of seventy years, the usual interpretation is that seventy "weeks" of years—490 years—is meant. Thus, too, in the Hebrew of the Dead Sea Scrolls, the word for "weeks" refers to a cycle of seven years. Explicating the notion of the jubilee, the year of release, the book of Leviticus also speaks of "seven weeks of years, seven times seven years, so that the period of seven weeks of years gives forty-nine years" (Lev. 25:8). That period is the maximum length of time when the ancestral property of an Israelite may be in the hands of outsiders and the maximum period when slaves may be held in captivity. After that period, the property, if it has already been alienated, must be returned to Israelite control and slaves must be released. The Chronicler had already interpreted Jeremiah's prophecy of the seventy-year period in the light of the theology of jubilee, loosely based on Leviticus 26:34–35, 43 (see 2 Chr. 36:21). The Chronicler viewed Jeremiah's prediction as a time for the years of sabbaths to run their course, until the land is returned to Israelite hands. That, for the Chronicler, meant the time when the temple was rebuilt in 516 B.C.E.—literally seventy years after the exile of 586 B.C.E. had begun. The book of Leviticus, though, does not refer to a seventy-year period before the release, and for the recipients of Daniel's message, the exile has certainly not come to an end at the end of seventy literal years. The land is still in foreign hands and the people are still in captivity. Daniel 9, therefore, reinterprets the prophecy of Jeremiah, perhaps in the light of the view expressed in Leviticus 26:18 that, if the people continue to sin, God would punish them sevenfold—seven times seventy years, that is, seven sabbatical years, which is ten jubilee periods (of forty-nine years each).

Such a periodization of history in terms of seven and seventy is not at all unique, and is actually typical of apocalyptic literature. Readers should not take the seventy years in Daniel 9 literally. That datum is probably to be interpreted symbolically, in the light of the concept of the jubilee, a time when the land is to be returned to Israelite hands and captives set free.

According to Gabriel's interpretation, the period has been decreed in order to allow for several objectives to be met: (1) "to finish the transgression," (2) "to put an end to sin," (3) "to atone for iniquity," (4) "to bring in everlasting righteousness," (5) "to seal both vision and prophet," and (6) "to anoint a most holy place" (Dan. 9:24). Noteworthy in the first objective is the presence of the definite article: "*the* transgression." The only other time that the book of Daniel mentions "the transgression" is in 8:13, where the atrocious attack on Jerusalem and the desecration of the temple are meant. Certainly that particular attack on Jerusalem by Antiochus was the most infamous of his many atrocities—indeed, *the* transgression. That event probably also explains the allusion in 9:24. The desolation brought about by Antiochus would be permitted for a time, but an end to it will come.

The certainty of the end is reiterated in the second objective. The Hebrew infinitive here—*hātēm*, "to put an end"—is used only one other time in the Old Testament. In Daniel 8:23, the verb is used in reference to divine intention in allowing the offenses of the foreign aggressor to run their course. Here the singular probably refers to the quintessential sin of Antiochus, *the* transgression par excellence: the desecration of the temple in 167 B.C.E.

After the first two objectives, which are negative and refer to the end of the destructive activity of Antiochus, comes a series of positive ones. The third objective is likely a reference to Israel's iniquities, given the language of atonement and that the preceding prayer mentions the iniquities of God's own people twice (vv. 13, 16). The implication is that the end will be at once retributive and redemptive. The purveyor of "the transgression," the foreign perpetrator of the sin, will be destroyed, but redemption will also come for people who have already suffered for their iniquities (compare Isa. 40:2).

The text then speaks of bringing in "righteousness." The term "righteousness" recalls several references to God's rightness (Dan. 9:7, 14, 16, 18). Because righteousness is to be brought in, however, one should probably think of the restoration of the temple's rightness—its legitimacy—after the transgression (see also 8:14). In contrast to the transgression, sins, and iniquity, all of which will have an end within the 490 years, this rightness will be eternal.

The fifth objective is the sealing of "vision and prophet." In the first place, this objective echoes the mention of the sealing of Daniel's vision in 8:26. Certainly, given the number of probable links to the vision of chapter 8—"the transgression," human sins running their full course, the restoration of legitimacy of the temple—the allusion to the sealing of vision is entirely appropriate. Such a sealing means that the vision is authentic (see 1 Kgs. 21:8; Jer. 32:10, 11, 44). The point is that Daniel's vision of the previous chapter is authentic.

The final objective, arguably the climax of them all, is the anointing of "a most holy place" (Dan. 9:24). The term used here is, literally, "holy of holies," the designation for the inner sanctum of the sanctuary. This language corroborates the view that at issue is the restoration of the temple following its desecration by the forces of Antiochus (8:13–14). As the sanctuary was anointed at its inception (Exod. 30:26; 40:9), so it will again be anointed, the text here referring probably to the reconsecration of the sanctuary by Judas Maccabee in 164 B.C.E. (see 1 Macc. 4:36–59).

Daniel 9:25–27 provides details of the prediction regarding the seventy weeks of years, dividing the period into a series of time periods: (1) seven sevens, (2) sixty-two sevens, (3) one seven. The first period begins with "the time that the word went out to restore and rebuild Jerusalem." Daniel is called upon to "know" and "understand" this message (v. 25), even as he is told in verse 23 to "consider the word and understand the vision." The text is alluding either to Jeremiah's prediction of the seventy years of captivity (Jer. 29:10) or the prophecy of Jerusalem's restoration following its destruction in 586 B.C.E. (Jer. 30:18–22; 31:38–40).

In any case, that first period of seven sevens (forty-nine years) would last "until the time of an anointed prince." The translation "prince" is also far from certain. While the term may, indeed, refer to an actual prince (so 1 Sam. 2:10, 35; 9:16; 10:1), it may also be used of a priest (Lev. 4:3; 2 Macc. 1:10; Neh. 11:11; Jer. 20:1). This period will be seven sevens (forty-nine years), that is, one jubilee period. For many scholars, the "anointed prince" must be Cyrus, who is called an "anointed" in Isaiah 45:1 and who first came to power some forty-nine years after 605 B.C.E., the date given for the prophecy in Jeremiah 25 (see Jer. 25:1). For others, the "anointed prince" is more likely the high priest Jeshua (Ezra 2:2; 3:2; Hag. 1:1–14; Zech. 6:9–14), who came to his position about a jubilee period (49 years) after the exile of 586 B.C.E. had begun and who, together with the governor Zerubbabel, was one of the "anointed ones" (Zech. 4:14).

Be that as it may, the first jubilee period is only the beginning. After that, there would be sixty-two more "sevens," that is, 434 years, before there would be the restoration and the rebuilding of the city "with streets and moat, but in a troubled time" (Dan. 9:25). The expression "streets and moat" is puzzling. The first term refers to the plazas that are the centers of lively economic and social activities in the city. To some extent, these "streets" are the ancient Near Eastern equivalent of shopping malls in modern American culture. As for the second term, it is unique in the Old Testament, although it is attested in some Aramaic inscriptions and in the Dead Sea Scrolls with the meaning "trench." In the Copper Scrolls from Qumran, for instance, one reads of "Solomon's trench," which appears to be part of the city's defense system (*DSST*, 462). Accordingly, the feature has been explained as "a trench cut into the rock outside a city's walls in order to increase the exterior height of the walls" (Hartman and Di Lella, *The Book of Daniel*, 244). The expression of "streets and moat," therefore, indicates the complete restoration of the city proper—its socioeconomic infrastructures and its defensive system. The point is that the city will be fully restored, even during what the Hebrew text calls, literally, "the stress of times" (NRSV "in troubled times"). The reference is probably to the pressures during the reign of Antiochus Epiphanes, but is perhaps meant also to recall the reconstruction of the walls of Jerusalem in the time of Nehemiah, a task that was carried out under pressure.

After the sixty-two "sevens"—that is, 434 years—"an anointed one" will be "cut off." The years are symbolic and, at best, only approximate historical periods. They are probably not literal and precise years.

The NRSV has it that this second anointed one "shall have nothing, and the troops of the prince who is to come shall destroy the city and the sanctuary" (v. 26). A number of interpretive moves are made in this rendering. In the first place, the translation "he shall have nothing" is little more than a guess at the enigmatic Hebrew; indeed, one should expect a different Hebrew construction, if that were the meaning intended. Moreover, the word interpreted as "troops" in the NRSV is the one normally used for "people." Also, what the NRSV takes as the object of the action of the "troops" in fact appears at the beginning of the sentence, not the end. One should perhaps punctuate the Hebrew text a little differently and read, "an anointed one shall be cut off and shall have neither the city nor the sanctuary; the people of the leader who is to come will behave corruptly."

The second "anointed one" (v. 26) is probably an allusion to the high priest Onias III, who happens to be a distant successor of the first "anointed one" at the end of the first jubilee period (v. 25), namely, Jeshua the high priest. Soon after Antiochus came to power in 175 B.C.E.,

Onias was displaced as priest by his traitorous brother Jason, who paid a large sum of money to Antiochus for the post, promising to establish a Greek polis in Jerusalem (2 Macc. 4:1–22). Jason himself was, however, betrayed by his henchman, Menelaus, who outbid his patron for the high priesthood (2 Macc. 4:23–28). Onias had to seek refuge in Daphne, near Antioch, an event that is perhaps alluded to in the reference to the anointed one losing the city and the sanctuary: he "shall have neither the city nor the sanctuary" (Dan. 9:26). In any case, Onias was tracked down and killed in 171 B.C.E., and the supporters of Menelaus plundered the temple and wreaked havoc in the city (2 Macc. 4:39–50). Menelaus, who is remembered as "the cause of all the trouble" (2 Macc. 4:47), was extreme in his promotion of Hellenism in the city. No Jew was more complicit in the atrocities committed by Antiochus than he (see 2 Macc. 13:4).

The "prince" in Daniel 9:26 is usually interpreted as Antiochus. Yet, the Hebrew term is the same as one used in verse 25 of the first anointed (NRSV "anointed prince"), and that word would be used again in 11:22 of an Israelite figure, "the prince of the covenant," which most scholars recognize to probably be an allusion to Onias III. If the leader (NRSV "prince") in verse 25 is the high priest Jeshua (see above), then the leader "who is to come" is probably Menelaus. The verb translated in the NRSV as "destroy" (v. 26) may also be taken to mean "cause trouble" (1 Chr. 21:12; Ps. 78:45) or "behave corruptly" (Deut. 4:16, 25; 31:29; Isa. 1:4), and the people of Menelaus, the "leader" of this sinful revolt, certainly "behaved corruptly" (see 2 Macc. 4:39–5:20). The "leader" of the Jews turns out to be a surrogate for the evil Antiochus and the chief troublemaker for the Jews!

The suggestion of the end coming "with the flood" is tantalizing, for in some ways it recalls the destruction of the world through a great deluge on account of human corruption. According to Genesis 6, the earth had become so hopelessly corrupt that God was determined to bring an end to it all by a great flood (Gen. 6:11–13). So here, too, because of the corrupt behavior of "the people of the leader," God would bring about an end through a flood of another sort, and "desolations are decreed." Literary and theological connections to the flood story, however, are not developed here. The two texts appear to share only the imagery of the destructive power of the flood in the face of corruption. More compelling, perhaps, are the linguistic affinities with Isaiah 10:22–23, a text that speaks of a destruction that is decreed like a flood (the Hebrew word is related to the one used in Dan. 9:26) because the Lord is bringing an end, "as decreed in all the earth." Although Isaiah used that language and imagery to speak of the destruction of Israel, Gabriel's interpretation applies them to the destruction of the wicked leader who is to come.

The renegade followers of the "leader," Menelaus, the surrogate of Antiochus, would "make a strong covenant with many" for a week of years. This text no doubt alludes to the alliance that the Hellenizing Jews forged with the foreign aggressors (see 1 Macc. 1:11), contrary to Israelite law (Exod. 34:11–16; Deut. 7:1–6). Menelaus, of course, formed many such alliances, not least with Antiochus himself. With the connivance of Hellenizing Jews like Menelaus, Antiochus then took drastic steps to hinder sacrifices and offerings at the temple, indeed putting in their place "an abomination that desolates" (Dan. 9:27), a reference no doubt to the ultimate desecration of the temple—the sacrifice of a pig to Zeus Olympius, which occurred in the year 167 B.C.E., roughly halfway through the period from the death of Onias in 171 B.C.E. to the rededication of the temple in 164 B.C.E., a period of seven years. The decree of the end will be "poured out upon the desolator" (v. 27). Here the "desolator" (Hebrew *šōmēm*) is at once an allusion to the Jewish renegade, to Antiochus, but also to the god whom Antiochus worshiped, Baal Shamem (2 Macc. 6:2). Read in light of the prayer, one gathers that Daniel's prayer will be answered. Even though the curse and the oath have been "poured out" upon God's people on account of their sins (so Dan. 9:11), God will finally "pour out" the decreed end upon *šōmēm*, the desolator.

# 10. The Final Revelation: Prologue
## *Daniel 10:1–19*

1 In the third year of King Cyrus of Persia a word was revealed to Daniel,
who was named Belteshazzar. The word was true, and it concerned a great
conflict. He understood the word, having received understanding in the
vision.

2 At that time I, Daniel, had been mourning for three weeks. 3 I had eaten
no rich food, no meat or wine had entered my mouth, and I had not
anointed myself at all, for the full three weeks. 4 On the twenty-fourth day
of the first month, as I was standing on the bank of the great river (that is,
the Tigris), 5 I looked up and saw a man clothed in linen, with a belt of gold
from Uphaz around his waist. 6 His body was like beryl, his face like lightning, his eyes like flaming torches, his arms and legs like the gleam of burnished bronze, and the sound of his words like the roar of a multitude. 7 I,
Daniel, alone saw the vision; the people who were with me did not see the
vision, though a great trembling fell upon them, and they fled and hid
themselves. 8 So I was left alone to see this great vision. My strength left me,
and my complexion grew deathly pale, and I retained no strength. 9 Then I
heard the sound of his words; and when I heard the sound of his words, I
fell into a trance, face to the ground.

10 But then a hand touched me and roused me to my hands and knees.
11 He said to me, "Daniel, greatly beloved, pay attention to the words that
I am going to speak to you. Stand on your feet, for I have now been sent to
you." So while he was speaking this word to me, I stood up trembling. 12 He
said to me, "Do not fear, Daniel, for from the first day that you set your
mind to gain understanding and to humble yourself before your God, your
words have been heard, and I have come because of your words. 13 But the
prince of the kingdom of Persia opposed me twenty-one days. So Michael,
one of the chief princes, came to help me, and I left him there with the
prince of the kingdom of Persia, 14 and have come to help you understand
what is to happen to your people at the end of days. For there is a further
vision for those days."

15 While he was speaking these words to me, I turned my face toward the

**ground and was speechless. 16 Then one in human form touched my lips,
and I opened my mouth to speak, and said to the one who stood before me,
"My lord, because of the vision such pains have come upon me that I retain
no strength. 17 How can my lord's servant talk with my lord? For I am shak-
ing, no strength remains in me, and no breath is left in me."**

**18 Again one in human form touched me and strengthened me. 19 He
said, "Do not fear, greatly beloved, you are safe. Be strong and courageous!" When he spoke to me, I was strengthened and said, "Let my lord
speak, for you have strengthened me."**

This passage is really the prologue of a much longer unit extending through all or most of the last three chapters of the book. This prologue sets the context for a long report of a vision about the end of desolation for the Jewish people. Scholars frequently identify a tripartite structure for the extended unit: prologue, vision-report, and epilogue. That the vision of chapter 10 is a prelude to the vision-report of chapter 11 can hardly be in doubt. The more difficult question is where the first unit ends and the second begins, given that the former seems to just flow into the latter. Because 10:20 begins to give the explanation for the epiphany, however, using 10:19 as a marker for the end of the prologue seems like a reasonable approach.

## INTRODUCTION
## Daniel 10:1

As one has come to expect, the literary unit begins with a chronological notice: the third year of the reign of King Cyrus of Persia, that is, 536 B.C.E. This date may come as a bit of a surprise, since 1:21 reports that Daniel remained in Babylonian captivity until the first year of Cyrus, that is, 539 B.C.E. Yet, Daniel has apparently not been repatriated to Palestine. Rather, he is on the bank of the Tigris (v. 4). One may understand the adverb "there" in 1:21, however, to refer not to the city of Babylon per se but to the "whole kingdom" (1:20)—that is, the Babylonian Empire, which technically ceased to exist in the first year of Cyrus. Thus, Daniel could have been "there" geographically, even though the kingdom of Nebuchadnezzar was certainly not "there" anymore when Daniel received this vision in the third year of Cyrus, whose designation as "king of Persia" suggests that a new era has, in fact, dawned.

Still, Daniel continues to be known by the name assigned by his Babylonian captors, Belteshazzar, a name that appears a number of times in chapters 1–6 all set in the historical context of the Babylonian captivity

(1:7; 2:26; 4:8, 9, 18, 19; 5:12), but only here in the latter half of the book. Despite the fall of Babylon, therefore, Daniel is still known by this captive name in the third year of Cyrus, 536 B.C.E., seventy years after the date of the beginning of Babylonian captivity presumed by the introduction of the book, 606 B.C.E. (see 1:1). The prophecy of Jeremiah regarding the seventy years of desolation should have been fulfilled (Jer. 25:11–12; 29:10), if seventy literal years were meant by the prophet. Moreover, the third year of Cyrus means that the prophecies of Isaiah 40–55 should have been fulfilled, for Jerusalem has indeed paid her dues and "her conflict" has ended (Isa. 40:2, NRSV "her term"). The Jewish exiles should have been repatriated to Palestine two years earlier to begin the restoration of the temple in Jerusalem (Ezra 1:1–3). Yet, as one learns from the preceding chapter, the desolation is not over. Even in the restoration period and beyond, the Jews remained a captive people and Daniel's captive name, Belteshazzar, is a reminder of that fact. Hence, with this introduction, one should not be surprised by the author's reflection on history down to the reign of Antiochus IV Epiphanes and the suffering that he caused the Jewish people. In some sense, every Jew in Palestine during the reign of Antiochus was still a "Belteshazzar," a captive and an exile.

It was in that year that "a word was revealed to Daniel" (v. 1). The Hebrew idiom used here for the revealing of the word occurs only one other time in the Bible, in reference to the call of Samuel (1 Sam. 3:7). The revealed "word" in Samuel's case referred to his visionary experiences (compare 1 Sam. 3:1). So, too, the revealed "word" in Daniel 10 probably refers to Daniel's visionary experience, the report of which is to follow. Interestingly, the previous chapter refers to the "word of the LORD" which Jeremiah received (9:2), the "word" that went out to Daniel at the beginning of his supplication (9:23) and the "word" that he was to perceive (9:23). Now apocalyptic vision is apparently understood as something on a par with the prophetic word. Each is the Word of God revealed. The vision is the message, the Word of the Lord. This vision that Daniel describes is not, therefore, the wild fantasy of a deranged person; it is "the word" and that word is, as the Hebrew has it literally, "truth" (v. 1). Daniel understood "the word," one is told, for he had received understanding in the vision. Hence, the text will explicate that understanding that he has been given.

The NRSV takes the subject matter of the vision to be "a great conflict," presumably the warfare that is being described in the vision, which is actually of several conflicts, both terrestrial (11:5–45) and celestial (10:13, 20; 12:1). That interpretation of the Hebrew is certainly possible. Also possible, however, is that the Hebrew word rendered as "conflict" is an ironic allusion to Isaiah 40:2, where that same word is used for the struggles of

Jerusalem in captivity, "her conflict" (NRSV "her term"). If so, that "conflict" that should have already ended has not, and Daniel is going to learn more about the "conflict" that is still forthcoming. The exile is still not over; true restoration has still not been achieved, which is why the text still calls attention to Daniel's exile name, Belteshazzar. Yet, the Hebrew word for "conflict" is the same one used elsewhere in the book for "host"—either the heavenly host or an earthly host (see Dan. 8:10, 11, 12, 13). Thus, the word of "truth" (v. 1) explicated in this context may not be so much about the conflict itself, whether of the past (the exile) or the future. Rather, the truth is about the host, as manifested on earth and in heaven. The truth is about the macrocosmic host, the manifestation of divine power. At the same time, it is about the microcosmic host, the people of God and their fate.

## THE SETTING
## Daniel 10:2–4

After the introduction, expressed in the third person (v. 1), the narrative is given entirely in the first person, that is, as a direct quote from Daniel. The seer says that he has been in mourning, literally, "in those days" (v. 2, NRSV "at that time"). The reference is to the period when the Jews were still, even after the restoration in the Persian period, amid desolation. The time was not unlike that in the previous chapter, when Daniel, as a proper response to Jeremiah's prophecy about the seventy-year desolation, expressed contrition with his people through fasting, sackcloth, and ashes. Now the text says Daniel has mourned for three weeks. He has consumed no delicacies, no meat or wine, and he has not anointed himself with oil. This vigil echoes the abstinence that he and his friends exercised during their initial captivity in the Babylonian court, both as an expression of their identity and a statement of faith (see 1:8, 12, 16). Refraining from anointing with oil marks the act of mourning (see 2 Sam. 12:20; 14:2).

Daniel mourns in this fashion for "the full three weeks" (so NRSV in v. 2). The Hebrew text has, in fact, "three weeks of days," thus distinguishing the period from the "weeks (of years)" that are at issue in the preceding chapter. At all events, the period of three weeks is a much longer period than the three-day vigil that the Jews in the Persian period kept when they faced the possibility of a pogrom (Esth. 4:16). It is also longer than the three days of preparation that the people of Israel undertook as part of the preparation for their encounter with God on Mount Sinai (Exod. 19:10–15). So the stakes must be very high in this case. Indeed, verse 4 implies that mourning lasted till "the twenty-fourth day of the first month," that is, the month of Nisan (March/April), during which the Passover Festival was celebrated between the fifteenth and the twenty-first days (Lev. 23:5–6; Deut. 16:3). Thus, Daniel mourns right through the quintessential festival commemorating the exodus, God's liberation of Israel from oppression. Although the Passover had been reinstated at the time of Ezra and Nehemiah, and Jewish documents found in Egypt of that period indicate that the festival was celebrated publicly then, there could be no such celebration for the original readers of Daniel in their time, for they were still enslaved and still in need of liberation. Daniel was still called Belteshazzar. In fact, Antiochus IV Epiphanes had even desecrated the temple and forbidden all festivals at the temple, so that the feasts of the Jews were "turned into mourning" (1 Macc. 1:39).

Daniel finds himself standing on the bank of "the great river." In 8:2, Daniel envisioned himself by the Ulai river in Susa, the old Elamite capital that had been reestablished as a Greek polis by the Seleucids. Presently he is by "the great river," the designation usually reserved for the Euphrates (Gen. 15:18; Deut. 1:7; Josh. 1:4), except that "the great river" is now the Tigris, not the Euphrates. The designation of the Tigris as "the great river" implies the end of Babylon, which was built on the Euphrates. The focus is now on the Tigris, the river on which the first Seleucid ruler established the city of Seleucia in the fourth century B.C.E. Daniel is still in the diaspora, as it were, only now the dominant power is no longer Babylonian.

## AN EPIPHANY
## Daniel 10:5–19

On the bank of the Tigris, Daniel has a vision, even as he did on the bank of the Ulai (8:3). What he saw was "a man clothed in linen," a description that echoes Ezekiel's vision of a mysterious holy assistant to God (Ezek. 9:2, 3, 11; 10:2, 6–7). The New Testament, too, describes angels as beings clothed in bright linen, a sign of holiness (Mark 16:5; Rev. 15:6). The being that Daniel saw was also girded with a belt or sash made of gold from Uphaz, an exotic region renowned for its gold (see Jer. 10:9). The rest of the description—his body being like some kind of gleaming stone, face like lightning, eyes like flaming torches, arms and legs like the gleam of burnished bronze, voice like the sound of a multitude—all suggest a supernatural presence, something like the presence that Ezekiel envisioned by the river Chebar (Ezek. 1).

The book of Revelation, no doubt under the influence of various passages from the book of Daniel, also describes in similar terms an encounter with "the Son of Man" (Rev. 1:13–16). This similarity has prompted some Christian interpreters to identify the "man" that Daniel saw with the glorious coming of "the Son of Man," namely, the Christ. The propriety of that way of appropriating the imagery in Daniel at a later time should not, however, be confused with the message intended for the original audience of the book. Daniel's vision was hardly framed as a specific prediction of the future coming of Christ. Rather, one should probably look to the literary antecedents for Daniel's description in one's search for the meaning of the vision. Indeed, one may point to a number of significant parallels with Ezekiel's encounter with holy presence. As Ezekiel was by a river, the river Chebar (Ezek. 1:1–3), Daniel is by a river, the Tigris. What Ezekiel saw gleamed like jewels and flashed like fire. So the being that Daniel saw also gleamed like jewels and flashed like fire. Indeed, virtually every expression in verses 5–6 echoes something in the description of Ezekiel's vision: special girding at the waist (Hebrew "loins," Ezek. 1:27), gleam like beryl (Ezek. 1:16), face being like lightning (Ezek. 1:14), brightly shining torches (Ezek. 1:13), limbs shining like burnished bronze (Ezek. 1:7), and the sound of a multitude (Ezek. 1:24). Straining to characterize the essence of what he saw, Ezekiel could only say what the form approximated: "something that seemed like a human form" (Ezek. 1:26). Daniel, however, simply characterizes the sight as that of "a man." Yet, in the light of the parallels with Ezekiel's vision, one can hardly take that characterization literally. Already in previous chapters, one finds the angel Gabriel called a "man" (8:15; 9:21). This "man" remains unidentified, while another angel, Michael, is named in verse 13. In any case, Daniel is certainly having an extraordinary encounter, an experience of the numinous.

The text is emphatic that Daniel alone saw the vision, as the redundancy in the Hebrew text shows. It says, literally, "I saw—I, Daniel, by myself—the sight, but the people who were with me did not see the sight, even though a great terror fell upon them and they fled in hiding" (v. 7). Daniel's aloneness is reiterated in verse 8, again with the redundancy evident in Hebrew: "But I, I remained, by myself, and I saw this great sight." Daniel alone is given the special privilege of divine revelation, just as he alone of all mortals had been given the gift to interpret dreams and portents. At the same time, the assertion implies that Daniel's description of his vision is his sole responsibility, not a concoction invented through conspiracy with others. In any case, the very visible reaction of the others who were with him corroborates the event, despite the fact that these people did not experience the phenomenon firsthand. Similarly, the prophet Elisha alone had a vision of the heavenly hosts as his Elijah was being taken up to the heavens; the others who were with Elisha were not privy to the vision, although they, even standing afar, knew that something phenomenal had happened (2 Kgs. 2:11–18). In the New Testament one finds an account of how Saul (Paul) had a vision on the road to Damascus, a vision that he alone had, although others who were present knew that something phenomenal had occurred (Acts 9:1–7). In Daniel's case, he alone remained at the scene, although he is drained of all strength, turns "deathly pale," and is unable to summon any energy (Dan. 10:8).

Then, upon hearing the sound of the divine being speaking, he falls into a trance, yet managing to remain in a posture of worship, his "face to the ground" (v. 9). That reaction echoes his earlier encounter with "the man Gabriel" (8:18). As before, too, Daniel is touched and given physical assistance (8:18); he is set on his hands and knees (v. 10), although whose hand touched him is not clear. Perhaps it is the hand of the one seen in the vision in verses 5–6. Perhaps it is the hand of another celestial being, possibly "the man Gabriel," who in a previous vision of Daniel had touched him and helped him up (8:18). Daniel is addressed again as one "greatly beloved" (see 9:23), and he is told to perceive the words of the angel (v. 11).

As the seer tries to collect himself, albeit still trembling, he receives an assurance—one that elsewhere also introduces epiphanies: "Do not fear!" (v. 12; see Gen. 15:1; 26:24; Judg. 6:23; Luke 1:13, 30). Thus, the prophet Ezekiel, upon his encounter of divine presence in his inaugural vision, falls to the ground and, after the spirit has set him on his feet, is given a similar assurance not to be afraid (Ezek. 1:28–2:6). Now Daniel, too, receives assurance that his earnest quest to gain understanding had been favorably received and that the angel has come to him on account of his "words," presumably meaning the words of his prayer (Dan. 10:12). Prayer has not been mentioned thus far in Daniel 10, so perhaps one is to infer that the period of mourning mentioned in verse 2 included a prayer. Such a prayer would no doubt be similar to the confession found in 9:4b–19, a prayer that is an appropriate response to the prophetic word of judgment that the desolation would continue for a long time yet. That prayer would be entirely fitting in the third year of the reign of Cyrus, namely, seventy literal years after the destruction of Jerusalem and the exile of 586 B.C.E. The end of desolation has apparently been deferred.

In 9:20–23, one learns that Gabriel had been sent to Daniel immediately as a divine response to Daniel's prayer of confession. Indeed, a word was sent out at the very beginning of his prayer. Now one learns of an instance when even one sent by God from on high may be hindered (v. 13). The angel's delay in responding to Daniel was reportedly caused by the opposition of the “prince of the kingdom of Persia,” the word “prince” here being a translation of the Hebrew word that is elsewhere used also of a military commander. Earlier in the book of Daniel, that very term was used of divine beings: “the prince of the host” (8:11) and “the Prince of princes” (8:25). It will also be used later of Michael as the “great prince, the protector” of the people (12:1). Here in Daniel 10, the prince/commander of the kingdom of Persia, who is able to delay the angel from his assignment, is clearly not an earthly being but a patron angel of Persia. Meanwhile, the angel who had been sent to Daniel receives additional help from a certain Michael, who is said to be “one of the chief princes,” that is, one of the leading “commanders.” He had been left to deal with the celestial patron of the Persians (v. 13).

Michael is known in 1 Enoch 20:1–8 as one of seven archangels, which is probably what “chief of princes” means in Daniel 10:13. He is mentioned many times in 1 Enoch and in the Qumran scrolls, along with the other angels. In the book of Daniel, however, he is portrayed simply as Israel’s commander, fighting on their behalf against the patron angels of other nations (vv. 20–21) and protecting the people of God (12:1). Every nation, it seems, has its own celestial counterparts to their earthly commanders.

The background for this concept of a celestial patron for a nation lies in the ancient Near Eastern belief that the divine council consists of celestial beings representing various nations. Such a view is reflected also in Deuteronomy 32:8–9, which depicts the Lord as the supreme deity of the divine council, who assigns all the gods their territorial lots. That perspective is evident, too, in Psalm 47:2–4 and Sirach 17:17. Moreover, in light of the notion that the Lord has a commander of the heavenly host (see Josh. 5:13–15), the other nations having their own commanders of hosts that mirror earthly realities is an understandable concept. Certainly the Bible does not deny the possibility of “principalities and powers” beyond the earthly realm. In fact, early Israelite religion did not present the Lord, Israel’s God, as the only deity who existed but rather as the only One who should be worshiped by Israel, the only One with whom Israel is to be related through a covenant. Hence one finds the confession of Israel that “the LORD is our God, the LORD alone” (Deut. 6:4). The Israelites subscribed to the command to have “no other gods” before the Lord (Exod. 20:3). The existence of other gods is implicitly recognized, although they are not to be worshiped and no allegiance should be paid to them; they are not considered before the Lord. Indeed, the other gods are viewed as subservient to the Lord, who is the Most High, the supreme deity of the divine council (see Pss. 82:1–8; 89:5–18; 97:1–9).

In ancient Near Eastern mythology, hegemony in the divine council was something that had to be achieved again and again; the deity who takes the place at the head of that council is by necessity a divine warrior, a god who fights against the other deities and becomes victorious again and again. Chaos is a persistent threat in the cosmos and is kept in abeyance only through the intervention of the ever-vigilant and benign divine warrior. This mythic worldview lies in the background of much of the Old Testament understanding of God, who is known by the common epithet of a divine warrior, Yahweh Sabaoth, "the LORD of hosts." This martial epithet of God reminds us that someone powerful counters the persistent threat of chaos on our behalf. Battle for the safety and well-being of the cosmos, indeed, for the salvation of humankind, is waged not only on human terms. Rather, God the warrior, the Lord of hosts, fights in ways that people do not even begin to comprehend. Thus, too, one of the documents from Qumran imagines a perpetual conflict between the forces of light and those of darkness. Likewise, the New Testament pits "Michael and his angels" against "the dragon and his angels" on the other side (Rev. 12:7). The conflicts of the world are not only earthly problems, it seems; they touch the heavens and involve God and the angels, for nothing less is needed to deliver humans from the overwhelming threat of evil. In this sense, the words from Luther's *Ein' feste Burg* ("A Mighty Fortress") are still an eloquent reminder that there is help for mortals struggling against the dangers wrought by the "principalities and powers," a struggle that they cannot overcome by their own strength:

> Did we in our own strength confide,
> Our striving would be losing,
> Were not the right Man on our side,
> The Man of God's own choosing.

For Luther, the chief threat comes from the "prince of darkness," but that prince and all his wicked forces will be countered by the "Man of God's own choosing," namely, Jesus Christ whose name is, indeed, "Lord Sabaoth." Daniel does not, of course, go so far; he does not name Jesus Christ as the representative of the people of God. Rather, Michael—whose very name in Hebrew ("who is like El?") attests to the incomparable power of God, the Most High—fights for God's people as their commander of host, their "prince."

This point of view challenges the all-too-common tendency among people to recognize only earthly powers, either of good or of evil. Postenlightenment people tend to discount the threat of unseen, extramundane forces of evil and count only on their own ability to fend for themselves and, when they are unable to overcome the forces of evil in the world, they despair. Daniel's vision, however, points beyond earthly realities to the conflict in heaven that in some ways mirrors that on earth. The revelation in Daniel 10 suggests that God's purpose may be threatened and momentarily thwarted. It affirms at the same time, however, that powerful if invisible forces are fighting on the side of God and good.

To be sure, Daniel does not have a fully developed demonology as in the Qumran documents and in the New Testament. The text speaks of a "prince of the kingdom of Persia" (10:13, 20) and a "prince of Greece" (10:20), but little is known about what they did, except that they are opposed to the powers on the side of Israel. They are mentioned only in passing and largely to account for the delay of the angel friendly to Israel. Nevertheless, the book has an angelology that is far more elaborate than anything found anywhere else in the Old Testament. Not only do we have here an angelic patron of Israel, we have another angel whose primary task appears to be as messenger and interpreter. Although hindered for twenty-one days (v. 13), presumably during the three weeks of days of Daniel's mourning (v. 3) and having left the threat of the "prince of the kingdom of Persia" in the hands of Michael, the angel reaches Daniel (v. 14).

The mission of that angel is to help Daniel understand what is about to happen to his people. The NRSV translation ("at the end of days") may foster the idea that the end of history is meant. Yet, that same expression occurs in 2:28 simply meaning sometime in the future, a meaning common elsewhere in the Old Testament (see Gen. 49:1; Num. 24:14; Deut. 4:30; 31:29). Set in the third year of Cyrus, the account stipulates that the vision is for the future, that is, sometime beyond the reign of Cyrus. The language echoes the words of Habakkuk, who prophesied at the end of the seventh century: "For there is still a vision for the appointed time; it speaks of the end, and it does not lie. If it seems to tarry, wait for it" (Hab. 2:3).

Daniel's reaction is one of utter awe. He puts his face to the ground, as he had previously done (10:9), and becomes speechless (v. 15). His loss of speech echoes in various ways the call narratives of Moses (Exod. 4:10–17), Jeremiah (Jer. 1:6–9), and, especially, Isaiah (Isa. 6:5, 7). This feature of the call narratives effectively suggests that the prophets do not speak on their own account; they speak only because they have been divinely enabled. Thus, for example, the Lord touches Jeremiah's mouth, putting words in his mouth, as it were (Jer. 1:9). Daniel's experience parallels Isaiah's call vision, too, for Daniel is touched upon his lips by someone who resembles a human being, apparently a divine being, even as Isaiah was touched upon his lips by one of the celestial creatures round about him (Isa. 6:7). With his speech restored, Isaiah was in anguish about his task, wondering how long it will all last (Isa. 6:11). Daniel's response is even more dramatic. His first utterance upon his recovery of speech is an outright admission of his debility in the face of the anguish of his vision (Dan. 10:16). He is completely drained of his strength, as before (see v. 8), and he is out of breath (v. 17). Thereupon, Daniel is touched again, now for the third time. He had been touched first by a mysterious hand (v. 10), then by someone with some semblance of human form (v. 16, Hebrew, "like the likeness of mortals"), and now by one "like the appearance of a mortal" (v. 18). Whether the third someone is the same as the second is not clear. The Hebrew terms are somewhat different, the second term being very similar to the description of Gabriel in 8:15 and identical to the depiction of the vision of divine presence in Ezekiel 1:26. Even so, a divine being is clearly meant. Daniel is told again not to fear (see also v. 12) and he is earnestly encouraged, the Hebrew text saying, "be strong, yea, be strong!" Indeed, various forms of the verb "be strong" appear four times in verse 19, thus offering a powerful counterpoint to Daniel's loss of energy and spirit in verse 17. Daniel needed to be properly assured, mentally prepared, and otherwise fortified to receive the revelation to follow.

# 11. The Final Revelation: Back to the Future
## *Daniel 10:20–12:4*

10:20 **Then he said, "Do you know why I have come to you? Now I must return to fight against the prince of Persia, and when I am through with him, the prince of Greece will come. 21 But I am to tell you what is inscribed in the book of truth. There is no one with me who contends against these princes except Michael, your prince.** 11:1 **As for me, in the first year of Darius the Mede, I stood up to support and strengthen him.**

**2 "Now I will announce the truth to you. Three more kings shall arise in Persia. The fourth shall be far richer than all of them, and when he has become strong through his riches, he shall stir up all against the kingdom of Greece. 3 Then a warrior king shall arise, who shall rule with great dominion and take action as he pleases. 4 And while still rising in power, his kingdom shall be broken and divided toward the four winds of heaven, but not to his posterity, nor according to the dominion with which he ruled; for his kingdom shall be uprooted and go to others besides these.**

**5 "Then the king of the south shall grow strong, but one of his officers shall grow stronger than he and shall rule a realm greater than his own realm. 6 After some years they shall make an alliance, and the daughter of the king of the south shall come to the king of the north to ratify the agreement. But she shall not retain her power, and his offspring shall not endure. She shall be given up, she and her attendants and her child and the one who supported her.**

**"In those times 7 a branch from her roots shall rise up in his place. He shall come against the army and enter the fortress of the king of the north, and he shall take action against them and prevail. 8 Even their gods, with their idols and with their precious vessels of silver and gold, he shall carry off to Egypt as spoils of war. For some years he shall refrain from attacking the king of the north; 9 then the latter shall invade the realm of the king of the south, but will return to his own land.**

**10 "His sons shall wage war and assemble a multitude of great forces, which shall advance like a flood and pass through, and again shall carry the war as far as his fortress. 11 Moved with rage, the king of the south shall go**

out and do battle against the king of the north, who shall muster a great multitude, which shall, however, be defeated by his enemy. 12 When the multitude has been carried off, his heart shall be exalted, and he shall overthrow tens of thousands, but he shall not prevail. 13 For the king of the north shall again raise a multitude, larger than the former, and after some years he shall advance with a great army and abundant supplies.

14 "In those times many shall rise against the king of the south. The lawless among your own people shall lift themselves up in order to fulfill the vision, but they shall fail. 15 Then the king of the north shall come and throw up siegeworks, and take a well-fortified city. And the forces of the south shall not stand, not even his picked troops, for there shall be no strength to resist. 16 But he who comes against him shall take the actions he pleases, and no one shall withstand him. He shall take a position in the beautiful land, and all of it shall be in his power. 17 He shall set his mind to come with the strength of his whole kingdom, and he shall bring terms of peace and perform them. In order to destroy the kingdom, he shall give him a woman in marriage; but it shall not succeed or be to his advantage. 18 Afterward he shall turn to the coastlands, and shall capture many. But a commander shall put an end to his insolence; indeed, he shall turn his insolence back upon him. 19 Then he shall turn back toward the fortresses of his own land, but he shall stumble and fall, and shall not be found.

20 "Then shall arise in his place one who shall send an official for the glory of the kingdom; but within a few days he shall be broken, though not in anger or in battle. 21 In his place shall arise a contemptible person on whom royal majesty had not been conferred; he shall come in without warning and obtain the kingdom through intrigue. 22 Armies shall be utterly swept away and broken before him, and the prince of the covenant as well.
23 And after an alliance is made with him, he shall act deceitfully and become strong with a small party. 24 Without warning he shall come into the richest parts of the province and do what none of his predecessors had ever done, lavishing plunder, spoil, and wealth on them. He shall devise plans against strongholds, but only for a time. 25 He shall stir up his power and determination against the king of the south with a great army, and the king of the south shall wage war with a much greater and stronger army. But he shall not succeed, for plots shall be devised against him 26 by those who eat of the royal rations. They shall break him, his army shall be swept away, and many shall fall slain. 27 The two kings, their minds bent on evil, shall sit at one table and exchange lies. But it shall not succeed, for there remains an end at the time appointed. 28 He shall return to his land with great wealth, but his heart shall be set against the holy covenant. He shall work his will, and return to his own land.

29 "At the time appointed he shall return and come into the south, but this time it shall not be as it was before. 30 For ships of Kittim shall come against him, and he shall lose heart and withdraw. He shall be enraged and take action against the holy covenant. He shall turn back and pay heed to

those who forsake the holy covenant. 31 Forces sent by him shall occupy
and profane the temple and fortress. They shall abolish the regular burnt
offering and set up the abomination that makes desolate. 32 He shall seduce
with intrigue those who violate the covenant; but the people who are loyal
to their God shall stand firm and take action. 33 The wise among the people shall give understanding to many; for some days, however, they shall fall
by sword and flame, and suffer captivity and plunder. 34 When they fall victim, they shall receive a little help, and many shall join them insincerely.
35 Some of the wise shall fall, so that they may be refined, purified, and
cleansed, until the time of the end, for there is still an interval until the time
appointed.

36 "The king shall act as he pleases. He shall exalt himself and consider
himself greater than any god, and shall speak horrendous things against the
God of gods. He shall prosper until the period of wrath is completed, for
what is determined shall be done. 37 He shall pay no respect to the gods of
his ancestors, or to the one beloved by women; he shall pay no respect to
any other god, for he shall consider himself greater than all. 38 He shall
honor the god of fortresses instead of these; a god whom his ancestors did
not know he shall honor with gold and silver, with precious stones and
costly gifts. 39 He shall deal with the strongest fortresses by the help of a
foreign god. Those who acknowledge him he shall make more wealthy, and
shall appoint them as rulers over many, and shall distribute the land for a
price.

40 "At the time of the end the king of the south shall attack him. But the
king of the north shall rush upon him like a whirlwind, with chariots and
horsemen, and with many ships. He shall advance against countries and
pass through like a flood. 41 He shall come into the beautiful land, and tens
of thousands shall fall victim, but Edom and Moab and the main part of the
Ammonites shall escape from his power. 42 He shall stretch out his hand
against the countries, and the land of Egypt shall not escape. 43 He shall
become ruler of the treasures of gold and of silver, and all the riches of
Egypt; and the Libyans and the Ethiopians shall follow in his train. 44 But
reports from the east and the north shall alarm him, and he shall go out
with great fury to bring ruin and complete destruction to many. 45 He shall
pitch his palatial tents between the sea and the beautiful holy mountain. Yet
he shall come to his end, with no one to help him.

12:1 "At that time Michael, the great prince, the protector of your people, shall arise. There shall be a time of anguish, such as has never occurred
since nations first came into existence. But at that time your people shall
be delivered, everyone who is found written in the book. 2 Many of those
who sleep in the dust of the earth shall awake, some to everlasting life, and
some to shame and everlasting contempt. 3 Those who are wise shall shine
like the brightness of the sky, and those who lead many to righteousness,
like the stars forever and ever. 4 But you, Daniel, keep the words secret and
the book sealed until the time of the end. Many shall be running back and
forth, and evil shall increase."

Continuing the vision of 10:1–19, this long passage offers first an overview of history from after the fall of Babylon in the sixth century B.C.E. to the reign of Antiochus IV Epiphanes in the second century. Cast in the form of a preview of history, much of it is really a review (11:2–39). That is, the narrator reviews the past as if previewing it, before engaging in some genuine predictions of what may lie ahead in the near future (11:40–12:4). Such a use of history is not unique. What we have here is a literary device that is well known in Mesopotamia, Egypt, and Greece. Indeed, one roughly contemporaneous example from Mesopotamia, the Akkadian "Dynastic Prophecy," provides a particularly suggestive parallel. The text bears close resemblance to Daniel 11:2–45 inasmuch as it casts as prophecy a review of history from the Assyrian to the Seleucid periods, including a genuine prediction of the fall of the Seleucids and a notice about keeping the prophecy secret (see A. K. Grayson, *Babylonian Historical-Literary Texts* [Toronto: University of Toronto Press, 1975], 13–37). In the case of Daniel's overview, the author's provenance is betrayed by the uneven coverage of history and the varying accuracy of the details. Over two centuries of the history of the Persian Empire are covered in a single verse, all the reigns telescoped under the rubric of just four kings (11:2). The momentous reign of Alexander is given only two verses, including his rise and the breakup of his empire (11:3–4). The conflict between the Ptolemies in the south and the Seleucids in the north, a history of 148 years, is treated in considerable detail in sixteen verses, virtually all of which may be coordinated with what is known in other records (11:5–20). Then the reign of Antiochus IV Epiphanes, which lasted less than a decade, is treated in 25 verses, 11:21–45. This period is obviously of greatest interest to the narrator and the original readers.

Yet not all of the details regarding the reign of Antiochus Epiphanes may be corroborated by the records; verses 29–39 may be documented by other records, but verses 40–45 actually contradict what we know from other sources. Contrary to the predictions in verses 40–45, for instance, no renewed attack on the Seleucids by the Ptolemies took place in the time of Antiochus Epiphanes, and he did not die in Palestine, but in Persia. The author apparently knows about the desecration of the temple in mid-December 167 B.C.E., but not the rededication of it or the death of Antiochus, both events occurring late in 164 B.C.E. Given that Antiochus launched his eastern campaign sometime around the late spring or early summer of 165 B.C.E., the passage most likely was completed shortly before that time.

Despite the amount of historical detail, the interest of the passage is first and foremost theological. The entire account is couched as an angel's report of what has already been recorded permanently in a register of "truth" (10:21), the word "truth" here being the same one used in 8:26 and 9:13 for God's reliability. One may deduce, therefore, that God's reliability is at issue in the history to be presented. Moreover, although Michael seems to have been mentioned only in passing in 10:21, his presence may be implied through the overview, for he is mentioned again at the end of the overview (12:1). Most importantly, as one reaches the end of the account, expressions of time recur (11:24, 27, 29, 35 [twice], 36, 40), all indicating that, contrary to the impression that events in the historical arena give, mortals are not in control of their destiny but God, who alone determines times and seasons. Reading the historical overview, one might be tempted to think that history is being determined on earth by wars, political alliances, and intrigues. Surprisingly, God is not mentioned in the entire historical overview, except in a passing reference to the Jews who are "loyal to their God" (11:32) and a mention of the "horrendous things" spoken by Antiochus against "the God of gods" (11:36). The impression that the overview creates, therefore, is that history moves on without divine intervention—as if everything were determined by human decisions and actions. Yet, the history is bracketed by references to God's intervention brought about through the activities of God's celestial hosts (10:20–11:1; 12:1), and the history is a "register of truth," a record of God's reliability.

## INTRODUCTION
## Daniel 10:20–11:1

The angel asks Daniel if he recognizes the purpose of the epiphany (10:20). That question is rhetorical, of course, for that purpose is already given in verse 14: the angel says he has come to help Daniel understand events that will occur in the future. That assistance apparently has to be given to Daniel immediately, indeed, before that angel returns to fight against "the prince of Persia" and "the prince of Greece" (10:20). Daniel and his people should know that God has not left them forlorn, even as the exile is extended beyond the Babylonian period well into the periods of the Persians and the Greeks—into the time of Antiochus Epiphanes. Now the angel gives an overview of historical events.

That message has been recorded in the "register of truth" (10:21, NRSV "the book of truth"). The existence of a written record implies authenticity, for what is inscribed therein may be verified. Elsewhere in the ancient Near East, too, one finds references to "tablets of destinies," essentially divine records of the human fates (*ANET*, 67, 112)—permanent, indelible records. The content of the revelation in Daniel's vision is called "truth," the same term used at the beginning of the prologue of the larger literary unit, namely, 10:1. That word is used in 8:26 for the authenticity of "the vision of the evenings and the mornings" (compare also Rev. 19:9; 21:5; 22:6). The word is also used for God's fidelity in Dan. 9:13. Ultimately the historical overview is a record of God's fidelity in the historical arena.

One is to read this information from that indelible record of truth with the assurance that powerful forces are fighting sight unseen on behalf of God's people. Even though the enemies of Israel seem to have supernatural powers on their side, the people of Israel, too, have their supernatural protectors, most notably Michael, who is explicitly identified as Israel's "prince," their heavenly commander. The attribution of such a protective, even salvific, role to Michael is sometimes considered at odds with the view expressed in Isaiah 63:9 that "it was no messenger or angel but [God's] presence that saved [God's people]." Yet, Israel has long affirmed God as a divine warrior, the Lord of hosts, who is assisted by the members of his heavenly hosts. Already in Joshua 5:14, one encounters the unnamed "commander of the army of the LORD" (or "prince of host of the LORD"), who is surely a reflex of the reality of divine presence in Israel's holy wars. The individuation of angels in the book of Daniel, indeed, represents a development of Old Testament angelology; earlier texts do not have named angels, as does this book, yet the functions of angels as described in the book do not contradict earlier traditions. In any case, to the narrator God is still the true protector and savior of people, although a representative of divine presence appears in the person of Michael.

The revealing angel—possibly Gabriel—claims to have stood by and strengthened Darius the Mede in the first year of the king's reign (11:1). The date troubles many interpreters, because the revelation is set in the third year of the reign of Cyrus (10:1). Yet the reference makes sense, for the problem that this unit concerns—namely, the ongoing experience of exile and desolation despite the end of the Babylonian Empire seventy years after the destruction of 586 B.C.E.—is precisely the issue Daniel considered during the first year of the reign of Darius the Mede (9:1). Divine assistance for the people of God began even at the very beginning of the end of the Babylonian power, and not only after the order for the restoration of Jerusalem had been given and restorative work had begun (see Ezra 1:1–3; 3:8; 4:24).

## THE PERSIAN EMPIRE
## Daniel 11:2

The overview of history is called "truth" (11:2), not only because it is authentic and reliable (the same Hebrew word in 8:26), but also because it reflects God's "true" character, God's reliability (the same Hebrew word in 9:13). From here on, the narrator gives a detailed "preview" of what will happen during the Persian and Greek periods—from the Persian rulers to Antiochus Epiphanes. The detail of the account as a whole is noteworthy. For the ancient readers, the presence of such precise details must have been comforting, for it is evidence of the narrator's knowledge of their history, their real-life experiences. The modern reader may also take comfort to know that the narrator is no esoteric theologian who expounds on theological ideas with nary a thought about the historical arena in which the audience lives and has its being. Rather, this author writes with attention to otherworldly realities (of divine beings working in the background) on the one hand, and to the events of the world on the other. Indeed, the account bears witness to the "both-worldliness" of apocalyptic texts: concern with this world as with an other world that mortals cannot see.

The account begins with "three more kings" of Persia who will come after Darius, followed by a fourth who will exceed the others in wealth and power, a king who will stir up others against Greece (11:2). In fact, thirteen Persian kings ruled between the fall of Babylon in 539 B.C.E. and the conquest of Alexander the Great in 331 B.C.E.: Cyrus (539–530), Cambyses (530–522), Smerdis (522), Darius I (522–486), Xerxes I (486–465), Artaxerxes I (465–424), Xerxes II (424), Sogdianos (424–423), Darius II (423–404), Artaxerxes II (404–358), Artaxerxes III (358–338), Arses (338–336), and Darius III (336–331). The Bible, though, mentions only four Persian kings by name—Cyrus, Darius (I), Xerxes (I, Ahasuerus), and Artaxerxes I (Ezra 1:1; 4:5–7; 7:1; Neh. 2:1; 12:22). Some scholars conclude that these four are meant in Daniel 10, but the history of these four will lead the reader down only to the mid-fifth century B.C.E. Moreover, if one takes at face value the comment that the fourth king is far richer and stronger than his predecessors and that he had stirred up others to fight the Greeks, that list would be odd, for historically Xerxes I, the third king on that list, was far more powerful than Artaxerxes I, not the other way around, and Xerxes was the most well-known of the Persian kings who fought the Greeks. Jerome proposed long ago that the four kings here refer to Cambyses, Smerdis, Darius I, and Xerxes I, but that accounting ignores the fact that the text suggests four kings after Darius the Mede, the first of which should, by the chronology presumed in the book, be Cyrus. In any case, that way of reckoning takes one only to the Persian-Greek wars in the early fifth century, skipping over the rest of the Persian period up to the conquest of Alexander that is the subject of Daniel 11:3. The most sensible reading of the text may be to see the history proffered here as one that has been telescoped, just as history is also telescoped in 1:1. In fact, the stylized nature of this "history" may be suggested by the reference first to three kings, then to a fourth, a style reminiscent of "numerical sayings" found elsewhere in the Old Testament (see Prov. 6:16; 30:15–33; Eccl. 11:2; Amos 1–2; etc.) and in various Canaanite and Aramaic inscriptions. The numbers in such sayings somehow aid the oral preservation of the material and the details do not necessarily add up. Perhaps a simplified oral history merely included the four prominent names, possibly the only four names of Persian kings known in the Bible, without any distinction made for the names that are shared by more than one king. In any case, the generalization and imprecision are indicative of the distance between the historical setting of the story, its stage, and the actual historical context of the narrator, its provenance.

## ALEXANDER'S EMPIRE
## Daniel 11:3–4

The "warrior king" of the kingdom of Greece in verse 3 is no doubt an allusion to Alexander the Great, whose rise has already been anticipated in an earlier vision (8:5–8, 21). So, too, is the allusion in 11:4 to the fourfold fragmentation of his empire (8:8). Alexander died in 323 B.C.E., while still in his prime—"while he is rising in power" (compare 8:8)—and his kingdom was carved up among the *Diadochi*, his immediate successors. Philip III, a half-brother of Alexander, was assigned nominal rule over Macedonia in the west, Antigonus took Asia Minor and most of Syria in the north, Seleucus retained Babylon in the east, and Ptolemy chose Egypt in the south. The kingdom was, thus, "divided toward the four winds" by Alexander's generals, while his own scions were at best mere pawns in their hands. Accordingly, then, the great kingdom was passed on to others, although "not to his posterity" (v. 4). The empire was certainly not like that which Alexander ruled (v. 4; see also 8:22), for there were, besides the four main regions, lesser claimants to power and minor political entities, like Armenia and Cappadocia, that continued to resist assimilation for over a century. The empire was forever broken, as the generals constantly fought one another. So the empire went "to others besides these" (11:4). By 312 B.C.E., however, two centers of power—one in the north under the Seleucids and one in the south under the Ptolemies—were established that would dominate the region for the next century and a half.

## NORTH VERSUS SOUTH BEFORE ANTIOCHUS IV EPIPHANES
## Daniel 11:5–20

The "king of the south" in verse 5 is clearly a reference to Ptolemy I Soter, who was given control of Egypt when Alexander died. He ruled as satrap of Egypt from Alexander's death until 305 B.C.E., when he declared himself king and reigned there until 285 B.C.E. In the year 316, Ptolemy gave refuge to Seleucus I Nicator, the satrap of Babylon and eventual founder of the Seleucid dynasty, who was forced to flee to Egypt by Antigonus, the ruler of most of Asia Minor and for some time also Syria. With Ptolemy's help Seleucus was able to regain Babylon in 312, following Ptolemy's victory over Antigonus in the Battle of Gaza. Hence, Seleucus may rightly be regarded as "one of his [Ptolemy's] officers" (v. 5). Seleucus, however, later won extensive territory on his own, extending his domain eastward as far as northwest India. Thus, the observation is correct that his realm would become greater than that of his former patron in the south (v. 5).

The alliance alluded to in verse 6 is the marriage of convenience that was forged "after some years" of conflict between the two centers of power, the Seleucids in the north and the Ptolemies in the south. Both the founders of the Ptolemaic and Seleucid dynasties—the subjects of verse 5—have by this time passed away. Now the narrator is concerned with another generation. Ptolemy II Philadelphus gave his daughter Berenice to Antiochus II, the grandson of Seleucus I, around the year 250 B.C.E. After years of struggle over the control of Palestine, the Ptolemies had finally defeated the Seleucids, but Ptolemy II thought it was in his own interest to form a marriage alliance with the vanquished Seleucids. Antiochus II had to repudiate his first wife Laodice and her sons in favor of Berenice and any heir that might come from their marriage. The purpose of that deal was, of course, to give the Ptolemies eventual control over the Seleucid domain.

Ptolemy was killed a few years later, in 246 B.C.E. In that same year, Antiochus II also died in the home of Laodice, who had allegedly poisoned him and then claimed that he had, on his deathbed, chosen their son as his successor. The infant son of Berenice, whom she had with Antiochus II, and Berenice herself were later murdered, along with a number of her Egyptian attendants. Thus the text says of her, "she shall not retain her power, and his offspring shall not endure. She shall be given up, she and her attendants and her child and the one who supported her" (11:6). The NRSV translation, which presumes slight emendations of the Hebrew text, is probably interpreting the reference to be the demise of Berenice, her child who is to be heir to the throne, and her attendants who accompanied her to the Seleucid court. The last phrase in verse 6, though, is enigmatic as the NRSV has it. The text is unclear to whom "the one who supported her" refers. The Hebrew should perhaps be interpreted as "the one who obtained her," that is, her husband. If so, verse 6 refers to the elimination of Antiochus, his queen Berenice, their son, and her Egyptian escorts, reportedly by Laodice, the spurned wife. So her son came to the throne as Seleucus II Callinicus.

Meanwhile in Egypt, Ptolemy III Euergetes, brother of Berenice, had ascended the throne in 246 B.C.E. He is surely the "branch from her roots" mentioned in verse 7. The text is confusing at this point, however, for it seems to imply that this "branch" arose to take the place of the child or the murdered husband, which makes little sense; Ptolemy III did not rise to take the place of the ruler in the Seleucid court instead of the husband of Berenice or their son. The word translated as "place" is, in fact, the word for position or office, in particular, a legitimate office. A more likely interpretation, then, is that Ptolemy Euergetes assumed his own legitimate position as the heir to the throne in Egypt; he arose to take the position that was his. In any case, Ptolemy immediately took action to punish the Seleucids, launching a series of successful campaigns against Seleucia, "the fortress of the king of the north" (v. 7).

Rumors of a rebellion apparently forced Ptolemy to return to Egypt, however, but he took with him large quantities of booty (see v. 8), including the divine images that had been captured by the Persian king Cambyses in Egypt and brought to Mesopotamia two centuries before. Indeed, the richness of the spoils of war that he brought back to Egypt resulted in his name of Euergetes ("Benefactor"). The tide was turned, however, when Seleucus II attempted to invade Egypt in 242 B.C.E., although whatever success he had was short-lived, as he was forced to "return to his own land" in 240 B.C.E., his army significantly reduced (see v. 9).

The account then turns to the sons of the king of the north (v. 10), that is, the sons of Seleucus II: Seleucus III and Antiochus III. The Hebrew text begins with verbs in the plural (they "shall wage war and assemble a multitude of great forces"), but it suddenly switches to the singular in the rest of verse 10: "he shall come and flood, and cross over, and he shall again wage war as far as his fortress." This switch may not be accidental. It may, indeed, reflect the fact that Seleucus III had reigned only a very short time, for he was murdered in the third year (223 B.C.E.). The focus here instead is on the exploits of one of the sons of Seleucus II, that is, Antiochus, who aspired to be a new Alexander and whose successful long reign (223–187 B.C.E.) allowed him to become one of the great Seleucid rulers.

Verse 10b characterizes his seemingly unstoppable advance in terms almost reminiscent of Alexander. He rapidly suppressed rebellions in the satrapy of Media and in Asia Minor and poised himself to reconquer Coele-Syria (that is, southern Syria west of the Euphrates, including Palestine), the accession of the weak and despised Ptolemy IV Philopator

(221–203 B.C.E.) in Egypt increasing the prospect of Antiochus's success. He began by recapturing Seleucia in 219 B.C.E., then waged extensive campaigns in the Transjordan and Palestine, "as far as his fortress" (v. 10). The meaning of "his fortress" is not entirely clear, however. Perhaps the phrase is an allusion to one of the strongholds of his Egyptian counterpart, possibly Gaza or Raphia, both on the seacoast of Palestine, just north of the border of Egypt.

At Raphia in the year 217 B.C.E. the "king of the south" went out in rage against the "king of the north" (v. 11). The two armies fought a pitched battle, which the Egyptians won, Antiochus reportedly losing some seventeen thousand men. The Ptolemaic ruler, however, failed to capitalize on his victory. Despite the massive defeat of the Seleucid forces and the recovery of his territories in Coele-Syria, Philopator "did not show himself strong" (v. 12; not as the NRSV has it, "he shall not prevail," for he did prevail, though he did not pursue his victory further).

The battle at Raphia had been won by the Ptolemies with the help of mercenaries as well as, for the first time in Egypt, conscripts. The latter now became involved in a series of insurrections. The king was caught in various court intrigues and eventually died in 203 B.C.E. under mysterious circumstances. He was succeeded by Ptolemy V Epiphanes, who was then only five years old. Meanwhile, between 212 and 204 B.C.E. (v. 13, "after some years"), Antiochus recuperated much of his territory and even waged new campaigns. He rose again. By the time of Philopator's death, Antiochus was ready for revenge against Egypt (see v. 13).

The Ptolemies certainly had many enemies both within and without (see v. 14a). Endless rebellions took place in the provinces and insurrections even in Egypt proper, and, of course, the Ptolemies still had the old nemesis in the north, Antiochus. The Jews, as often in their history, were caught between two foreign powers, one in the north and one in the south. Some of them preferred to cast their lot with the Seleucids in the north, while siding with the Ptolemies in the south. A tantalizing allusion is made in verse 14b to the "lawless" ones who would elevate themselves in order to fulfill "the vision" but would not succeed. The "lawless" ones are probably members of a pro-Seleucid faction who entertained visions of liberation from Ptolemaic rule when Antiochus annexed Judea in 201 B.C.E. The Jewish historian Josephus reports that some Jews of their own accord offered Antiochus their support, joined his forces in surrounding the Ptolemaic garrison, gave provisions for his army, and openly welcomed him into their city (*Ant.* 12.3–4 §§138–46). Accordingly, Antiochus returned the favor by promising to restore Jerusalem and its temple. He also granted the Jews tax exemption for three years and reduced their taxes by a third. The high priest, Simon the Just, was apparently a leader of this faction that comprised many of the aristocrats, including the rich and powerful Tobiads. The narrator's designation of the pro-Seleucid faction as "lawless" indicates an anti-Seleucid bias. Jesus ben Sira, by contrast, was more sympathetic to that party, and so Simon the Just is listed among the faithful (Sir. 50:1–24). In any case, whatever favor the pro-Seleucid faction received from the Seleucid government was short-lived, for the Ptolemaic general, Scopas, soon recaptured the city, which is the failure to which verse 14b alludes.

The ever-resilient Antiochus would once again recuperate, however (v. 15). Around 200 B.C.E., the armies of Antiochus defeated the Ptolemaic army at Paneas (modern Baniyas), Caesarea-Philippi in New Testament times. Scopas, the Ptolemaic general, had to flee to the well-fortified Phoenician city Sidon with an elite corp of mercenaries, but Antiochus soon besieged the city and captured it, an event alluded to in verse 15. The victorious Antiochus stood in what the Hebrew text calls, literally, "the land of the Beauty"—that is, Judea (compare 8:9)—all of which would now come into the control of the Seleucids (v. 16). Ptolemaic control over Judea was ended once and for all.

The wily Antiochus then decided to consolidate his power. In an ironic reprise of an earlier alliance marriage between the Seleucids and the Ptolemies, he gave his daughter Cleopatra in marriage to Ptolemy V, with the wedding celebration being held at Raphia, where the Seleucids had been humiliated over two decades earlier. The word for "alliance" in verse 17 echoes the word in verse 6, where the earlier diplomatic marriage is mentioned. The word is derived from a root suggesting evenness, thus implying the alliance was one between equals. The use of the term in verse 17 may suggest, too, that this marriage was the payback to the Ptolemies for the earlier deal. Antiochus was getting even, as it were. Furthermore, the Hebrew text may be taken to suggest that the purpose of the marriage was to overthrow the kingdom through her—she whom the text calls "the daughter of women," probably an idiom meaning she was an exceptional woman. No doubt, Antiochus was hoping to gain influence or control over the Ptolemaic throne, just as Ptolemy II had tried to gain control of the Seleucid kingdom through the marriage of Berenice to Antiochus II. But the ploy would "not succeed or be to his advantage" (v. 17). Cleopatra cast her lot with her husband, and she in fact became the regent of Egypt upon the death of her husband in 182 B.C.E. until her own death in 173 B.C.E.

Undeterred by this diplomatic failure and encouraged by the weakness of Philip V of Macedon and Ptolemy V, Antiochus turned to the western coast of Asia Minor and the islands beyond, seizing many Macedonian and Egyptian territories (v. 18). He reached Thrace in 196 B.C.E. He was, however, defeated in 191 B.C.E. at Thermopylae in Greece and then the following year in Magnesia by the Roman consul, Lucius Cornelius Scipio, the "commander" to which verse 18 alludes. Antiochus had dismissed the warnings of the Romans to stay out of the region, but he was utterly humiliated, unable to requite the challenge issued him by his victor (v. 18).

Soundly defeated, Antiochus was forced to withdraw from Asia Minor, "back toward the fortresses of his own land" (v. 19). At Elymais (Elam), while attempting to raid the temple of Bel to pay his heavy indemnity to the Romans in 187 B.C.E., he was assassinated. The ignominy of his death is expressed in the imagery of his stumbling and falling (v. 19). Antiochus the Great vanished like a fleeting reality—"he shall not be found" (v. 19; compare Job 20:6–8; Ps. 37:36).

Antiochus was succeeded by Seleucus IV Philopator (187–175 B.C.E.), who inherited the enormous financial consequences of his predecessor's many wars. One source of funding came to his knowledge through Simon, a Tobiad of the pro-Seleucid faction who no doubt had political aspirations of his own (2 Macc. 3:1–40). Simon passed the information about the existence of a substantial sum of money stashed away at the temple. Hence the king dispatched one of his chief ministers, Heliodorus, to the city to seize the fund. Heliodorus, the royal commissioner, is surely the one who was sent, according to verse 20, although the word translated neutrally as "official" in the NRSV should be understood more precisely as "an oppressor" or "an exactor" (of taxes or tribute). Indeed, the precise Hebrew idiom used here—literally, "to cause an oppressor/exactor to pass over"—is reminiscent of Zechariah 9:8: "no oppressor/exactor shall again pass over them" (NRSV "no oppressor shall again overrun them"). At all events, Heliodorus soon plotted against the king and installed the king's young son on the throne. Thus, Seleucus died not in the heat of battle (v. 20), but in secret, at the hand of a trusted courtier, which in ancient Near Eastern culture was regarded as a particularly ignominious way for a king to die.

## ANTIOCHUS IV EPIPHANES
## Daniel 11:21–39

The climax of this history, told in considerable detail in verses 21–39, is the reign of Antiochus IV (175–164 B.C.E.). He is said to be a "contemptible" person (v. 21), and he certainly is the object of much contempt in the book of Daniel, where he is derogatorily dismissed as "a little horn" (7:8; 8:9), a man who speaks arrogantly (7:8, 11), and a man who is full of deceit and intrigues (8:23, 25). Elsewhere, too, he is derided as "a sinful root" (1 Macc. 1:10) and remembered as "an arrogant and terrible man" (4 Macc. 4:15). What's more, some of his contemporaries reportedly referred to him as Epimanes ("Mad"), mocking his self-designation as *Theos Epiphanes* ("God Manifest").

Verse 21 also notes that "royal majesty had not been conferred" upon him, that is, he was not heir designate, but rather, he had come unexpectedly to seize kingship through "intrigues" (the Hebrew noun is plural, contrary to the NRSV). The Hebrew word translated by the NRSV as "without warning" appears three times in the book of Daniel, always associated with activities of this Antiochus (8:25; 11:21, 24). The word perhaps suggests stealth, possibly even implying deceit, as the Greek versions understood the word in 8:25 (so the NAB, "by stealth"). At any rate, Antiochus rose to power through an improbable series of apparent coincidences. Although he was sent to Rome as hostage in 189 B.C.E., after his father Antiochus III was defeated at Magnesia, he was subsequently released when his nephew, the crown prince Demetrius, was inexplicably sent by Seleucus IV to take his place. Then his brother the king was murdered by his chief minister, Heliodorus, leaving the throne to the next-in-line, who was a minor, whom Heliodorus conveniently removed. Antiochus himself was already in Athens living it up as a Hellene at that time. King Eumenes II of Pergamum, with his own political agenda, decided to back him for the Seleucid kingship, furnishing him with money and troops for the expedition home, ostensibly to reclaim the throne in the name of his family. Heliodorus mysteriously disappeared from the scene at that time. Hence, Antiochus assumed co-regency with another son of Seleucus, nominally ruling with him. Within five years, however, the younger co-regent was murdered, leaving Antiochus IV as the sole ruler of the Seleucid domains. If Antiochus was complicit in the various incidents that led to his rise, no proof has survived. The text says simply, if cryptically, that he had come, literally, "in quietness," and that he seized kingship through "intrigues" (the Hebrew meaning also "smooth things").

Whatever opposition forces were left, both within and without Seleucia, fell before him. This probably explains the allusion in verse 22, where the Hebrew expression translated as "armies" in the NRSV is, literally, "arms of the flood." Among those who fell victim to him was one called the "prince of the covenant," probably an allusion to the High Priest Onias III, who apparently had pro-Ptolemaic sympathies (see 2 Macc. 4:1–6). Jason, a brother of Onias, backed by the rich and powerful pro-Seleucid Tobiad family, was able to bribe the king for the position of High Priest (2 Macc. 4:7–10). Antiochus agreed to the deal, but only until a better one came along—in this case, from Menelaus, who would later offer a higher bid for the office. Verse 23 probably alludes to the deal with Jason, but surely not to that alone. The Hebrew word for "alliance" in 11:23 is an abstract noun; it may refer not to any particular event but to various means of connection. The point is that Antiochus is able to use such means (the Hebrew says, literally, "from connection") to advance his purposes through deceit. Thus, this verse calls attention to shady deals such as the one he made with Jason, but also to deals that he forged with Eumenes of Pergamum, with Menelaus, with various political allies and would-be enemies. Bluntly put, Antiochus was a wheeler-dealer who came to power from disadvantageous positions and with limited resources.

Verse 24 is obscure as the NRSV renders it, for the text is unclear as to what "the richest parts of the province" might refer. This translation perhaps reflects a common view among interpreters that the text is referring to Antiochus's first campaign against Egypt, but it seems far-fetched to say that Egypt was in any sense a "province" of the Seleucids. The NRSV translation also disregards the conjunction ("and") after "without warning" (literally "with quietness"; see also 8:25; 11:21). Moreover, in the Hebrew text, "province" is without the definite article. An editorial note in the NRSV suggests an alternative translation that may, in fact, be the better one, namely, the fact that the reference may be to rich people (as in Isa. 10:16; Ps. 78:31) rather than to rich places. If so, one may take the beginning of verse 24 to mean that Antiochus came "with quietness and with rich ones (people) of a province."

In part through the alliance with Jason, the immediate referent in verse 23, Antiochus forged ties with the rich and powerful Tobiad family in the province of Judea. The king lavished gifts in unprecedented fashion upon his allies, no doubt to buy their affection and loyalty. Indeed, his liberality is well attested in the ancient sources. First Maccabees 3:30 and Josephus (*Ant.* 12.7.2 §294) corroborate the fact that he was more generous in his giving than preceding kings, even to the point of fiscal irresponsibility. A Hellenistic historian attests to his extreme generosity to individuals, even to strangers (Polybius 26:10), while another writer, commenting on his generosity to various cities and peoples, concludes that he surpassed all preceding kings in this regard (Livy 41.20), as alluded to in the observation that Antiochus would do what none of his predecessors had ever done.

So, on the one hand, Antiochus could be exceedingly generous with his allies, as he apparently was with the pro-Seleucid Hellenizers like Jason and the Tobiads in Judea, "lavishing plunder, spoil, and wealth on them." On the other hand, as various sources corroborate, he could be ruthless and tyrannical. Verse 24 attests to both extremes of his nature. One may see the end of the verse as an anticipation of his establishment of the Akra, a fortress overlooking the temple mount and garrisoned with Jewish renegades and Gentile mercenaries (1 Macc. 1:33–36), a move designed in part to support his rich allies in Judea. Yet, one may also take that reference to anticipate Daniel 11:25–28, which concerns his invasion of Egypt (compare 1 Macc. 1:19).

Manifesting an anti-Seleucid bias, the narrator presents Antiochus as the aggressor against Egypt, the one who "stir[s] up his power and determination against the king of the south with a great army." This view is supported by other Jewish sources (1 Macc. 1:16; Josephus, *Ant.* 12.5.2 §242). The origin of the war with Egypt is much more complicated, however. Despite their defeat at Raphia in 198 B.C.E., the Ptolemies had never given up hope that Coele-Syria would be returned to their control someday. The Ptolemies had voiced a number of threats to retake Coele-Syria by force, but things came to a head when, upon the death of Cleopatra in 173 B.C.E., powerful court officials began to push for a more aggressive stance. Indeed, tentative moves for an invasion seem to have been made. Antiochus's envoy, a man by the name of Apollonius, sent to represent the Seleucids at the coronation of Philometor in Egypt, noted strong anti-Seleucid sentiments in the Ptolemaic court (2 Macc. 4:21–22), and Antiochus himself later complained to Rome of Egyptian aggressions against him (Polybius 27.19). Still, Antiochus no doubt harbored hopes of conquering Egypt and restoring glory to the Seleucids after their humiliation at the hands of the Romans at Magnesia in 190 B.C.E. Hence, on the pretext of this Ptolemaic aggression, he made preemptive strikes against his enemy, invading in 169 B.C.E. "with a strong force, with chariots and elephants and cavalry and with a large fleet" (1 Macc. 1:17). According to Daniel 11:25, the "king of the south," no doubt referring now to young Ptolemy VI Philometor, raised an even greater force to fight him. But Philometor would not be successful, "for plots would be devised against him." The text alludes here to the bad advice that he was receiving from the anti-Seleucid courtiers, specifically two men known from other historical accounts, the eunuch Eulaeus and the Syrian Lenaeus, among "those who eat of the royal rations" (v. 26). These foolish and treacherous courtiers later fled to Alexandria, where they cast their support behind Philometor's younger brother. In 169 B.C.E., Antiochus marched into Memphis (see 1 Macc. 1:16–19), where he made a great show of magnanimity toward his nephew Philometor, who by now was fighting for his own hold on kingship. The two were united in the common cause of maintaining Philometor's kingship, in Antiochus's case so that he could have a puppet that he could manipulate.

The diplomatic niceties at the Memphis summit are recognized as the farce that they were: "The two kings, their minds bent of evil, shall sit at one table and exchange lies" (v. 27). That meeting would not end the matter, however, "for there remains an end at the time appointed" (v. 27). To the narrator, the time was not yet ripe for God to intervene in history (compare 8:19, 23). So Antiochus left Memphis "with great wealth" (v. 28; see also 1 Macc. 1:19). He then tried to capture Alexandria, where the Greek population had installed Philometor's brother as king. In this attack, Antiochus was casting himself as the champion of right and protector of the interests of the legitimate king. But the siege failed and Antiochus withdrew his forces, setting his heart on an easier target—the Jews, the people of "the holy covenant" (v. 28; see also 1 Macc. 1:15, 20–23, 63). With them, he seemed to have been able to do whatever he wished. So he raided the treasure of the Jerusalem temple, an act that various ancient historical sources concluded was motivated largely by his financial needs. In any case, Antiochus claimed victory, minting new coins that bore an additional epithet for himself: "Victorious."

Within the year, the Ptolemy brothers were reconciled and united in their opposition to their treacherous uncle. The narrator implies again that history was being worked out in due time according to the sovereign will of God: "at the time appointed" (168 B.C.E.), Antiochus again invaded Egypt, although it would "not be as before" (v. 29). Antiochus scored initial victories, but as he was preparing to attack Alexandria again, a Roman fleet ("the ships of Kittim" in v. 29) suddenly showed up. The historian Polybius reports that the Roman envoy, Gaius Popilius Lenaeus, presented Antiochus with a demand from the Roman senate to withdraw immediately. Antiochus hedged, but the Roman officer drew a circle in the sand around him, demanding that he decide there and then, before he left the circle. Antiochus paused for a while, but eventually backed down.

Meanwhile, rumors reached Palestine that Antiochus had been killed. Jason, who had been deposed as High Priest by Antiochus in favor of Menelaus, led a group of rebels to storm Jerusalem, forcing Menelaus to retreat to the citadel to join the mercenaries (2 Macc. 5:5–10). The timing of the rebellion could not have been worse. Already humiliated by the Romans, Antiochus unleashed the fullness of his anger upon the Jews, (Dan. 11:30; see 2 Macc. 5:15–24). Whether he was personally present in the attack on Jerusalem is not clear, but the orders and the blame were no doubt his. He supported "those who forsake the holy covenant" (v. 30), that is, Jewish renegades like Menelaus and the Tobiads. Antiochus capitalized on the internal strife among the Jews, backing the Hellenists (see 1 Macc. 1:11–15).

His troops occupied and desecrated the temple (2 Macc. 5:23–27), abolished the daily offerings (compare Dan. 9:27; 1 Macc. 1:54), and set up "the abomination that makes desolate," an allusion to the erection of an altar to Zeus Olympius, upon which he sacrificed a pig (Dan. 11:31). The temple at Jerusalem was fortified at that time (see v. 31a; compare 1 Macc. 4:60; 6:7), but the invaders tore down the fortification and built in its place the Akra, a citadel overlooking the temple mount that was defended by renegade Jews and Gentiles (1 Macc. 1:33–35).

Antiochus tried to seduce the Jews with "intrigue" (literally, "smoothness"), perhaps an allusion to his use of flattery, an approach that he tried with some Jews (see 1 Macc. 2:17–18). Those "loyal to their God" (literally, "the people who know God")—that is, people like the loyal Mattathias—were resolute in their resistance (1 Macc. 2:19–22). The Hebrew text may be understood to mean that these loyal Jews "show strength and act" (Dan. 11:32), which may imply not only quiet resolution but active resistance, like that shown by the sons of Mattathias.

Alongside these active resisters who "show strength and act" are "the wise among the people," who "give understanding to many" (v. 33). The word translated as "the wise" in the NRSV is based on a root that occurs a number of times in Daniel. In 9:13, it is used in reference to faithful reflection on the fidelity of God. Elsewhere in the book, the word is associated with the possession of extraordinary insights (so 1:17; 9:22, 25; 12:10). So it is not surprising that these people are associated with the task of helping people understand. To judge by the usage of the term and the content of the book, one may infer that these people translate to the public their insights of dreams and visions, their understanding of the faithfulness of the Sovereign God. Interestingly, too, apart from their instructive role, these people are described in entirely passive terms: they fall (three times in vv. 33–35), they are in captivity and plunder for days (v. 33), they are helped a little (v. 34), they are joined by others (v. 34), and they are to be refined, purified, and cleansed (v. 35). This characterization stands in stark contrast to the depiction of those loyalists who show strength and take action (v. 32).

Perhaps here are recorded two responses of people who are faithful to the covenant in those critical times when Antiochus persecuted the Jews. On the one hand, some people were determined to act with strength, like the Jewish freedom fighters who acted forcefully, even violently, to resist the policies of the Seleucids (see 1 Macc. 2:42–48). On the other hand, some people chose the alternative approach of imparting insights—people like the author of the book, who probably belonged to such a group (see 1:17; 9:22, 25). Insufficient evidence is available to conclude that these people were strictly pacifists, but they did seem to respond to the crisis not with force but with quiet manifestations of faithfulness: the promotion of understanding of the faithfulness of the sovereign God and their willingness to suffer for their convictions. For a while at least, some of this group would have to pay a high price for their stance (v. 34). Three times in verses 33–35 the text speaks of these people stumbling, indicating probably the reality of their martyrdom. Indeed, some Jews in the time of Antiochus preferred death rather than compromising their faith (see 1 Macc. 1:31–38, 57–63; 2 Macc. 6:11; 7:1–41). Some scholars suggest on the basis of several common idioms that this portrayal of faithfulness has been inspired by the depiction of the suffering servant in Isaiah 40–55. The servant of God, according to that view, will "act wisely" (Isa. 52:13; the Hebrew root there is the same as for "wise" in Dan. 11:33, 35) so that the "many" who see his suffering will "perceive" or "understand." Moreover, the suffering servant of the Lord will stumble (see Isa. 59:10, 14), but he will bear his suffering quietly for others' sake. This approach may have provided a model for the portrayal of quiet faithfulness in Daniel.

Among faithful Jews, two responses to the atrocities of Antiochus were apparently available: active resistance (v. 32) and passive resistance (vv. 33–35). These alternatives were chosen, respectively, by the *ḥăsîdîm* (1 Macc. 2:42) and apparently the *maśkîlîm*, the group to which the author of Daniel belonged. One may find analogies, too, in more recent history in the courageous resistance of nationalist freedom fighters on the one hand and the morally compelling resistance of nonviolent civil disobedience. Mahatma Gandhi of the Indian independence movement, for instance, was among those in his generation who imparted insights and taught understanding, while advocating passive resistance, and he and many of his supporters had at times to pay a heavy price for their cause. In the American civil rights struggles, similarly, one may find analogies to the two Jewish responses to oppression: the approach of active resistance of Malcolm X on the one hand, and the passive resistance of Martin Luther King Jr. on the other. Each paid a heavy price for his resistance. Also, Martin Luther King Jr.'s authority revolved around his insights and his ability to interpret dreams and visions to many.

The text in Daniel 11 passes no judgment on the active resistance movement, the *ḥăsîdîm*, but it seems to advocate the approach of the *maśkîlîm*, "the wise among the people." The narrator is blatantly honest about the possible consequences for the faithful: they will suffer for a while at least, their lives may be endangered in various ways, and they may not even survive. They will also have "little help," which probably refers not to any particular group of individuals, but to the general vulnerability of these faithful ones. Their cause would not be advanced by the many who would ally themselves with them "insincerely" (so NRSV in v. 34), the Hebrew term here being exactly the same as that translated in the NRSV as "through intrigue" in verse 21, where it refers to the deceitfulness of Antiochus. The term is also similar to a term used of Antiochus's "intrigue" in verse 32. The Hebrew word, as mentioned earlier, means something like "smooth things." At issue here, it seems, are those who flatter the would-be martyrs with smooth talk and purport to be on their side but who do little else to indicate their commitments. These people talk a good talk but give in when the chips are down. Many people like that are in every generation—people who praise others for their stance and encourage them, whether sincerely or not, but whose own actions do not reflect their smooth words. For the narrator, the situation is an interim one, however, that will not last forever. Indeed, an end time to this bleak history will come, for "an appointed time" is still to come (v. 35).

Verses 36–39 appear to be a recapitulation of the offenses of Antiochus as a summary judgment of his character. He is depicted as an autocrat who does whatever he pleases (v. 36; see also v. 16). In that he is hardly unique, of course, for people in such positions of power are often like that, and the book of Daniel in fact characterizes other rulers that way (8:4; 11:3). Antiochus, though, is said to have elevated himself so much so that he considered himself superior to any god, and even against "the God of gods" he dared to speak "horrendous things." His boasting has already been noted before (7:8, 20), but here one gains a further insight into the nature of his boasts. The word rendered as "horrendous things" in verse 36 is used also in 8:24 of Antiochus's destructive power. Extremely bitter irony appears in this vocabulary, for that Hebrew term is used elsewhere for God's wondrous deeds. Forty-three times in the Old Testament the word appears in reference to God's wonderful works of creation and salvation (e.g., Exod. 3:20; 34:10; Josh. 3:5); only twice—in Daniel 8:24 and 11:36, both times in regard to Antiochus—is the word used of anyone other than God. The boasting of Antiochus, it appears, was nothing short of blasphemy: not only had he the audacity to destroy the results of God's awesome work, but he purportedly boasted about his own awesome power, as if he exacted this awful destruction and then had the temerity to speak of the destruction as his miracles and wonders.

Such an assessment of his arrogance has already been anticipated in 8:10–12, which draws upon the ancient Near Eastern myth of a rebellion in heaven against the supreme deity in the divine council, an imagery evident also in Isaiah 14:3–21 and Ezekiel 28:2–19. The pretensions of Antiochus have implications not only in the realm of earthly conflicts. They have implications also beyond the mundane (see also Dan.

8:10–12). He had been getting away with this attitude because the predetermined end time had not yet come. Antiochus was even prospering. Indeed, he had boasted about his successes in increasingly pompous terms, as evident on coins struck during his reign, which culminated with his claim to be "God Manifest, Victorious One."

The offenses of Antiochus were not limited to the earthly atrocities intimated, however. They touch even the realm of the divine, and the concern with that realm is evident in the fact that the word for "god" appears eight times in three verses (vv. 36–39). According to the narrator, Antiochus had no consideration of the god of his ancestors, meaning probably the god Apollo, the patron deity of the Seleucids. The appearance of Zeus instead of Apollo on some of the coins minted during his reign may have suggested to some in his time that he was favoring Zeus at the expense of the god of his forebears. That may not have been Antiochus's intention in depicting Zeus, but it made for good polemics. Moreover, the king is said to have no respect for "the one whom women loved," a probable reference to Adonis, a god long venerated in Mesopotamia as Tammuz (Ezek. 8:14) but now also favored in Ptolemaic Egypt. He had respect for neither the gods of the Seleucids nor the gods of the Ptolemies. Indeed, according to the narrator, Antiochus had no consideration of any god whatsoever because he had magnified himself above every god (Dan. 11:37). Yet, he honors a god "in his place" (NRSV "instead of these"), the expression here being the same one used in the overview of history for succession (see vv. 7, 20, 21). In Canaanite mythology, the supreme deity of the divine council was the one who assigned the gods their places; in Israelite theology, their God was the Most High, assigning to the gods their allotments (Deut. 32:8–9), but Antiochus was acting as if he had this role, demoting or promoting the gods as he saw fit, making choices to suit his political agenda. The god whom he presently favored was "the god of fortresses," a god whom his ancestors had not known. This god must be Zeus, whom Antiochus had honored on some of his coins, although not strictly the same Greek Zeus Olympius, whom his Seleucid ancestors surely knew. Rather, the god appears to have been a bastardized version of Baal Shamem, the deity worshiped by the predominantly Syrian mercenary troops garrisoned at the Akra, the fortress that Antiochus had established in Jerusalem. This god was a warrior, the god of power, who could be identified generally with any number of deities, including for Hellenist Jews, their God. This god was a god of the mixed multitudes of all the fortresses, including the Akra. This god was a god that all of his troops at the Akrea could agree on and, hence, a god that served the political agenda of Antiochus well. Apparently, religion was to Antiochus nothing but a tool, a convenient means to an end.

The beginning of verse 39 is somewhat obscure as the Hebrew text stands. It reads, literally, "and he shall act for the strongholds of fortresses with a foreign god . . ." (NRSV "he shall deal with the strongest fortresses"). A number of commentators have proposed repointing the text slightly to read, "And he shall act for those who fortify the fortresses, people of a foreign god . . ." This reading makes good sense in the context, and it emphasizes, again, the crafty manipulation of religion by Antiochus. He favored a god whom his mercenaries (those who fortify the fortresses) could conveniently worship. Yet, he did not merely attend to the "spiritual needs" of his denizens. Ever the pragmatic politician, Antiochus also provided material benefits for those who recognized his authority. He increased their stature, granted them more power over others, and allotted them property "for a price" (v. 39; compare 2 Macc. 7:24). Thus, in Judea, Antiochus blatantly promoted his allies and allowed them to acquire property seized from his opponents (1 Macc. 1:34–35; 3:36), no doubt in a manner similar to his reassignments of the high priesthood to his highest-bidding supporter.

## AN END OF ANTIOCHUS
## Daniel 11:40–45

Verse 40 returns to the theme of an "end time" that has been anticipated earlier, in verses 27 and 35. Thus begins a section (11:40–12:4) depicting an end-time scenario, first concerning the death of Antiochus (11:40–45) and then concerning the resurrection of the dead (12:1–4). Unlike the preceding overview of history, which is corroborated by historical happenings often to a remarkable degree, the events in this climactic section cannot be so coordinated. The accounting of truth (see v. 2) has, in fact, moved from a review of the past, to a view of the present condition of the narrator and the audience, and now to a daring preview of the future. The present is a time when arrogant Antiochus is able to work his will, as if he is completely in charge of earth and heaven, because the time of the end is not yet come, the period of divine wrath is not yet complete (vv. 32–39). Now the narrator will offer a scope, as it were, for how the end of that history might come to pass.

The narrator expects the difficult situation to continue for just a little while longer. With little doubt the antecedent of "him" in verse 40 must be Antiochus (see vv. 35–39), since no indication is given that the subject has been changed. Clearly at issue is an "end time" for the trial of suffering that the Jewish people must undergo (v. 35), the completion of the "period of wrath" (v. 36). This end will not be in the distant future, the author assures his readers. Antiochus had been turned back by the Romans from his invasion of Egypt (v. 30). The author now predicts that the Ptolemies will launch a new attack on their old enemies in the north and that Antiochus will undertake a massive retaliation (v. 40), in the course of which Judea will once again suffer significant loss of life, while the Transjordanian states of Moab and Edom and Ammon, traditional enemies of Israel, will escape, no doubt because they will ally themselves with Antiochus (v. 41). Egypt will be conquered and, even beyond Egypt, the Libyans and Ethiopians will submit to his will (vv. 42–43). Yet some news from his homeland in the north and east, presumably rumors of insurrection, will come that will prompt Antiochus to withdraw and he will die en route home, somewhere between the Mediterranean coast and Jerusalem, but not before bringing destruction to many (vv. 44–45).

Unlike the preceding review of history, the details in vv. 40–45 are not in accord with historical records. There is no extant historical report concerning yet another battle between the Ptolemies and the Seleucids during the time of Antiochus Epiphanes. Jerome did note that the anti-Christian polemicist Porphyry had thought that there was yet another Egyptian campaign by Antiochus after 168 B.C.E., but it seems likely that verse 40 was in fact the source for Porphyry's conclusion. Moreover, all other accounts of Antiochus's demise suggest that he died in Persia, soon after looting a temple in Elymais (Polybius 31.9; 1 Macc. 6:1–17; 2 Macc. 1:14–16), and not in Palestine.

Needless to say, the contradictions have greatly troubled interpreters who have been embarrassed by the inaccuracy of the details. Yet, the hallmark of biblical prophecy has never been the precise fulfillment of predictions to their last detail. Biblical prophecy is not clairvoyance but the interpretation of the will of God in the sociopolitical and historical arena. The biblical writers paid attention to history and carefully observed all that occurred in their generation and interpreted the will of God in the light of the traditions that they received. They were not soothsayers. They were considered inspired in their ability to shape the community of faith's response, not because of the precision of their predictions. Thus, the author of Daniel, as a close observer of events in history, believed that history will repeat itself, that the affliction that the Jews have had to endure would last a little longer, that the faithful would continue to suffer and die, perhaps even in greater numbers than before, that those who have been traditional enemies against them would escape the calamity that seems to befall everyone else. The gist of that prediction has arguably been validated in history, although not in precisely the way that the author had envisaged. Antiochus did engage in military campaigns, as he always had, but this time in the northeast, rather than against the "king of the south." He was about to launch a new campaign in the east when news came of widespread revolt in Judea headed by Judas Maccabeus. History repeats itself on that score, too, for centuries before Sennacherib of Assyria was besieging Jerusalem when rumors of insurrection at home forced him to withdraw. More recently, Ptolemy III Euergetes was forced to withdraw from his attacks when he received news of insurrection in his homeland (v. 8). Antiochus did not return to Palestine himself, but he did give orders to deal harshly with the Jewish rebels. He himself would soon die—not in Palestine, however, but in Persia. He had not learned his lessons from history, it seems, for he looted a temple in Elymais, just as his father had before. He died soon after that event, late in 164 B.C.E. To the end, Antiochus was arrogantly dismissive of divine realities, but his appointed time had finally come: "He shall come to his end, with no one to help him" (v. 45).

## RESURRECTION OF THE DEAD
## Daniel 12:1–4

The linkage of 12:1–3 to the previous chapter is suggested in the first instance by the setting given twice in verse 1, "at that time," meaning no doubt the time of the end mentioned already in 11:40. Michael, who has been introduced first in 10:13 and named again in 10:21, now is in focus. In 10:21, just before the historical overview, he is mentioned almost in passing. Now, at the end of that historical overview, he reprises his role as Israel's guardian angel. The historical overview in 11:2–45, then, is framed by the presence of Michael who, one is told already in 10:21, joins other unseen powers in the fight on Israel's behalf against the supernatural patrons of the world empires, Persia and Greece. He is, in fact, subliminally present throughout that historical recitation.

According to the NRSV translation, Michael is Israel's "protector." That translation rightly conveys Michael's martial character, for he has been portrayed as a commander of hosts, fighting on behalf of God's people on earth. The Hebrew text here suggests one who stands up "over" or "beside" or "for" the people (the Hebrew preposition can mean all three). Hence, inasmuch as Michael is called "the great commander" (NRSV "the great prince"), one may think immediately of the commander of the heavenly host whom Joshua long ago saw "standing before him" (Josh. 5:13). Michael is the celestial commander standing over the people. At the same time, however, the language here may have juridical connotations. Michael as the chief angel is one who stands up in the divine council for his people, Israel. Certainly he plays such a role as an advocate in the celestial court in the pseudepigraphical *Testament of Daniel* (6:1–5) and in the New Testament (Jude 9). Here in Daniel 12, Michael apparently stands in the divine assembly (compare 7:10), presumably to advocate for those registered "in the book" as members of the covenant community and, hence, destined for life not death (see Exod. 32:32; Pss. 69:28; 87:6; Isa. 4:3; Ezek. 13:9; Mal. 3:16; Rev. 20:12, 15). These people will be delivered from "the time of anguish" they have experienced under Antiochus's reign of terror, a period when God's wrath was still being worked out.

Daniel 12:2 is clearly referring to a resurrection of some sort. That resurrection is to take place not in the distant future, not at the end of world history, but in the period twice identified in verse 1 as "at that time," that is, the end time (11:40). Although it had always been axiomatic in Israel that those who die cannot be raised from the dead (see Job 14:12; Jer. 51:39, 57; Amos 5:2), biblical writers from time to time entertained the notion of miraculous revivification. Among the legends of the prophet Elisha, for instance, one records his revival of a child who had already died (2 Kgs. 4:18–35) and one that tells of corpses becoming enlivened when they come into contact with the prophet's own corpse in the grave (2 Kgs. 13:20–21). The prophet Hosea in the eighth century spoke of the possibility of national revival thus: "After two days he will revive us; on the third day he will raise us up, that we may live before him" (Hos. 6:2). The imagery there, though, may be that of someone who has been deathly ill but wonderfully revived (compare 2 Kgs. 4:31). More dramatically, Ezekiel would later envision the possibility of life even for bones so thoroughly bleached out by the sun that life seems impossible (Ezek. 37:1–14). The "resurrection" in that context, as in Hosea, is a historic and communal one. In each case, resurrection is a metaphor for the restoration of the people of Israel after a period of destruction (see, especially, Ezek. 37:11). In the "Isaianic Apocalypse," too, one finds the metaphor of resurrection applied to the covenant community: "Your dead shall live, their corpses shall rise. O dwellers in the dust, awake and sing for joy! For your dew is a radiant dew, and the earth will give birth to those long dead" (Isa. 26:19). So, too, one may surmise that the seer in Daniel 12 is using the imagery of resurrection to convey hope in the revival of the Jewish people after a history of suffering and death.

The text does not speak of the resurrection of all humanity, but only of "many of those who sleep" (Dan. 12:2). Who the "many" are here is not immediately evident. Perhaps the text refers to the "many" whom the wise would instruct (11:33), or the "many" over whom Antiochus would appoint his cronies as rulers (11:39), or the "many" whom he would kill

(11:44). They are, perhaps, the "many" who may be brought to righteousness by the wise (12:3). Thus, the "many of those who sleep" may be Jews, specifically those who have been registered "in the book" but who have died. This conclusion is all the more compelling when one considers the presence of the Hebrew conjunction ("and"/"but") before the "many," a conjunction that is not reflected in the NRSV translation. That conjunction, in fact, links verse 2a to verse 1b, contrasting those who are alive to be delivered by Michael (v. 1b) and those who are not (v. 2a). Thus, one may better translate the text: "at that time your people shall be delivered, everyone who is found in the book. But many of those who sleep in the dust of the earth shall awake." If this view is correct, the seer's notion is a development beyond the vision of national revival and restoration that one finds in earlier biblical texts, for not all of those so resurrected will in fact live. The people as a whole will be delivered. But as for those who have already died, some will be awakened to everlasting life, while others to shame and everlasting contempt. The two groups refer, respectively, to the Jews who have been faithful to the covenant at all cost and those who have betrayed the covenant by siding with and otherwise aiding Antiochus (see 11:32–35). The seer has in effect qualified the earlier notion of resurrection of the nation to suggest that those in the covenant community who are resurrected will not be equally treated, for some within the community have, in fact, betrayed the covenant. There is individual accountability in this notion of resurrection.

As before (11:33), those who are "wise" are singled out (12:3). They are the ones who, like the suffering servant portrayed in Isaiah 40–55, accept their suffering and even death with quiet courage in order that "many" might be brought to understanding (see comment above at 11:33). The seer had suggested that some of these would fall or otherwise suffer so that "they may be refined, purified, and cleansed, until the time of the end" (11:35). Now in the description of the time of the end, the seer envisions that these people will "shine like the brightness of the sky" (12:3). This text presents a dramatic reversal of the situation described in 8:10, where the arrogant "little one" (Antiochus) is depicted as one who ascends the heavens, casting down some of the hosts thereby. The mythological background of that description is the rebellion in heaven—the myth of one who would ascend to the heights of heaven in an attempt to take the place of the supreme deity of the divine council. The seer now envisions, however, the vindication of the fallen *maśkîlîm*, the "wise," in terms that are reminiscent of the hosts of heaven assuming their rightful stations in the sky after they have been cast down by Antiochus. Thus we have here the motif of the exaltation of the lowly and the humiliation of the arrogant. The one who attempts to ascend to the stars (8:10;

11:36–37) is brought down, while whose who are fallen (8:10; 11:33–35) are exalted. Such a reversal of destiny and vindication of the fallen is in accord with the promised exaltation of the suffering servant who will "act wisely" (Isa. 52:13). Moreover, even as the suffering servant is expected to lead many to righteousness (Isa. 53:11), "those who lead many to righteousness," presumably a parallel description of "those who are wise," shall be like the stars forever and ever (12:3). The parallel with Isaiah 53:11 is even more suggestive according to readings in the Qumran manuscripts and the Greek translation of that text: "Out of his suffering one will see light" (author's translation). Or, as Matthew puts it in the New Testament, with echoes of Daniel, "the righteous will shine like the sun in the kingdom of their Father. Let everyone who has ears listen!" (Matt. 13:43).

Daniel is told, as before (see 8:26), to keep the words a secret and to seal up the vision until the time of the end. Given the sixth-century setting presupposed for the book, the obvious implication is that the revelation is meant not for that time in the past (the sixth century) but for the book's present—for the original readers in the second century B.C.E. The book concerns the imminent future ("the time of the end") for Daniel's readers. Presumably, the seal would be broken in their time, the words made relevant. For the reader of the book in the second century B.C.E., the very existence of the book before them is testimony to the fact that the end is nigh, the words are being revealed as truth. For the reader of the book in every generation, too, the very act of reading the book unseals it, calling one to participate with the ancient reader in making sense of the visions that are now revealed, though still in many ways remaining a mystery.

The last part of verse 4 is obscure in large part because of the lack of connection with what precedes it. Does it indicate what will happen when the seal is broken at the "time of the end"? Or does it suggest what will happen in the interim, before the mystery is finally revealed? The NRSV translators apparently follow many modern critics in assuming that the latter is the case. According to this view, a desperate need for divine guidance will arise before the disclosure at the end, as many run to and fro seeking a divine word (compare Amos 8:12), only to be faced with the increase of evil instead. That interpretation, however, requires an emendation of the Hebrew text, partly on the basis of the view proffered by the Old Greek version that the land will "be filled with wickedness." Yet, all the other textual witnesses support the Hebrew text as it stands, which refers to an increase not in "evil" but in "the knowledge." Assuming the correctness of the Hebrew text, one may take Daniel 12:4b to be referring to events when the truth of the vision is revealed at the end. In that case, the situation represents a dramatic reversal of the gloomy vision of Amos 8. Instead of people roaming about in a desperate-but-vain search for the word of God, now "many"—perhaps the "many" who are resurrected from the dead (12:2) or the "many" who have been led to righteousness by the resurrected servants of God (12:3)—will roam the earth and knowledge will be increased (12:4). Indeed, the destruction of "many" by Antiochus (11:44) will not preclude the prospect of this scenario, for "many" will be raised and "many" will be led to righteousness. Now, because of the "many" who go to and fro to teach understanding, "the knowledge"—that is, the knowledge of God—will be increased. So the situation described in verse 4b is what one is supposed to find when the vision is disclosed. Then many will range the earth and "the knowledge" will be increased. The vision corroborates the prophecy in Isaiah 53:11 that the suffering servant, who will "act wisely" and lead many to righteousness, "will find satisfaction through his knowledge."

The resurrection as envisioned by the seer in Daniel 12, thus, is not an end in itself, but rather an expression of confidence in the faithfulness of God, whose salvation extends not only to those who are alive (v. 2), but also to those who have died (v. 3). The resurrection is an expression of hope of vindication for the faithful and retribution for the unfaithful—hope as traditionally expressed in Israel's corporate and individual worship life (see Pss. 6, 32, 38, 69, 130, 143). Even more importantly, the resurrection is an expression of hope that the power of God manifested in the resurrection would enable many to roam about the earth so that "the knowledge"—surely meaning here the knowledge of God—might increase. Death will not prove to be the ultimate triumph of evil, for in the possibility of resurrection, the will of God promises to be worked out. The seer in Daniel 12 envisions that this resurrection hope will be fulfilled in the near future of the book's implied reader.

# 12. The Final Revelation: Postscript
## *Daniel 12:5–13*

**5 Then I, Daniel, looked, and two others appeared, one standing on this bank of the stream and one on the other. 6 One of them said to the man clothed in linen, who was upstream, "How long shall it be until the end of these wonders?" 7 The man clothed in linen, who was upstream, raised his right hand and his left hand toward heaven. And I heard him swear by the one who lives forever that it would be for a time, two times, and half a time, and that when the shattering of the power of the holy people comes to an end, all these things would be accomplished. 8 I heard but could not understand; so I said, "My lord, what shall be the outcome of these things?" 9 He said, "Go your way, Daniel, for the words are to remain secret and sealed until the time of the end. 10 Many shall be purified, cleansed, and refined, but the wicked shall continue to act wickedly. None of the wicked shall understand, but those who are wise shall understand. 11 From the time that the regular burnt offering is taken away and the abomination that desolates is set up, there shall be one thousand two hundred ninety days. 12 Happy are those who persevere and attain the thousand three hundred thirty-five days. 13 But you, go your way, and rest; you shall rise for your reward at the end of the days."**

The preceding passage, 12:1–4, would have constituted an appropriate denouement of the book. It envisions a decisive deliverance brought about by none other than Israel's own guardian angel, Michael; it holds that even those who are already dead will not be left out of the final vindication. Moreover, Daniel is told to shut up the words and seal the book until the end. Yet, one more passage in the book (12:7–13), as the text stands, constitutes a postscript not only to the report of the final revelation in 10:1–12:4, but also to the visions of the second half of the book (chaps. 7–12) and, indeed, to the whole book of Daniel. This final unit is not presented as a report of an entirely new encounter for the seer, for no chronological notice introduces the vision, as one finds elsewhere. Some signs, too, indicate that the passage postdates the preceding materials. Verses 11–12, for instance, evidence a historical knowledge of events at the end of 164 B.C.E. in a way that the preceding unit, 11:40–12:4, does not. Indeed, the discrepancy is so stark that many historical critics are inclined to view verses 11–12 as glosses inserted later into the text as revisions of earlier erroneous calculations. These putative glosses, some scholars contend, represent two different attempts to deal with the problem of the delayed fulfillment of prophecy—first in verse 11, then in verse 12. Be that as it may, the passage as a whole appears to be appended to the preceding materials, indeed, now functioning as an epilogue to the account of the final revelation.

The vision finds Daniel at a water channel, presumably the Tigris, on a bank of which he had been standing since the beginning of the revelation of the end (10:4). The extended literary unit of chapters 10–12 thus begins and closes with a vision at a river; the prologue (10:1–19) parallels the epilogue (12:7–13). Curiously, however, the water channel is not called "the great river" as the Tigris is in 10:4. Rather, another term is used, one that the NRSV renders as "the stream." Indeed, some scholars prefer to associate this scene with the vision at the Ulai canal in chapter 8. They observe that in the vision of chapter 8 Daniel overheard celestial beings in conversation with one another, deliberating over the question of how long the atrocities perpetrated by Antiochus would last (8:13–14), precisely the issue addressed in 12:5–13. Yet, the word translated as "the stream" in verse 5 is also different from that used for the Ulai canal. The term in verse 5 is most often used of the Nile in earlier biblical texts, although it later became a general term for a channel (see Isa. 33:21; Job 28:10). The use of this ambiguous, even odd, term should perhaps prompt one to recall both the visions in 8:1–27 and 10:1–12:4. In fact, elements in this passage echo both visions, as well as chapters 7 and 9. Thus, this final passage was probably composed as a conclusion to, or a postscript of, the visions in the second half of the book of Daniel.

Daniel sees "two others" in the vision (v. 5), meaning two more celestial beings besides the one clad in linen first mentioned in 10:5. The NRSV locates that linen-clad man "upstream" (v. 6), but the Hebrew should probably be understood to mean that the person was "above the waters of the channel." In 10:5, Daniel is said to have lifted up his eyes to see that linen-clad one. The conversation presently echoes the one between celestial beings in 8:13–14, where the question is the duration of the situation under Antiochus: "How long is this vision concerning the regular burnt offering, the transgression that makes desolate, and the giving over of the sanctuary and host to be trampled?" (8:13). The question is phrased differently here, however: "How long shall it be until the end of these wonders?" (v. 6). The word translated as "wonders" in the NRSV refers to things that are hard to comprehend. It is usually used of God's awesome works of salvation (Exod. 15:11; Pss. 77:11, 15; 89:5; Isa. 25:1), but occasionally also of God's awful acts of judgment (Isa. 29:14; compare Lam. 1:9). The word is related to a word that appears twice before in reference to the awfulness of Antiochus's destructive acts (8:24; 11:36). Here in verse 6, it seems to refer to Antiochus's extraordinarily arrogant rebellion against the most high, notably the atrocities that he wrought in Jerusalem (see 8:13).

The response comes from the mysterious linen-clothed one (v. 7), who gives a sworn testimony as his answer, an oath duly witnessed by the required "two or three" (see Deut. 19:15). The vehemence of the oath is indicated by the fact that both hands are lifted, as opposed to just one, which is the normal practice (see Deut. 32:40; Rev. 10:5–6). The oath is sworn in the name of the one who is eternally living, that is, the eternal God (see Dan. 6:26), the one who is over times and seasons (see 2:20–23). The promise of the divine being is that the situation will last, literally, "for a time, times, and a half" (12:7), a phrase that echoes the Aramaic expression in 7:25, literally, "period, periods, and a portion of a period." In both cases, scholarly consensus suggests that three and a half years are meant.

The further specification is that all these extraordinary events will be finished "when the shattering of the power of the holy people comes to an end" (12:7). The Hebrew is somewhat awkward, however. The reference to the "power of the holy people" seems completely out of place and meaningless. It would perhaps make more sense if one assumes the transposition of a couple of words and repoints the text to read, "when the power of the shatterer of the holy people is brought to an end," that is, when the power of Antiochus Epiphanes is finally destroyed. Yet, the vision here does presume some mystery. Daniel himself would admit that he "heard but could not understand" and he still wanted to know what the future (NRSV "outcome") would be (v. 8). Revelation, even a direct one like that which Daniel receives, does not mean the end of mystery. One may gain some insight as to divine will and hear a word of judgment or find a word of hope, but much will remain mysterious and ambiguous despite revelation from on high. Daniel is simply instructed to keep on going, for the mysteries and ambiguities will be preserved until "the time of the end" (v. 9); the present situation of trials and uncertainties—as articulated already in chapter 11—will remain for a while yet (v. 10).

Even though verse 10 echoes 11:35, a subtle difference is of note. Whereas the text has said that some of the wise will be tripped up and be refined, purified, and cleansed (11:35), while they try to make many understand (11:33), now many will be purified, refined, and cleansed. The implication is that the suffering of the wise will not have been futile after all, for redemption will be extended to many—the many who will be led to righteousness (see 12:3). Meanwhile, "the wise"—the group with which the author of Daniel is associated—will understand, but the wicked, namely, the renegade Jews who abandoned the covenant, will still fail to understand. In any case, the text does not claim too much, such as that all mysteries will be resolved once and for all. So the wise ones, like Daniel, will understand (v. 10), even if they do not fully understand (v. 8).

The end is not far away but imminent, and a projected schedule is spelled out in verses 11–12. Two perplexing calculations, though, must have made sense to the original readers of the book but have thoroughly confounded modern interpreters. Along with the other predicted schedules in the book—the three and a half years (7:25; 9:27; 12:7) and the 2,300 days and nights (8:14)—the reader is now presented with two more figures: 1,290 days (v. 11) and 1,335 days (v. 12). One difficulty in interpreting these dates is that the modern interpreter cannot be sure which calendar is presumed. There were three in use during the second century B.C.E.: a solar calendar of 364 days, a lunar calendar of 354 days, and a lunisolar one of 360 days. The greatest problem in the case of the dates in verses 11–12, though, is the fact that the particular events that will occur at the end of the 1,290 and 1,335 days are not spelled out. Fortunately, the starting point of the calculation is given, namely, the taking away of the burnt offerings and the desecration of the temple, that is, December 7, 167 B.C.E. (the fifteenth of Kislev, according to 1 Macc. 1:54). Assuming a solar calendar, a period of 1,290 days would correspond to roughly three and a half years, the probable meaning of the expression "time, times and a half" in verse 7 (also 8:13; 9:27). That calculation would mean a date around the beginning of the summer solstice, June 21, 163 B.C.E., although the text does not say what precisely will transpire at that time. By contrast, 8:14 indicates that the temple will be restored after the cessation of sacrifices for 2,300 days and nights, a period of seven years, possibly dating from the murder of Onias by Menelaus in 171 B.C.E. Menelaus was the one who conspired with the enemy for "one week" of years (that is, seven years), a connivance that led eventually to the desecration of the temple in 167 B.C.E., and the temple laid desolate for half a week of years, that is, three and a half years, before Judas Maccabeus led the cleansing and rededication of the temple on the twenty-fifth of Kislev, 164 B.C.E. (9:27; see also 1 Macc. 4:36–61). Taking the calculations at face value, then, one may infer that the event implied in verse 11 must be something after that rededication of the temple. But what could that be?

Antiochus died in late 164 B.C.E., about the time of the rededication of the temple by Judas Maccabeus. However, news of his death apparently did not even reach Antioch till the end of December 164 B.C.E. or the beginning of the next year, 163 B.C.E. Antiochus V, the young son and successor of Antiochus Epiphanes, subsequently wrote a letter announcing the death of his father and officially restoring to the Jews their right to worship at the temple and to otherwise practice their faith (2 Macc. 11:22–26). The Jewish resistance forces under Judas Maccabeus had meanwhile gained strength enough to besiege the Akra in Jerusalem (1 Macc. 6:18–20). Successes like these might have led to a conviction that Seleucid power was near its end. So the author of Daniel 12:5–13, probably some time early in 163 B.C.E., predicted the total collapse of the Seleucid dynasty by the middle of the year—1,290 days after the desecration of the temple, that is, around June 21, 163 B.C.E. However, the real climax of the vision will be in yet another 45 days, that is, 1,335 days after the desecration of the temple. That date would be the twenty-fourth of Ab (August 5, 163 B.C.E.), possibly on the anniversary of the public reading of the Torah (compare 2 Macc. 2:14), when it was expected that the Gentile laws would be abrogated and the Jews would once again be judged by their own law. With the successes of the Jewish resistance, the author of this postscript dared to imagine that all foreign domination would end soon and that the reign of God in the form of a restored and renewed Israel would be ushered in, which may be what those who persevere would be fortunate to witness (Dan. 12:12).

Such a reconstruction makes sense. Yet, if that is what the text meant, the original readers were no doubt disappointed, for those events did not in fact come to pass. On the contrary, after a few initial setbacks at the hands of the Jewish forces, the new king Antiochus V amassed a great army, defeated the Jews, and successfully took Jerusalem (1 Macc. 6:21–48; 2 Macc. 13:1–19). A remnant of the resistance movement fled to hide in the mountains. The wait for the end had to continue, it seems, for the ultimate triumph of God would not yet be manifest.

That is the way history has been. Centuries after the book of Daniel was written, the faithful must still cope with the trials and tribulations of a world dominated by evil and terror. They must still live with ambiguities and uncertainties. They can hear the Word of God revealed to them and hearing that Word they may begin to understand (v. 10), and yet they do not yet fully understand (v. 8). Nevertheless, the faithful are called to believe in a God who acts not only on earth but in realms mysterious and unseen, a God whose ultimate triumph may be manifest not in one's lifetime but at an end time to be determined by the sovereign God alone. Until that time, the reader can only hear and perhaps appropriate the command given to Daniel, the seer. According to the Hebrew text, Daniel is told to keep on going to the end (the NRSV omits "to the end" with the Greek translations). He may also die. Yet he knows that he, as one of the wise, will be resurrected in due time. Simply put, people to whom this revelation is given may take courage in the difficult journey of living, even though the end time is still to come, for if they are alive when the time comes, they will be delivered (v. 1). Even if they die, as the faithful and hopeful of Daniel's time did indeed, they may rest assured, for they will be among those who will be resurrected (v. 2). Herein, too, is a message for the reader of the book at any time: one must keep on going in life despite the overwhelming presence of evil, despite the ambiguities, terrors, and travails of one's time. One keeps on going, trusting only in the power of God to deliver the faithful who are alive and even to resurrect those who are not, for God's power is not limited to this life and to this world that one sees and knows. For Christians, this resurrection hope culminates in the resurrection of the Christ (1 Cor. 15:12–58). His victory over death makes it possible for every believer, long past the end time of Daniel's vision, even long past the age of the New Testament, to affirm with the faithful in times past in the words of the Nicene Creed: "We look for the resurrection of the dead, and the life of the world to come. Amen."

# Select Bibliography


Anderson, R. A. *Signs and Wonders: A Commentary on the Book of Daniel.* International Theological Commentary. Grand Rapids: Eerdmans, 1984.

Baldwin, J. G. *Daniel.* Tyndale Old Testament Commentary. Leicester, England: Inter-Varsity Press, 1978.

Berrigan, D. *Daniel: Under the Siege of the Divine.* Farmington, Pa.: Plough, 1998.

Collins, J. J. *Daniel.* Hermeneia. Minneapolis: Fortress, 1993.

———. *Daniel, with an Introduction to Apocalyptic Literature.* Forms of Old Testament Literature 20. Grand Rapids: Eerdmans, 1984.

Collins, J. J., and P. W. Flint. *The Book of Daniel: Composition and Reception.* 2 vols. Vetus Testamentum Supplement 133. Leiden: Brill, 2001.

Davies, P. R. *Daniel.* Old Testament Guides. Sheffield: JSOT, 1985.

Driver, S. R. *The Book of Daniel.* Cambridge Bible for Schools and Colleges. Cambridge: Cambridge University, 1900.

Fewell, D. N. *Circle of Sovereignty: A Story of Stories in Daniel 1–6.* Journal for the Study of the Old Testament Supplement 72. Sheffield: Almond, 1988.

Gammie, J. G. *Daniel.* Atlanta: John Knox, 1983.

Goldingay, J. E. *Daniel.* Word Bible Commentary 30. Dallas: Word, 1988.

Gowan, D. E. *Daniel.* Abingdon Old Testament Commentaries. Nashville: Abingdon, 2001.

Hartman, L. F., and A. Di Lella. *The Book of Daniel.* Anchor Bible 23. Garden City, N.Y.: Doubleday, 1978.

Heaton, E. W. *The Book of Daniel.* Torch Bible Commentary. London: SCM, 1956.

Lacocque, A. *The Book of Daniel.* Trans. David Pellauer. Atlanta: John Knox, 1979.

Montgomery, J. A. *The Book of Daniel.* International Critical Commentary. Edinburgh: T. & T. Clark, 1927.

Miller, S. R. *Daniel.* New American Commentary, 18. Nashville: Broadman & Holman, 1994.

Porteous, N. W. *Daniel, A Commentary.* Old Testament Library. Rev. ed. Philadelphia: Westminster, 1979.

Redditt, P. L. *Daniel, A Commentary.* The New Century Bible Commentary. Sheffield: Sheffield Academic Press, 1999.

Russell, D. S. *Daniel.* Daily Study Bible. Philadelphia: Westminster, 1981.

Smith-Christopher, D. L. "The Book of Daniel," in *New Interpreter's Bible* VII. Pp. 19–152. Nashville: Abingdon, 1996.

Towner, W. S. *Daniel.* Interpretation. Atlanta: John Knox, 1984.

van der Woude, A. S., ed. *The Book of Daniel in the Light of New Findings.* Louvain: Leuven University Press, 1993.